THE GEOPOLITICS OF FEAR

THE GEOPOLITICS
OF FEAR

FROM SECURITY TO SOLIDARITY
AT EUROPE'S RACIAL BORDERS

BERNA TURAM

STANFORD UNIVERSITY PRESS
Stanford, California

Stanford University Press
Stanford, California

Printed in the United States of America

Library of Congress Cataloging-in-Publication Data
Names: Turam, Berna author
Title: The geopolitics of fear : from security to solidarity at Europe's racial
  borders / Berna Turam.
Description: Stanford, California : Stanford University Press, 2025. | Includes
  bibliographical references and index.
Identifiers: LCCN 2025003421 (print) | LCCN 2025003420 (ebook)
  | ISBN 9781503643529 cloth | ISBN 9781503643703 paperback |
  ISBN 9781503643710 epub
Subjects: LCSH: Solidarity—Greece—Athens | Solidarity—Italy—Palermo |
  European Union countries—Emigration and immigration—Government
  policy | Athens (Greece)—Emigration and immigration—Psychological
  aspects | Palermo (Italy)—Emigration and immigration—Psychological aspects
  | Athens (Greece)—Emigration and immigration—Political aspects | Palermo
  (Italy)—Emigration and immigration—Political aspects
Classification: LCC JV7590 .T867 2025 (ebook) | LCC JV7590 (print) | DDC
  325.4 23/eng/20250—dc16
LC record available at https://lccn.loc.gov/2025003421

Cover photograph: Jamestown, Accra, Ghana, 2022. From the Pray for Seamen collection. © Francesco Bellina

The authorized representative in the EU for product safety and compliance is: Mare Nostrum Group B.V. | Mauritskade 21D | 1091 GC Amsterdam | The Netherlands | Email address: gpsr@mare-nostrum.co.uk | KVK chamber of commerce number: 96249943

To my son, Sean S. Whitney, who accompanied me to several refugee-receiving borderlands and brought along his big heart.

CONTENTS

PREFACE

This ethnography was not intended but triggered. It did not start with a hypothesis or an argument to be proved. It was not sparked by intellectual conversations or the leading academic and analytical debates in my fields. The motivation for my field research arrived on a silver plate as I was taking a respite from world affairs on the Greek islands bordering mainland Turkey. The research was prompted by the rapid shift of perceptions and feelings about the refugees arriving mostly, but not only, from Syria via Turkey. The swift change of emotions was driven by the closure of the Greece-Turkey border upon the agreement between Turkey and the European Union in 2016.

After the outbreak of the Syrian civil war, masses of refugees were arriving every day from Turkey to the Greek islands. Before they passed in a few days to Athens, the capital city of Greece, the displaced people were densely populating the squares, streets, and parks of the border islands. These islands at the periphery of Greece were inundated by refugees as they ate, slept, and waited for the transfer to mainland Greece with the goal of settling in Northern Europe. The largely unhindered flow peaked in 2015. The islanders were saddened as they faced the misery of people running from the war in Syria. The locals did their best to facilitate the refugees' difficult journey, saved lives at the sea, helped refugees with food, blankets, clothing, medicine, and so on before sending them off to their intended destinations in Europe. The relatively humane border management was in alignment with the negative view of securitization of migration by the radical-left SYRIZA government. SYRIZA regarded border securitization as a threat to European integration (Stivas 2021). The period of "desecuritization" did not last long (Skleparis 2018). Things changed rapidly after the 2016 Turkey-EU agreement, which aimed to slow down and eventually stop the refugee flow.

With my last book just off the presses, I had no urge to begin a new research project in that geography at that moment. I was simply breathing the air of the Aegean Sea on these islands so close to Turkey that I could sometimes hear the music from the clubs on the Turkish shore. Unsurprisingly, my honeymoon as an ethnographer staying away from the mischief of the world did not last long. I slowly found myself drawn into a geopolitical agony caused by the "new borders" of Europe (Vradis et al. 2019). Border security was being reinstitutionalized on the basis of a new hot-spot approach, which led to the entrapment and detainment of refugees and asylum seekers in camps on the border islands.

How did these islands, where people lived peacefully, turn into globally infamous red lines at such a pace? As some of the world's most inhumane refugee camps were created on five Greek islands, intense emotions became the modus vivendi shaping everyday life in these violent border zones. This is how I unintentionally came across the impact of the securitization of borders, the "independent variable" of this research that prompted and shaped a wide range of responses and reactions.

The same refugees who had been welcomed warmly and empathetically turned rapidly into objects of the islanders' fear, suspicion, and distrust. Little by little, through pushing buttons of threat and hostility and digging out the historical memory of troubling border politics with Turkey, the fear of a "Muslim invasion" became contagious.[1] But unsurprisingly, the tightening of borders following the Turkey-EU deal did not deter refugees from arriving and accumulating in these peripheral islands, which were lacking resources and infrastructure to accommodate tens of thousands of refugees. Soon, a newly constructed dual reality sank into the lives of the islanders: On the one hand, they felt intimidated that their islands were being "invaded" by these "illegal" Muslim refugees arriving from the historically intimidating neighbor Turkey, which had a large military and a population more than six times that of Greece. On the other hand, the islanders despised the EU's new border regime and the hot-spot policies that were bending their little islands into detention camps for arbitrarily long periods. Intense negative emotions, fear in particular, rooted in history and embedded in Greece's border geography, surfaced in front of my eyes—emotions that changed the dynamics of everyday life, mundane practices, and discourses in Europe's border zones.

As I watched the dramatic shift in perceptions of the refugee from a vulnerable, good human to a feared criminal or terrorist, nothing could stop the ethnographer in me from getting her hands dirty. The shifting emotions on these border islands in such a short period were alarming, pointing to the emotional aspects and repercussions of securitization. This was the beginning of a multisited ethnography that traced refugee politics from the eastern to the central Mediterranean, from the border islands to the main arrival cities in Greece and Sicily. I spent the next seven years researching these two major entry points to Europe, one of the world's most dangerous doorways in the Mediterranean, referred to as "deathscapes" (De Genova 2017; Pezzani and Heller 2013; Heller and Pezzani 2017; Stierl 2016).

The unintentional unfolding of this project continued, even after my ethnographic research was initiated in 2017. From the start, experts and colleagues warned me to beware the "high-security" loci where my fieldwork was taking me. As an ethnographer who had conducted decades of field research in challenging sites in different countries and continents, I wondered what the high-security zone entailed for mundane, everyday life. In a casual interaction with a high-ranking security professional in the United States, I voiced my curiosity: Why were the EU's Mediterranean border islands and cities that have been neglected even by Europe falling under the radar of *global* security forces at that moment? Since when, and why, did the West care about the remote islands and poor port cities at the periphery of Europe? Not only has Europe treated Greece and Sicily as its problem children and ignored the rich historical heritage of both Athens and Palermo, Europeans also have largely neglected both places with prejudice and contempt. These cities were mostly perceived as underdogs, the result of a widely shared and historically formed stigma of Southern Europe as a burden on the EU.[2] Only after the establishment of the violent, hot-spot border regime did the border islands, particularly Lesvos and Lampedusa, and the border cities draw attention from all over the world.

The perfunctory links made between safety and security were puzzling. As the driving motivation of my research was the safety of refugees, it did not make sense for me to be invited to security workshops and to sit next to security experts and professionals on panels. I felt out of place. As I came to terms with the fact that the loci of my research were not only the heavily guarded and weaponized gateways to "Fortress Europe," but also entryways from the Middle East to the First World, the big picture became clearer.[3] The *safety issues* of the most vulnerable population in the world, the refugees who were stripped of everything they had, were being constructed as a major *security threat* to the Western world. The securitization of the borders with the Middle East and North Africa (MENA) became the primary deal-breaker in the electoral politics in Western countries, as the refugees and migrants turned into pawns of power politics in the EU and the United States.

Considering the two entry points in the eastern and the central Mediterranean, the irregular border crossers were too diverse to be categorized racially or ethnically, even though most of them were Muslims. On Europe's soil, a few dozen miles from Turkey or Tunisia, the Muslim or Black *stranger* had no business or right to be. Hence, the refugees and asylum seekers were targeted for their move regardless of the underlying reasons and conditions of their forced displacement—whether they were running from death, war, violence, torture, hunger, or famine. This is how the West abandoned its commitments to observe the international agreements of the 1951 (Geneva) Refugee Convention in a strikingly indifferent manner at the EU's southern borders.

The story was entirely different for the EU's northern borders. A different border governance prompted different emotions at the EU's border between Poland and Ukraine. When Russia waged a war on Ukraine, Europe opened its borders, observing international law and following the agreements of the refugee conventions signed after World War II. Baby strollers were left at Poland's open border to welcome refugee mothers, and selfies were taken with people making hand gestures symbolizing love for the Ukrainian refugees. The West showed its unlimited capacity for solidarity, sympathy, and compassion by standing up against war crimes. Many in the West celebrated their "humanity" by conveniently overlooking the fact that the EU's border regime was valuing human lives differentially in the north and the south depending on people's race, ethnicity, and religion. The extremity of Europe's dissimilar border governance left no legitimacy for its claims of "color-blind" liberal understandings of border security. The Ukrainian refugee appeared more deserving and was treated differently from the Muslim "stranger." Upon criticism, defensive explanations were offered indicating that Ukrainians and Europeans were *more alike*. I wondered, similar to which Europeans and in which way? The EU borders cover a large geography, with ethnically diverse people and various historical memories. Sicilians in the south, for example, have interacted throughout history more closely with North Africans and Black Africans than they ever did with Northern Europeans (for the power dynamics and affinities between Sicilians and Tunisians, see Ben-Yehoyada 2017). The Mediterranean Sea brought people of different racial and religious origins into contact throughout history whether by fishing boats or more recently by migrants' dinghies.

As the Mediterranean has become an increasingly contested and policed geography, the contrast between the fearful closure of southern borders to Muslim and Black migrants and the festive opening of the northern borders to Ukrainians presents a conundrum. At the center of this controversy, there seems to be a convenient belief about the "natural" inclination to welcome the ones who were "like us" and to fear the stranger who was not. From my field sites to academic conferences and classrooms, I listened to people arguing for the "innateness" of the fear of the stranger, the synonym of which is *xenophobia*.[4] The critics of such an idea, like me, who questioned and disagreed with the inherent nature of a fear of the stranger, were often dismissed or attacked with cultural or biological arguments. I have witnessed tremendous effort to *normalize and justify* fear of the stranger even by use of examples from the animal world. Yes, the good old biological reductionism that once weaponized fascism in Europe was back at center stage, arming anti-immigrant sentiments against the flow of Muslim and Black migrants.

Do human beings *innately* feel safe to open their doors and borders only to those who are racially, ethnically, or religiously alike or culturally similar? Do sharp cultural or other differences prevent or preclude safety and inclusion? Sociological research has refuted such cultural arguments, providing solid findings on the role of political institutions (Wimmer and Soehl 2014). Wimmer and Soehl argued that it was not the cultural distance of the Other—the Muslim migrant in this case—that made inclusion impossible, but the state's capacity for accommodation in the receiving country. Put differently, rather than sharp cultural differences, the ability of political institutions to accommodate the Other mattered. Recent ethnographic sociological accounts have complemented Wimmer and Soehl's quantitative analysis: Gowayed (2022) showed how possibilities of realizing human potential were structured (and hindered) by the receiving state and the policies of the host state. Presenting the migrants' journey from the eyes of the refugees, Gowayed's analysis challenged the understanding of human capital as an individual skill or a quality shaped by cultural baggage. In contrast, cultural or biological arguments justified the differential treatment of irregular border crossers by assigning different deservedness to people, thereby justifying the violations of human rights. Europe conveniently looked away from its formerly established principles that *all* refugees, including Syrians, Afghans, Iraqis, and Palestinians escaping from war zones, were human beings equally deserving of rights, freedom, and safety.

If a sense of safety and inclusion was primarily shaped by politics (rather than by culture), safety could not be an ahistorical concept or a noncontextual feeling, unaffected by geographical, spatial, and temporal manifestations of power and domination. Bluntly, would a human being feel unsafe in the presence of another race absent the securitization of that particular race? The question posits the utmost importance of resistance to securitization of migration (and hence also to racialization of migrants). Ethnographic accounts remind us that the designation of difference and relatedness in the Mediterranean is part of the same process (Ben-Yehoyada 2017). So, then, how would the Mediterranean Sea, which historically has both divided and linked for centuries, manage the human flow between difference and affinity if left alone by European security forces?

Unsurprisingly, "the history of the West was not always easy to separate from the East, especially around the easily traversed Mediterranean basin" (Makari 2021, 11). Yet, the Mediterranean region historically has been the heart of the construction of the fault lines between "the West and the rest." Although still debated, the origins of notions of the "West" and the "East" can be traced back to the split of the Roman Empire into two parts in the third century AD. Nevertheless, whether it was the Ottoman conquest of the Eastern Roman capital, Constantinople, and its renaming as Istanbul (the capital of the Islamic empire, or the European colonization of North and Sub-Saharan Africa, the borders of what is referred to as "Western civilization" have been heavily and repetitively (re)drawn in this geography.[5] The historical constructs of this separation are important, as they "helped justify Western colonial expansion as a benevolent effort to bestow civilization on the East" (Makari 2021, 11). Rather than sheltering benevolent acts, however, the Mediterranean "has long been a center of economic extraction, racist violence and imperial ambition—indeed today, the Mediterranean is immediately recognizable as the symbol of Fortress Europe's brutal border regimes" (Hawthorne 2022, 10). That is, EU policies rendered "the Euro-Mediterranean" an issue of security (Zardo and Wolff 2022, 690).

Having lived most of my life in this geography, I faced my own positionality as one of the border people in this hypersecuritized border zone. But for an Istanbulite, who in everyday life routinely crosses the Bosphorus channel, "normalized" as a geographical divide between Europe and MENA, there was *nothing natural* about the constructed fault line. Despite the bitter history and tense geopolitics of borders between Turkey and Greece, many Greeks and Turks have felt familiar with each other's intimate lifeworlds—cuisine, culture, architecture, music, humor, and so on. The linguistic familiarity owing to the widespread use of Turkish words in the Greek border islands was as striking as the use of Arabic words in the Sicilian dialect of Italian language. Is it surprising, then, that the so-called stranger may often not feel strange in the borderlands of the neighboring country, absent the securitization of the borders and the crossers? Owing to an intimate familiarity formed through centuries of crossing and interplay of trade, population exchange, war, conquest, and so on, border cities have been not only gateways and passages but also hubs of frequent interaction with what was politically construed as the feared stranger.

Emboldened by the feelings of such familiarity, on one occasion I accepted the invitation of my Greek activist friends to accompany them to a refugee camp on one of the Greek border islands. Although entrance to the camps was banned for everybody, including locals, I entered with a team that was delivering routine medicine and other basic needs, such as shoes, blankets, toothbrushes, shampoo, and so on. As my friends were cheerfully welcomed by the refugee children in the camp, I could not help taking photos. The misery in the refugee camp was not describable without the visuals of children playing in sewage; of migrants sleeping on the concrete under the sun due to lack of mattresses and tents; of people waiting the whole day in line in the intolerable heat for a cup of inedible food. Subsequently, I took more photos and got caught by the surveillance cameras. After seeing my multiple passports and making me erase all the pictures on my cell phone, the local police relaxed and were getting ready to let me go. But the situation worsened abruptly when a higher-ranking security official stormed into the camp's police station. Infuriated upon seeing my birthplace on my passport, she started screaming "Constantinople" at the police officers, creating a scene and terrorizing everybody in the police quarter. Reading the room carefully, I observed the swift transformation from the previous relaxed mood to fear in the officers' eyes. In highlighting the confusion, anxiety, and its "flip side, aggression" that the stranger may provoke, Makari (2021, 1–2) notes that "scared human beings are capable of terrible things. . . . Only later, often much later, may we discover that these victims had little to do with the fear that possessed us."

Before conducting seven years of field research in the border zones, I used to feel a naïve optimism and comfort there. I was comforted by the physical closeness (a short boat ride) and Greek cultural affinities to my homeland, as well as my multiple citizenships and my residence and work in the United States. But I was not mindful yet of the fact that even these documents of privilege, such as citizenship, would not make a difference to the aggrandized jurisdiction of border security.[6] The racialized strangers at the physical border are easily stripped of everything they have and everything they are. Once they are dehumanized, their entire existence becomes reduced to a trivial object of securitization.

Accordingly, for the high-ranking security professional in the camp, I was merely a threat, a feared Muslim from across the border. It took my activist friends a lot of explaining about who I was and that I had official permission to conduct research on the island, to try to convince the border police that I was not a human trafficker but an "innocent" professor. Even though I had not felt in danger in the border zones until that day, I realize now, looking back, that I was anything but safe in that place where pro-migrant activism and practices were criminalized arbitrarily as acts of collusion with human traffickers. Despite my legal documents and research permit, in that border site and at that time, I was the perfect stranger that Europe feared, targeted, racialized, and criminalized.[7] Yet, the persons who cross the border are not feared for who they are. Rather, they are made into objects of fear, targeted as dangerous as the result of border securitization and the acts and spectacles of the border regime. Europe's southern borderlands with MENA provide a perfect example. While securitization is not a new phenomenon, September 11 served to catalyze Islamophobia and racialization of Muslims (Furedi 2007; Fekete 2009; for the racialization of Muslims, see Barreto and Sindi 2020; Ali and Whitham 2020; Selod 2019). But the heightened control and closure of EU borders in the aftermath of the outbreak of the Syrian civil war marked the beginning of this project that contextualizes safety and (in)security through an in-depth inquiry of everyday life. Hence, the dehumanization of migrants by the EU's new hotspot regime triggered this ethnography.

ACKNOWLEDGMENTS

This book blossomed and developed during multiple political tragedies that shook up the world in the last decade starting with the outbreak of the Syrian civil war. It is in this worsening dire sociopolitical context that I repeatedly observed how emotions were pitted against reason and where emotions have been consistently dismissed and dissociated from world politics. This ethnography is a challenge to those who fail to realize that all (geo)politics are emotional. During the period of this research, I was first puzzled and then disappointed to watch the international left, including a sizable section of "democrats" who self-identified as defenders of human rights and justice, abandon their commitments to humanity and condemn emotionality as a menace. Watching injustice and violence with a cold heart, passively and nonreactively was rendered a cool skill that only the "nonemotional" could achieve.

Thankfully, the past decade also became the most blessed part of my social and academic life and research experience. This part of my life is unforgettable, because I got to know and developed deep gratitude to communities of people who worked and acted beyond their comfort zones and reached and cared for people outside ethnic and racial "tribes." I had the privilege of meeting and living among wonderful people who resisted the securitization and racialization of migrants with their hearts and minds, risking their own criminalization. I consider myself extremely lucky to be embraced and surrounded by migrants and their allies who pushed back and fought against the fear that has become the main defining characteristic of (geo)politics across the world. This book would not exist without these brave souls, who shared similar core values of justice and freedom for all, including the racialized migrants. I learned tremendously from their experiences, emotions, and skills. I found shelter in their company, as they shared sorrow and joy as well as despair and hope with open hearts at a time when the world was passively witnessing unlimited violence towards displaced Muslim and Black people. The migrant solidarity at Europe's southern border zone with the Middle East and North Africa is so embracing in its local, cross-border, and transnational reach that there is no way I could name all these displaced people and their allies. Owing to confidentiality, I am not able to name any of my migrant interlocutors and friends, whose courage, integrity, and determination I greatly admire. To them: I love you all with all my heart in this violent world that encroaches human dignity and criminalizes layers of human potential piece by piece.

The research for this project could not have been conducted without the cooperation of the pro-migrant municipalities in Athens and Palermo, as well as many local politicians in solidarity. My special thanks go to Mayor Leoluca Orlando and Vice Mayor on Migrant and Refugee Affairs Lefteris Papagiannakis, who generously and consistently shared not only their time for many years but also their experience, thoughts, reactions, and emotions with me. I continued meeting with both Orlando and Papagiannakis for many long hours between 2017 and 2024. Together with their municipal teams, the support they offered me was precious. Dionysia Lambiri in Athens municipality and Alessandro Lombardi in Palermo municipality connected me with large numbers of nongovernmental organizations and activists. Papagiannakis helped me reach the mayors of the Greek border islands. The mayors of Leros, Chios, and Samos kindly responded to my requests for interviews. Lampedusa's mayor Toto Martello spent half of the day with me, answering all my questions in detail. Pietro Bartolo, Lampedusa's famous doctor of arriving migrants and a member of the European Parliament for two successive terms (2019–present), shared his experiences and challenges about his work both as a doctor and as a politician. Erasmo Palazzotto, former member of the Italian Parliament and a founder of Mediterranea

Saving Humans, kindly offered his views on several puzzles that motivated my research. Luigi de Magistris, mayor of Naples, gave me an interview and helped me understand his alliance with Mayor Orlando and the solidarity between Palermo and Naples in resisting securitization of migration. It is impossible to name all the municipal actors that I interviewed and collaborated with border cities and islands. I thank Maria Stragaki, a former vice mayor of Athens, Mariangela Di Gangi, a member of the City Council of Palermo, Fausto Melluso, a former member of the City Council of Palermo, Adham Darawsha, a former vice mayor of Palermo, and Ermioni Frezouli, member of the city council of Chios. I traveled to Geneva to interview four officials of the UN Refugee Agency (UNHCR). Many thanks go to Denise Garcia for hosting me and connecting me with them in Geneva.

I am indebted to Alessandra Sciurba, the former president of Mediterranea Saving Humans, Italy, and a founder of the law clinic at the University of Palermo, and Nadina Christopoulou, the founder of Melissa Network, Greece, two passionate and unstoppable women who became my good friends and academic and activist allies. Thank you so much for fighting so many injustices and crimes against humanity, both masked and blatant, that remain unpunished and for sharing your secrets for remaining strong and undeterrable even in the face of evil. Lidia Tilotta, anchorperson at RAI Italia in Palermo and the author of two books, became a dear friend, a reliable source of trust and truth, a political ally, and emotional bulwark against an increasingly anti-immigrant and inhumane world and brutal borders.

I am grateful to Francesco Bellina, a talented Sicilian photojournalist and research photographer, who generously allowed me to use his stunning photos, one of which became the cover of my book. Over many years, I learned a lot from his adventurous critical mind, love for humanity, and meaningful collaboration. I am also thankful for the pleasure to work with Francesca Guarino. In May 2024, she became the teaching assistant for the field research course I taught in Palermo on borders, security, and migration. Even though we met towards the very end of my book project, it was wonderful to learn about her admirable politics, adorable character, and critical ideas. Fausto Melluso kindly hosted my class in the youth center of Palermo, which provided a dynamic venue for interacting with migrant and native (non)activists in Palermo. Since we met in 2019, Fausto has always been there to talk, discuss, and update me on all aspects of city, solidarity, and migrant politics in Palermo and beyond. Claudio Arestivo, one of the founders of Moltivolti in Palermo, was consistently available and collaborative since the beginning of this project.

This book benefited vastly from numerous long, rich conversations with Maurizio Di Lucchio, a journalist of RAI, Giorgio Ruta from rescue teams in Palermo, Sotiria Kyriakopoulou and Dina Vardaramotou from pro-migrant civil society organizations, and Anastassia Papakonstantinou, a United Nations representative in the Greek border islands. In Leros, Ilay Örs, Cengiz Aktar, Lavanta Milona, Elektra Kostopoulou, and her mother, Matina Katsiveli, generously offered me their time and hospitality. In Chios, Erminoni Frezouli hosted me in her home, introduced me to solidarity and invited me to activists' meetings. Carlo de Marco, a researcher of Lampedusa, connected me with solidarity and municipality in Lampedusa. There, Francesco Piobichi and Chloe Haralambous from Seawatch helped me reach out to newly arriving migrants, locals, and Lampedusa's Mayor Toto Martello.

In Palermo, Chiara Giubilaro and Alessandra Di Maio have generously shared their critical minds with me and my students. Kathrin Zippel, Alessandra Ciucci, Nina Silvanus, and Gordana Rabrenovic connected me to key interlocutors who played crucial roles in my research in Athens and Palermo. I consider myself very lucky to have these great colleagues in my life, and I deeply appreciate their collegiality, support, and cooperation.

Parts of this book were supported by many fellowships. I was a Dahrendorf fellow at London School of Economics (2016), Erasmus Mundus scholar in 4CITIES at Vrejde University in Belgium (2017), Max Planck fellow at Göttingen (2018), and a visiting professor at Trento University (2019). During the year of my sabbatical in 2021–22, I was Fulbright Research Chair of Canada and spent the spring semester of 2022 at Carleton University in Ottawa and Montreal. I cannot give enough thanks for the hospitality and support I received during these fellowships from my hosts, Esra Özyürek at Cambridge University, Mario Diani at Trento University, Van der Veer at Max Planck, Bas van Heur at 4CITIES at Vrejde University, and Yiagadeesen Samy at Carleton University, as well as Elena Mandalenakis for her invitation and hospitality at Regional Stability in South East Europe workshops in Crete organized by the Austrian National Defense Academy, and Petros Vamvakas, who invited me to the annual seminars of the Institute of Eastern Mediterranean Studies in Boston. I am grateful for the multiple opportunities to share my work with experts in these intellectually vibrant environments.

My wonderful friends and colleagues Amílcar Barreto and Denise Garcia, were my rocks where I found comfort and support from the beginning to the end of this project. Denise and Amílcar never stopped encouraging me to continue my research through COVID-19, even when traveling became challenging, and when years of fieldwork in violent border zones had taken a toll on me. I was blessed by the collegiality, friendship, and cooperation of Julie Boudoukara, the program coordinator of International Affairs at Northeastern University. Julie not only traveled to Palermo for three successive years and helped me teach a one-month fieldwork course; she also supervised and orchestrated a high turnover of undergraduate students in Boston who transcribed my interviews. I appreciate the good work done by many students, particularly Yadah Ampofo. I am indebted to Julie for her hands-on attentive oversight of a highly complex logistics of transcription over many years.

My mentor and dear friend John A. Hall read drafts of several chapters and as always gave me precious comments helping me to flesh out the big picture. His questions pushed and encouraged me to expand the geographical and intellectual confines of my previous research and academic career. Yeşim Bayar, my intellectual soul mate, read the entire book and several drafts of some chapters. Without Yeşim, the edges of intellectual journeys would be a lonely place. Didier Fassin commented on and asked constructive questions about the second chapter. Tom Vicino read drafts of fellowship applications and the book proposal and gave me excellent feedback. Rawan Arar served as an excellent discussant at an ASA panel, engaging Chapter 2. Petros Vamvakas and Youly Diamanti-Karanou read Chapter 1 and gave wonderful comments. Denise Garcia made great points and critiques on Chapter 3 and the book proposal.

I benefited immensely from the comments of the anonymous reviewers of my solo-authored articles published in *Political Geography* and *Journal of Urban Affairs*. Chapter 1 is derived in part from my article "Refugees in Borderlands: Safe Places Versus Securitization," *Journal of Urban Affairs* 43, no. 6 (2021): 756–80, copyright © 2021 Urban Affairs Association, reprinted by permission of Taylor & Francis Ltd., https://www.tandfonline.com, on behalf of Urban Affairs Association. Chapter 2 is a revised version of my article "The Geopolitics of Fear: Pro-Refugee Resistance Against Europe's Racial Security," *Political Geography* 109 (2023): 103047, https://authors.elsevier.com/sd/article/S0962-6298(23)00225-1.

I had the privilege of having as the editor of my book Dan LoPreto, whose questions and comments left major impacts on the manuscript. From the start to the end, working with him was a great pleasure. The title of the book owes its charm to Dan. I was lucky to receive the constructive comments of the anonymous reviewers of Stanford University Press.

During my long stays and frequent travels to multiple research sites, many friends and family members paid visits from several countries. My high school friends in Istanbul, a group of amazing people with a deep and genuine connection, visited several times, and on one occasion, they even moved our class reunion to Athens so as not to deprive me from their precious company. Yeşim Bayar, Idil Elveriş, and Turgut Kışınbay my intellectual counterparts, have always been a phone call away. Harika Özkaya, my confidant in Boston, listened to me when I was on my game or not; when I was at the peak of my motivation or the lowest point and in all seasons. She also drove with me to my Fulbright sabbatical site in Canada. My invaluable yogi friends from Stil Studio have been an incredible source of energy, positivity, and light, even though the worsening border violence was dimming our light and hopes.

My wonderful parents, Batur and Sevim, and my big, loud, warm family, including Kuzey, Esra, Semra, Ahmet, Hasan, Nesrin, Melis, and Luca, traveled from Istanbul many times to visit me in my field sites when I was away for fieldwork for long periods. My son, Sean, spent a lot of time with me in the borderlands during his most formative ages between eleven and sixteen. His calm and pleasant presence made even the most challenging parts of my field research smooth and meaningful. My love for him lit me up during years of research and writing, when he was becoming a young adult and starting to argue politics with me. I am blessed for the abundance of love, kindness, warmth, and support poured out to me from these unique human bonds.

In a world of increasing political slipperiness and self-centered indifference to human suffering, this book could not be finalized without the genuineness, openness, reliability of these beautiful souls: native and migrant activists, family, and friends.

THE GEOPOLITICS OF FEAR

Introduction

The peak of refugee flow in the aftermath of the Syrian civil war culminated in the tightening of the EU's southern borders. Member states of the EU closed their borders at the cost of violating the 1951 Geneva Refugee Convention, when facing refugee influx from the Global South. My multisited ethnography began in the aftermath of the agreements between Turkey and the EU (2016) and between Italy and Libya (2017) that aimed to slow down and gradually stop the flow of *refugees* and *irregular migrants*.[1] The externalization of the EU borders to the MENA states by way of Europe's collusion with and funding of Turkey, Libya, and, in 2023, Tunisia turned the Mediterranean Sea into a mass graveyard. In weaponizing Libya and Tunisia against forced displacement, the EU has been sponsoring crimes against humanity, violence, and rape (see *The Guardian* 2024).

The violence at the EU's southern borders put a spotlight on Europe's "racial security" (Fassin 2005; Turam 2023) and "racial borders" (De Genova 2017, 2018a, 2018b; Jones 2021), which prioritized the "protection of a European, Christian, and white civilization against Third World, Muslim, or black populations" (Fassin 2005, 381).[2] Clearly, the explicit racial character of the EU's border management defeats the presumed "neutrality" of the notion of security. Considering that "the enforcement of border control [was] not the same for everyone" (Fassin 2020, 2), racial

1

borders were defined as "territorial and political border regimes that disparately curtail movement (mobility) and political incorporation (membership) based on race" (Achiume 2022, 449).[3] Racial borders maintain international migration and human mobility as racial privileges.

The Geopolitics of Fear delves into the most vulnerable, yet understudied, spot of racial security regimes, the border cities on major refugee routes in Europe. The locus of this book was motivated by a series of puzzles: While nativism, racism, and Islamophobia have been on the rise in Europe (Duyvendak et al. 2023; Ponce 2023; Armenta 2017; De Genova 2018b), I found vigorous day-to-day resistance to securitization of borders in the EU's gateway cities to the MENA region. In a geography where the EU (and national) security forces were pushing migrants back across the Mediterranean Sea to MENA countries, the resistance in arrival cities was pushing relentlessly against the EU's anti-migrant security regime. While the majority of Europeans from all political fronts increasingly perceived Muslim and Black migrants as "societal illness" and treated them as "threats" (Karyotis and Skleparis 2016, 266; De Genova 2010, 2018b), several disobedient southern European municipalities were confronting the EU's securitization of borders and migration.[4]

Dissecting the resistance against securitization, this book explores the underlying (f)actors that facilitated and contributed to the flourishing of a multiscalar solidarity reaching from local to transnational levels. What was the key to the rise of strong resistance in Europe's two major entrance points in the eastern and central Mediterranean? How did two capital cities, Athens in Greece and Palermo in Sicily, rise up to the challenge of resisting the racial security regime despite their difficult locations at Europe's hypersecuritized border zones? Paradoxically, how did these frontier port cities generate powerful solidarity despite common socioeconomic hardship, high unemployment rates, and austerity (Arampatzi 2017a, 2017b; Skleparis 2017)?

Beyond their similar issues of poverty and unemployment, Greece and Sicily (an autonomous region of Italy since 1948) differed in terms of the historical and geopolitical background of migration and border securitization, as well as in their ethnic and racial makeup. In scrutinizing connections and differences between the two cases, this book explores what the poor arrival cities of Athens and Palermo had in common to produce vital (pro) migrant solidarity. Through an in-depth inquiry of who, how, why, and where there was resistance to Europe's security regime, this book brings the two regions together by using a multisited ethnography. Even though pro-migrant resistance in both the eastern and central Mediterranean was generated against the same machinery—Europe's racial security—the two regions have been studied in disjunction from each other (for an exception, see Chouliaraki and Musaro 2017).[5]

Although Athens and Palermo dovetailed as two major gateways into Fortress Europe, similarities and differences between them have largely been neglected in existing literature. As migrant boats drifted away, got lost, were ignored, or pushed back by border security to international waters between Greece and Italy (for example, for the Phylos shipwreck, see Fallon et al. 2023; Simon 2023), the two border regions became more than just physically connected geographies. They are entangled geopolitically in their shared complicities and violations. Tightening and the closure of borders to irregular migrants in arrival geographics are complicit in generating violence. Contrary to the rhetoric used in justifying the war on terror, the new security practices are "the source of the violence, not a response to it" (Jones 2016, 5). Yet, the scholarly divides in studying the EU 's violent southern borders persist, and result in the partial understanding of the contextually different production of racial security. Consequently, these incomplete grasps of Europe's racial borders obscure the distinct racialization and criminalization of Muslim and Black migrants, as well as the overlapping and diverging challenges and strengths of solidarity in the eastern and central Mediterranean.

While recent critical scholarship on the "Black Mediterranean" has sparked a prolific debate (see, e.g., Proglio et al. 2021; Di Maio 2021; Pesarini 2021; Hawthorne 2022), its primary focus on the central Mediterranean largely left out the racialization of Muslim migrants from the MENA region in the eastern Mediterranean and beyond. The debate also dismissed the vastly overlooked fact that a large proportion of Black and Brown migrants were also Muslim in the increasingly Islamophobic Europe. The Mediterranean basin consists of many more forms of racism and racialization than have been implicated in existing debates (for a comprehensive analysis of anti-Muslim and anti-Black racism, see De Genova 2018b).

However, while the racialization of irregular migrants in the eastern and central Mediterranean was the result of the intertwined processes of the same inhumane border regime, the geopolitical dynamics were situated in different historical and geographic contexts. Hence, this ethnography considers the different regional players, with a focus on migrant-receiving Greece and Italy and their problematic collusion with different neighboring Muslim states—Turkey, Libya, and Tunisia. This is the first full-length book that bridges Europe's two southern peripheries: the Greek and Sicilian borderlands with the Middle East and North Africa. Together, the peripheries display the entwined processes of securitization and racialization of the Muslim and Black refugees and migrants.

The Catalyst from Security to Solidarity

The key to (pro)migrant resistance to the securitization of migration is the geopolitics of emotions. My ethnographic findings show that powerful geopolitical emotions shape native-migrant solidarity that is situated in distinct historical and geographical contexts. The book elucidates and analyzes the dialectics between a top-down securitization sustained by fear and intimidation and the bottom-up resistance empowered by emotions such as safety and local trust. Accordingly, I use *geopolitics of emotion* as an umbrella term that covers widely shared emotions incited in borderlands in response to the violent security regime.

Different from the primacy of "integration" issues and policies in destination countries, this ethnography reveals that migration rests upon the interwoven geopolitics of fear and safety in the everyday sites of arrival cities. The *geo* here enables me to situate emotions not only geographically in the border zones but also spatially in the urban sites of border cities. For example, I pit the feeling of safety, belonging, and local trust in migrant neighborhoods against the government-led fear and insecurity generated by violent borders nearby. My approach draws attention to how contrasting emotions coexist in striking proximity and shape everyday contestations in border cities. Parting ways with emotion-blind analysis in conventional studies of security, this research illuminates how the geopolitics of emotion manifest as a catalyst of local pro-migrant ways of life, practices, and discourses at Europe's violent borders. Despite roots in dissimilar historical and geographic background, the solidarity in both Athens and Palermo is primarily driven and empowered by geopolitical emotions. This finding shed light on why fear-mongering anti-migrant security regimes openly target feelings of empathy, undermine trust, and thereby, hammer the sense of safety.

My approach deviates from both international relations and the conventional understanding of geopolitics, which prioritize and confine their scope to power relations between states. The mainstream views of geopolitics have a major disregard for human dimension. Working against the persistent denial of the role of emotions in (geo)politics and world affairs, this book brings agency and emotion to the center of power relations.[6] My focus on emotions in geopolitics enables me to move beyond the global centrality of national security, which obstructs the importance of human security.[7] Demonstrating why people, their will, and their emotions matter tremendously in the context of securitization of borders and migration, my analysis pits human agency against the presumably passive audience or bystander that both security forces and theories take for granted.

Just as Europe's border regime capitalizes on the fear of a Black and Muslim invasion to fuel widespread support for the securitization of borders, other powerful emotions inspire and galvanize pro-migrant resistance and embolden solidarity against the security regime. A sense of safety, local trust, belonging, familiarity, camaraderie, dignity, hope, as well as anger exemplify some of the geopolitical emotions uncovered and analyzed in this book.

Geopolitical emotions *intervene* in the relationship between racial security and (pro)migrant resistance.[8] These intense emotions, I illustrate, *intrude* into the impact of the security regime by *guiding* local responses, reactions, and practices against the securitization of migration. My findings in both arrival cities reveal that geopolitical emotions are not given—they manifest as political choices. Both natives and migrants in Athens and Palermo temper, regulate, and rechannel geopolitical emotion in their mundane lives by making politically impactful choices, such as refusing fear, selecting whom to trust, channeling anger to assertiveness in protests, using art to fuel hope, and so on.

Importantly, however, like other subjectivities, geopolitical emotions do not transpire in a vacuum and are not chosen arbitrarily from an array of infinite emotions. They are rooted in past experiences and a collective selective remembering of a shared history, often referred to as historical or public memory (see, e.g., Özyürek 2007).[9] Collective remembering in this book includes the historical memory of relations of the peripheral border city not only with Europe (and later the EU), but also with the neighboring country in the MENA. Embedded in historical and geographical backgrounds, geopolitical emotions motivate present meaning-making and place-making, such as the making of safe places, migrant neighborhoods, and Black spaces. The ethnography contextualizes how these deeply situated emotions interrupt and disrupt the interplay between a racial security regime and solidarity. In this sense, the geopolitical emotions are the major instruments of the relationship between states with violent borders and irregular migrants.

Detailed ethnographic evidence discloses how the legacy of violence (Orlando 2001; Vradis 2020) and its current repercussions in the border city have affected natives and migrant newcomers differently and have constituted varying vulnerabilities. While natives have carried the memories of violent past, the migrants who ran from violence in their homelands went through other forms of violence during their journey across brutal borders. This project reveals and analyzes what happens after the violent journey, when they arrived in two city centers with violent legacies. "Both institutionalized and informal spaces of transit have become sites where people's mobility is regulated in a way that breaches their rights, renders them illegal and subjects to violent and protracted interventions that would be considered illegal in 'normal' circumstances" (De Vries and Guild 2018, 2164). One would expect that the intersection of these multiple layers of violence from homeland to entry points in the host land would reinforce the (geo)politics of fear. But my findings provided me with a puzzle. In these border cities, I found and documented substantial fear aversion and hatred of fear-based securitization.

Let me unpack this puzzle. Here, it is extremely important to note the different violent legacies of each port city: the lingering homegrown extralegality associated with anarchists in downtown Athens has nothing to do with the remnants of mafia-linked crimes in the city center of Palermo. Regardless of the difference, both violent legacies were capitalized on by securitizers to create an obscure sense of "global fear" and justify securitization. Concretely, the violent pasts of these cities were used to securitize migrants who were targeted, criminalized, and lumped in with local perpetrators—anarchists, traffickers, and the mafia. Even though violence and fear would typically be expected to ease and reinforce securitization, I found that the securitizers' strategies in both cities culminated in unexpected outcomes. My ethnography revealed an unnoticed dynamic: Arriving from a deadly journey with skillset of resilience and ample hope, irregular migrants played major roles in transforming the historically rooted insecurity of the city into safe places and trust relations of solidarity.

My ethnographic evidence also discloses distinct feelings and responses of natives and migrants in relations to violence in each border geography. Chapter 4 uncovers and examines how migrants tempered their responses to fear- and anger-inciting encounters with local perpetrators in Palermo. In alignment to this, mafia brutality, I argue, culminated in the political learning of a shared hatred of violence against *all* human beings in Palermo. Hence, past bloodshed had a major impact on local responses and sentiments towards vulnerable migrants. Different from widely shared sentiments in the anti-mafia movement in Palermo, anarchists' nonviolence towards civilians and their alliance with refugees contributed to a fear-aversive local politics in downtown Athens. Chapter 2 explores these local processes steered by powerful emotions, such as fear aversion, by documenting, for example, the *conditional* cooperation between anarchists and solidarity exclusively over refugee politics in Athens. In both cases, I illustrate the ways in which safe places and local trust were built and (pro) migrant activism thrived. Paradoxically, in-depth field research illuminates how solidarity rose from the ashes of a violent legacy, while also fighting against the brutal border security. A mountainous irony that deserves highlighting here is that the actors in the transitions from (in)security and local crimes to safety were the very migrants who were criminalized by the security regime.

Geopolitical emotions not only are formative of the mundane practices of nonstate actors but also play roles in the decisions and acts of state actors, policymakers, legislators, and even security forces and the police (see, e.g., Rozakou 2024; Lampredi 2024; Aradau 2004). Typical of security regimes, government-generated fear manipulates relations between ordinary people and political rule. My interviews with officials revealed the central place of emotions in decisions about local migration governance. For example, the book presents a notable contrast: I juxtapose the anti-immigrant New Democracy municipality in Athens that instrumentalizes the fear of the refugee and the radical left against Mayor Orlando's pro-migrant local government in Palermo that disobeys and confronts fear-ridden securitization by both Italy and the EU.

While the solidarity in both border cities resists manifestations of the EU's racial security, each is also positioned vis-à-vis historically formed institutional legacies—different types of nation-states, electoral and party politics, and relations with neighboring Muslim countries. *The Geopolitics of Fear* considers these different factors and how they figure in the securitization of borders as well in the interplay between political rule and geopolitical emotions. The capacity and propensity of political regimes and the political elite to generate and manipulate emotions have been theorized throughout history. Political emotions have been central to politics and political theory from Montesquieu's rule of fear by despots to Tocqueville's politics of envy, propagated by the kings to divide and rule and to turn people hostile to their fellow citizens (Hall 1992, 2013; see, Tocqueville [1856] 2008; Montesquieu [1721] 1973, [1748] 1977). The politics of fear— defined as "the strategic use and abuse of public fear for political gain" (Enroth 2017, 56)—is clearly not a new political tool. By ruling through emotions (de Wilde and Duyvendak 2016; Di Gregorio and Merolli 2016), states and regimes "promote, and legitimize what citizens must feel towards other citizens, towards themselves, towards non-citizens" (Lampredi 2024, 725). The sovereign power thereby aims to prescribe the parameters of hostility, distrust, and suspicion as well as national belonging, loyalty, and so on.

As part of the goal of controlling the reactions and practices of targeted groups, political regimes and rulers work to shape perceptions of familiarity versus strangeness (Ahmed 2000). These manipulative propensities and capacities render implausible the presumed *naturality* of who is a stranger. From this perspective, the postulated *normality* of emotions toward the so-called stranger, such as xenophobia, becomes also dubious and unpersuasive.

Despite the historical roots of the politics of fear, fear-based politics acquired a new gravity and became a catch phrase after the terrorist attacks in New York City on September 11, 2001. In the post–September 11 period, arbitrary security practices, including the securitization of migration, were largely justified by fear of the Muslim terrorist (Guild 2006). In this context, political fear has been used to refer to "people's felt apprehension of some harm to their collective well-being—the fear of terrorism, panic over crime, anxiety about moral decay—or the intimidation wielded over men and women by governments or groups" (Robin 2004, 2).[10] My findings further specify and narrow this definition by situating fear and other emotions in the racial borders. Spatially, political emotion proliferates in the violent border geography. Temporally, "affects are historically embedded" and link the past with contemporary experience (İşleyen 2023, 371).

The historical memory of Greeks and Sicilians, located at the periphery of Europe, is imbued with invasions and conquests.[11] Wide-ranging geopolitics of emotion emanate from the past and become selectively ingrained in present-day politics, such as the Greek loss of Constantinople to the Ottomans (Örs 2021) or the bitter awareness of Italy's annexation of Sicily followed by the economic and racial marginalization of the border island. Related geopolitical emotions can be found, for example, in Ilaria Giglioli's (2021) notion of "Not Being European Enough."

Greece, as Europe's economic underdog, and Sicily, as the racialized, impoverished Other, have both been perceived as lacking by European standards. But beyond their common estrangement from Europe, I also found that historical memory and feelings about Europe's colonial past differed in these two border zones. My interlocutors in Athens and Palermo reckoned Europe's complicity in more recent forced displacement rather differently. In the political imaginary of most of my Athenian interlocutors, neither Europe's economic exploitation of former colonies nor the United States' invasions of Afghanistan and Iraq were verbalized as precursors of what is referred to today as Europe's migration crisis (see Chapter 2). The Greek perspective on the refugee flow was largely obscured by the geopolitics of the eastern Mediterranean, tainted by border politics with Turkey as an imminent threat and the memories of its predecessor, the Ottoman Empire. In this sense, the Greek-Turkish relations presented an exception to the East-West power dynamics in this region, for non-European, Muslim Turkey featured as the former conqueror and current aggressor in Greek national imagery.

In terms of historical memory of borders and conquests, the case of Sicily differs from that of Greece. A widely shared Sicilian collective memory constructed centuries of successive conquests positively as the source of present-day diversity on the island. Further, many Sicilian activists were critical of Italy's colonial history, particularly its colonization of neighboring Libya, and regarded Italy's annexation of Sicily as a colonial act. But Europe's complicity in current migrations flows was voiced most vocally by Black activists and only some of their native allies in solidarity in Palermo.[12] Even though I observed that the shared feelings of marginalization and racialization facilitated bonds of native-migrant solidarity,[13] Black migrants were more assertive in their anticolonial and anti-racist articulation. Unlike in Sicily, native-migrant solidarity in Greece, one of Europe's most ethnically and religiously homogeneous countries, did not thrive on the basis of a shared sense of marginalization between Muslim refugees and Greek natives. Importantly, in both cases, their historically situated estrangement from Europe and peripheralization by no means prevented racism and Islamophobia, which surfaced in sporadic racial violence.

In addition to being rooted in historical background, emotions are also deeply embedded in present-day geopolitics. The EU's southern borders exemplify emotional geographies defined by a hectic cycle of arrival, detainment, criminalization, exploitation, deportation, and violence against racialized migrants. Yet there is no perfunctory association between violent borders and native-migrant solidarity, because not every border geography with a violent past or present produces solidarity against the securitization of migration. Unlike several southern port cities of Europe, such as Marseilles, Palermo, Naples, and Barcelona, Italy's economically better-off northern border cities, such as Trento or the northern port city of Genoa, did not stand out with comparable solidarities. In this sense, Athens and Palermo present curious cases. In proving wrong the idea that poverty is associated with the rise of (racial) violence and anti-immigrant sentiment (Karyotis and Skleparis 2016, 266), these cities embodied the cooperation between local activists, migrants, and pro-migrant municipalities.

Then, how do we explain the pro-migrant solidarity in gateway cities bordering MENA against all odds—poverty, austerity, peripheralization, racial marginalization, violent border geography, and so on. In response, my findings point to the role of geopolitical emotions. However, rather than presenting festive snapshots of sanctuaries and welcoming cities, this book dwells on the dynamics of high levels of contestation in daily life in the agentic border cities. From this perspective, pro-migrant practices in Palermo and the creation of safe places for refugees in Athens manifest not as peaceful and welcoming sanctuary activities but as daily struggles with the EU's security regime and local anti-migrant actors. My analysis exposes the leverage frontier cities have in resisting and dismantling the taken-for-granted "global fear" of Muslim and Black migrants. The book uncovers how the residents of (pro)migrant neighborhoods in the city centers of Athens and Palermo display an aversion to government-constructed fear. I claim that the geopolitics of emotion are integral in forming, transforming, contesting, interrupting, and even evading the securitization of migration in the least expected place that is the poor border city in the hypersecuritized borderland between Europe and MENA.

This book makes four major contributions. First, shifting the predominant focus from the global scale of fear and securitization (of migration) to the understudied local scale of pro-migrant resistance, my research shows the importance and leverage of everyday life and local politics. Second, the book reveals how geopolitical emotions intercede local responses and reactions to the security regime and its racial borders. While benefiting from existing research that shows how securitization (by walls, fences, guns, police raids) creates insecurity (Glück and Low 2017; Vallet 2014; Low and Maguire 2019), my findings complicate debates in critical security studies: Ethnographic evidence shows that geopolitical feelings of safety, local trust, hope, and so on thrive in proximity to the fear and insecurity cultivated by securitized borders. The geopolitics of emotions, I argue, disrupt and evade fear-based securitization while empowering trust-based solidarity.

Third, the book excavates the ambivalences of (extra)legality utilized in the criminalization of migrants and solidarity. Pointing to the governments' strategic conflating of migration with local crime, I problematize views and policies that present racialized migrants as threatening and dangerous regardless of the actual danger they pose (Karyotis and Skleparis 2016, 266). I document how solidarity struggles for decriminalization in daily life by disentangling the blur between legal and extralegal fields constructed by the security regime. Finally, a major finding emerged unexpectedly from the comparison of the city centers of Athens and Palermo. Putting the pieces of a large geopolitical puzzle together, I was happily surprised to find that the irregular migrant was a common spur of the shift from insecurity toward nonviolent (pro)migrant resistance in these border cities with violent legacies. Put differently, the unfairly criminalized racial migrant was the shared spark in the transformation from (in)security to solidarity in these gateways.

Decentering the Security Regime

This book decenters the predominant focus in the literature on the governance of migration and borders. First, I part ways with the prevailing interest in the policies and acts of the security regimes (see also Zardo and Wolff 2022; El Qadim et al. 2021), including the Eurocentric approaches to "integration."[14] Instead, I center on the geopolitics of fear and safety and local-migrant in solidarity in everyday life by giving them voice (see also Squire et al. 2021). Second, I denounce the terminology of refugee "crisis,"[15] a term that the EU has conveniently appropriated to justify the securitization of borders and migration. *Securitization* refers to the process in which "extraordinary narratives, means and procedures are employed to deal with *non-traditional* security challenges" (Stivas 2021, 3; Buzan et al. 1998, italics added) such as migration, pandemics, and converts to Islam.[16] Beyond this basic definition, scholarship on the securitization of migration is divided, mainly along the lines of focus, locus, and methodology. This book has an understudied locus (the border city on the major refugee route) and a methodology (multisited ethnography of everyday life in borderlands) that is rather marginalized in conventional security studies. Focusing on agency and geopolitical emotions, I bring political geography and critical security studies into a conversation with urban and border ethnographies.[17] Below, I discuss the three interdisciplinary debates that the book engages with: emotions in geopolitics, (de)criminalization of migration, and gateway cities at racial borders.

Primacy of Emotions and Agency in Geopolitics

In conventional security studies, an issue is deemed a matter of security only "when the elites declare it to be so" (Waever 1998, 6). Originally deliberated among international relations scholars, this state-centered approach generalized the totality of nonstate actors as "the audience." The Copenhagen school argued further that acceptance of the audience was a necessary precondition for successful securitization (Buzan et al. 1998), although the audience was not clearly defined in terms of identity, agency, or spatiality. Consequently, the concept remained underdeveloped (Côté, 2016; Stivas 2021).[18] Departing from the vague and sweeping use of the term *audience* to refer to the public (here, the "European public"; e.g., Stivas 2024), critical security studies later brought the individual to the center of analysis (Bigo and Guild 2005; Guild 2009; Balzacq and Carrera 2016; Bigo 2016; Bilgiç 2013). Benefiting from these works, my ethnography focuses on disobedient local actors who resist securitization not only by refusing to be lumped in as "the audience" but also by confronting the security regime and its policies, anti-immigrant ruling elite, and security professionals and their political acts.

Concretely speaking, pro-migrant neighborhoods in the city centers of Athens and Palermo display how local dissidents preempt the threat and rebuke the fear constructed by the securitizing elite. Just as crisis management is the key strategy of securitization (Bigo and Guild 2005; Guild 2009; Mountz and Hiemstra 2014), fear, danger, and threat are the building blocks of a state of emergency. Accordingly, the resistance to the "global enormity of securitization" (Hagmann 2017, 423) entails a rejection of crisis management, as well as the geopolitical emotions, such as fear and danger, underpinning the experience of the crisis.

In this respect, the politics of scale matters tremendously. The global magnitude of the securitization of borders and migration is coupled and backed up with another metanarrative: global fear. The securitization of borders and migration works best when it achieves wide-scale fear of the Muslim refugee and/or the Black migrant. By way of bloating discourses of a Muslim or African "invasion" of European geography (De Haas 2008; Turam 2023; Hawthorne 2022, 13) and the global fear of terrorism (Yuval-Davis et al. 2019, 2–3), the racialized migrant becomes the bread and butter of the securitization of borders and migration.

However, it is ironic that the bulk of scholarship on global fear makes "little or no reference to the feelings, perceptions, views, subjectivities or bodies of those who are *supposed to be* fearful" (Pain 2009, 471). Recent theories of global fear have largely neglected earlier works in sociology and criminology that linked vulnerability and marginality with fear, for example, in the context of racial and domestic violence (Pain 2001; Valentine 1989). As an outcome of the "War on Terror," the importance of geopolitics has risen drastically at the expense of disregarding the human dimension—emotions and everyday life (Pain and Smith2008, 5). One way of challenging the neglect of agency and emotion is to spatialize fear and safety. The circular process between space and fear complicates the issue of securitization. While securitized spaces generate fear, fear of the targeted Other reinforces the social and physical production of the securitized space (Low and Maguire 2019; Glück and Low 2017; Vallet 2014; Besteman and Gusterson 2010; Caldeira 2000). Referred to as "security scapes," these securitized zones, like borders, reproduce "racist social relations, institutional arrangements, architectural details, legal and symbolic encodings and affective structures of feeling" (Low and Maguire 2019, 13).

Deeply situating fear and safety in everyday life in border zones, my ethnography raises several questions: What happens when the presumably fearful and passive audience of securitization is unfearful of and indifferent or disobedient to the security regime, as in the case of residents of (pro)migrant neighborhoods in Athens and Palermo? What conditions and factors embolden and empower local pro-migrant resistance to securitization? What happens when the fifth-time mayor of Palermo, Mayor Orlando, confronts Italy's inhumane border policies by announcing to the world that he cannot be intimidated by the Italian government because he fought all his life with the Sicilian mafia? Like the macro theories of securitization that take for granted a receptive (and submissive) audience, theories of global fear largely assume a fearful society. Rapidly mushrooming theories of global fear have largely bypassed and dismissed *whose* fear is being discussed and how people respond and react rather differently to the constructed fear.

Beyond the sweeping theories of the universalization of fear, to which geographers have also sometimes contributed, we need a more attentive understanding of "what is happening on 'the ground' in the places and lives that people inhabit" (Pain 2009, 467). My research in Exarcheia, the historically insurgent anarchist corner of Athens, provides a perfect laboratory for studying *different* responses and emotions of pro-migrant residents to the security regime. Even under police raids and surveillance by security forces, the neighborhood displays an aversion to the government-led fear in resisting the criminalization of Muslim refugees and their allies. My in-depth analysis of Exarcheia challenges "the artificial scaling" (Sziarto and Leitner 2010, 160) of fear and its twin concept of securitization as global, all-encompassing phenomena. To analyze the fear-aversive urbanity in the context of security regimes, I bridge the rapidly growing literature on emotional geographies, affective geopolitics (İşleyen 2023; Gökariksel and Secor 2018; Askins 2016; Pain and Smith 2008; Stierl 2016) and urban ethnographies of (in)security (see Glück and Low 2017; Low and Maguire 2019).

The Geopolitics of Fear reveals wide-ranging local responses to an anti-immigrant security regime shaped by the geopolitics of emotions. For example, in Athens, I found deep frustration, contempt, and distrust of the conservative New Democracy government (2019–present), concurrently experienced with feelings of safety and local trust in (pro)migrant neighborhoods (Chapters 1and 2). Importantly, despite socioeconomic insecurities and government distrust, my interlocutors expressed feeling safe and no fear in the pro-migrant neighborhood even in the face of government crackdowns and police attacks.[19] In Palermo, my findings similarly show that the power of geopolitical emotions, such as local trust, a sense of belonging, and hope, gave rise to a dynamic Black activism. I maintain that solidarity, nurtured by geopolitical emotions, holds the key to evading and circumventing a fear-based securitization of migration.

The contextual analysis of emotions and agency differentiates this research from the bulk of works in migration studies. The predominant tendency in migration studies is to uncritically adopt the Eurocentric approaches, particularly the integration paradigm and policies. The integrationist rhetoric often flattens the deep contextuality by surpassing the human dimension manifest in people's sense of fear, safety, dignity, belonging, (dis)trust, hope, and so on (for critics of integrationist approaches, see Ciucci 2022, 4; Turam 2023, 2015; Spencer and Charsley 2021). In pointing to the problems and limitations of the integration paradigm, both empirically and conceptually, throughout the chapters, my primary interest remains in the link between sense of local trust and safety in everyday sites. As Askins (2016, 517) compellingly argues, the safety of migrants is explained better by "the emotional and embodied sense of being 'in place' and 'secure' " than by the "fixed and fixing notions of exclusion/inclusion."

Decriminalizing Migration

European Union policies present "the Euro-Mediterranean" as an issue of security on the basis of a fault line constructed between Europe and "the Other" (Zardo and Wolff 2022, 690; Bigo 2014). Subsequently, EU member states have adopted "crimmigration" laws that link discourses of crime to immigration by transforming "irregular" migrants into "illegal" persons (De Genova 2013, 2017; Bazurli and Delclós 2022; Bessant and Watts 2022; Fabini 2017; Sciurba 2017; Karyotis and Skleparis 2016; Briskman and Fiske 2016; Selod 2016; Armenta 2017; Cusumano and Bell 2021; Hagan and Bachelet 2024). In Italy, migration governance primarily "comprise[d] the police who manage[d] 'illegality' rather than controlling, punishing, or expelling illegal migrants" (Fabini 2017, 47). Referred to as "differential inclusion" (Fabini 2017, 49; Sciurba 2017, 101), Italy's migration governance does not "serve to exclude migrants from the national space, but to incorporate them in a subordinate and vulnerable position" (Giglioli 2021, 727). This system, referred to as an "illegality factory" by D'Angelo (2018), works like "machinery" and generates illegality by "releasing" migrants without documents. The system sets migrants "free to stay, provided they are first deprived of rights, including the right to work legally, the right to welfare, the right to be visible" (D'Angelo 2018, 2224).

By denying irregular migrants their rights as human beings, refugees, or asylum seekers, the system pushes migrants to the spheres of illegality and toward local illicit actors. Refugees and irregular migrants are left with no other option but extralegal venues, such as transportation by human traffickers, housing offered by anarchist squats in Exarcheia, and income by the informal historic market of Ballarò in Palermo.

How, then, does the border city resist this full-fledged system of crimmigration in local everyday life? Representing a politically meaningful instance, Palermo embodied a local effort of decriminalization under the leadership of Mayor Orlando, who became internationally famous for his efforts to convince the EU to lift the residency permit requirement—a major basis of criminalization. Against the background of the ambiguity and discretion in migration governance at the EU's borderlands (see for example, Heyer 2022), my findings illustrate how the peripheral border municipality took advantage of these ambiguities to create some room to turn the system of arbitrary criminalization upside down. Concretely, Chapter 3 shows how ambiguities created to punish and discriminate against migrants were reversed to be used to advantage them in Orlando's municipality.

I draw from a sociological approach to the constitution as a lived experience to showcase Palermo's municipal government and local supporters and how they used "everyday constitutionalism" as a shield (Abel 2018; Scheppele 2017). My findings disclose how a shared faith in the rule of law and reliance on the constitution in everyday life helped challenge and evade security decrees that violated human rights and international law. The case addresses how, under strong pro-migrant municipal leadership, the solidarity can put both the constitution and international law to work in the fight against the unlawful procedures of securitization. Importantly, however, the politicization of the constitution in everyday life functioned as an enabler, rather than a motor of change in challenging unfair criminalization of migrants. The main push comes from geopolitical emotions prompted by the city's past experience of mafia supremacy and injustices. That is, the agentic city manifests a shared contempt for arbitrary rule, violence, and violation of human rights.[20] My ethnography reveals that even under attack from the government that targets and securitizes Palermo, the pro-migrant municipal government and activists remain committed to and invest their trust in the constitution as a major protector of human rights.

In the context of immoral borders (El Qadim 2021), ethnographic evidence pits the unfair criminalization of migrants against actual homegrown crime and the historically rooted insecurity of each border city. Revealing differing local perceptions and discourses of (in)security, I explore how native-migrant solidarity is affected by and responds to local contestations over who and what is legal and illegal.

Why Do the Cities at Racial Borders Matter?

The UNHCR's estimation of forcibly displaced people in April 2024 was about 120 million.[21] Even though most of these displaced people reside in urban areas, the city as shelter for urban refugees has not received sufficient attention (Koizumi and Hoffstaedter 2018; Rabrenovic and Bunar 2021). Border cities on refugee routes stand out in this respect for their strategic proximity to the entry points and ongoing back-and-forth of solidarity actors between landing sites (in this case, border islands) and the frontier city. Owing to the continual irregular border-crossing, rescue and reception become routinized practices and impact the flow of everyday life in the city.

Second, the place and role attributed to border cities at securitized violent borders present a paradox. On the one hand, gateway cities are often misperceived as parts, if not boosters, of border security that help the sovereign power to govern migration. They are often lumped in with multiple instruments of states' national security and territorial jurisdiction mandates. These common misconstructions reduce the city's geopolitically formed and historically embedded agency to a one-dimensional functional understanding of security apparatus. The scholarly preoccupation with security regimes and their policies partly explains the scarcity of in-depth research on dissident gateway cities at racial borders.

On the other hand, because of their hybridity formed through their history of cross-border interaction, border cities are also perceived and stigmatized in conjunction with what is across the border, the racialized Other. Hence, depending on their proximity to the Global South, some arrival cities in the peripheral geographies have been racialized and even condemned as uncivilized, underdeveloped, or corrupt. These stigmatizations not only dismiss the importance of cross-border mobility in the historical evolution of these frontier cities (as manifested in architecture, art, cuisine, and so on); they also bypass the importance of transnational networks and local resistance to brutal border regimes in these urban centers. Even though the Dublin Regulation[22] complicated the role of border cities by assigning asylum processing to arrival countries (Ferreira 2019), this book shows how Athens and Palermo, with minimal resources, inventively maneuvered the flow of refugees on the ground and carved out safe spaces against the background of violent racial security. Hence, notwithstanding the tightening of border security and increasing encroachments of security regimes, this work challenges reductive understandings of the border city as an instrument of the security regime, by spotlighting the resistance and transformation they generate in the periphery.

Overall, southern Europe's arrival cities and municipalities are relatively understudied compared to rapidly growing interest in economically developed urban centers in the destination countries in the North, such as Milan, Paris, Berlin, Amsterdam, and so on.[23] Contrary to this academic trend, after conducting pilot studies in Berlin in 2018 and Trento in 2019,

I was drawn into the everyday dynamics of resistance in southern border cities. My findings pit the dynamics of bottom-up bonding and solidarity in these Mediterranean port cities against the top-down mandates and policies of integration.

In Palermo, I met many racially mixed couples over the years. Mixed couples were a common phenomenon in the city center of Palermo.[24] They shared with me instances of racism during their visits to northern Italy. For example, Sofia, an Italian border activist, told me how the Milanese talked to her in English in the street when she was with her baby and her partner, a Senegalese refugee. Sofia was the daughter of an Italian mother and a Libyan migrant father. Her parents were based in Milan. She felt offended and humiliated by the northerners' assumption that they were a British family, despite the high Italian proficiency of her Senegalese partner, which impressed native Italians. Hence, racialization vis-à-vis speaking English had nothing to do with an Italian accent; the postulation was that Italians "do not mix racially." This blatantly racist assumption did not align with everyday life in Palermo's city center.

When pro-migrant resistance and spaces were shrinking under repression and attack from securitizers across the world (e.g., Della Porta and Steinhilper 2022), migrant-led associations were multiplying in Palermo. Sofia and her Black partner felt cherished and respected in Palermo's migrant neighborhood in the city center, which was a hub of an interracial, transnational native-migrant solidarity. Their baby was communally embraced and spent her days with her parents and other activists in the migrant association, a space of warm sociability that welcomed people, music, cuisines, and more from all over the world. This explains why Sofia, who had previously worked in Greece and the Netherlands as a researcher and held an academic position in Britain at that time, was determined to spend her life in Palermo. I asked about her prospects of finding a job in Palermo besides volunteering at the association and answering emergency calls from the sea. She responded to me that the "treatment of her family with dignity was more important than her status and career."[25]

Nevertheless, I am not preaching here the sanctuary qualities of utopian "Pleasantvilles" at the borders. To the contrary, my findings illustrate high levels of contestation and erratic racial violence in these border cities. Clearly, there is no universal intrinsic quality to be attributed to the border city. Similarly, there is no common perfunctory characteristic of a place of refuge (Turam 2021; Darling and Bauder 2019). These cities have *no essence* that assures their residents a peaceful and anti-racist coexistence, legally or sociopolitically. Rather, they evolve as a result of the high turnover of migrants in these emotional geographies that themselves have deep roots in history, and by generating bottom-up practices of carving out some safe spaces for irregular migrants. However, these local processes are largely obscured by right-wing populist discourses, far-right anxieties, and acts of securitization.[26] Furthermore, even though there is nothing inherent in the fear of the irregular border crosser, the constructed fear and stigma of the racialized migrant is by no means trivial. Hence, a main goal of this book is to situate sites of resistance into broader racial security. Against the background of prima facie "neutral" legal categories of border regimes and international legal doctrine, E. Tendayi Achiume (2022, 445), elucidates that the borders of the First World are inherently racial and violent because they privilege whiteness and govern the racialized inclusion and exclusion of human beings (see also, De Genova 2017, 2018a, 2018b; Jones 2016, 2021). As "race operates as a means of enforcing liberal territorial and political borders . . . international migration governance is also a mode of racial governance" (Achiume 2022, 445).

But if border cities are neither de facto sanctuaries nor perfunctory vessels of racial border regime and racial security, why did they become the main loci of this book? These cities provide remarkable laboratories in which the geopolitics of emotions mediate most explicitly between the brutal racial security and a dynamic resistance in everyday life. Not only the geographical proximity between inhumane physical borders and pro-migrant resistance but also the historical memory of border conflicts and local violence foster intense geopolitical emotions in these arrival cities. Frankly, even though I did not launch this project with the goal of studying gateway cities, my interest in securitization of migration and the resistance have drawn me to highly emotional geographies of entry locations.

The spatialities and temporalities in these border geographies were captured and theorized best in critical border studies and political geography, which this book relies on (e.g., Johnson et al. 2011; Jones 2016, 2018, 2021; Jones and Johnson 2015; De Genova 2017; El Qadim et al. 2021; Mountz 2020; Vradis et al. 2019; Yuval-Davis et al. 2019; Dijstelbloem and Walters

2021; Nicholls 2015; Stierl 2017; Roberts 2015). Benefiting from these critical works on borders, I explore how the securitization of migration is experienced, felt, and reacted to from the bottom up in urban centers of border zones. The analysis zeros in on dissident places in border cities that are marginalized and often neglected by the top-down perspectives prevalent in international relations. While I draw from this rich literature on borders that deeply contextualizes responses, experiences, discourses, ethics and morality from borderlands, very little is known about the link between the heightened geopolitical emotion and border cities (see, e.g., Turam 2021, 2023; Örs 2021; Frazzetta and Piazza 2022).[27]

Hence, even though the *key* actors of international governance of migration are the central state and international organizations (Guild 2009, 69), the locus of this project is the relatively less explored everyday urban space and city life in borderlands. In this respect, my research benefited from the recent shift in interest in cities from the nation-state to the local—a shift often referred to as the "local turn" (e.g., Mollenkopf and Pastor 2016; Varsanyi 2010; Bazurli and De Graauw 2022; Ridgley 2013). Most works in this vein have primarily focused on policy-related issues. Instead, this book zooms in on the deeply contextualized, spatialized flow of everyday life.

Attention to contestation and resistance in border cities enables me to tell "different stories, identify new actors and connect them with less explored local urban geopolitical contexts" (Fregonese et al. 2020, 3). As the trajectory of my research unfolded across the gateway cities from Greece to Sicily, I figured out things on the road by observing, participating, and familiarizing myself with the people, places, practices, and emotions. My critical inquiries also took me to some European cities that drew a lot of attention and were praised for their "success" in migration governance. For example, my visit to Florence in 2023 was particularly eye-opening. Contrary to the overpowering visibility, participation, and activism of Black migrants in the city center of Palermo, migrants were largely invisible in the fancy streets of downtown Florence. In contrast to the historic migrant-led market in the city center of Palermo, the local governance of migration rendered Black migrants as unseeable as possible in Florence by housing them outside the city center. My conversation with a native local scholar of migration confirmed my impressions. While Palermo was often judged for its failures in governance of migration, Florence was considered a successful case. I wondered: Since when has keeping migrants "out of sight" been a measure of success in migration governance?

My long stays in other border cities, such as Trento, near Italy's border with Austria, made me question whether some cities that were praised for their local governance of migration were in fact victors of segregation and xenophobia. Was the Black space in Palermo despised and judged as a failure from the fear-ridden xenophobic perspectives of the security regime? This controversy about the "success" of local management of migration gave me a strong incentive to write this book. Using border cities as the loci, this book presents a historically and geopolitically situated analysis of resistance by decentering the Eurocentric views about securitization of borders and racialization of migrants.

The Background of Migration and Securitization

Unlike northwestern Europe, which has received guest workers since the 1960s, southern Europe remained for a long time a migrant-sending region due to poverty. Italy and Greece did not receive much migration flow until the 1980s and 1990s and have not mastered the politics and policies of integration that northwestern European countries experimented with for decades. In the context of the "refugee crisis," European public discourses criticized Greece and Sicily as unreliable arrival countries for their "inadequate" asylum practices. While Greece was regarded "as an insufficient guardian of EU borders or as an inadequate host for newcomers" (Rozakau 2012, 563), Sicily ironically was disparaged for its receptivity even by Italian political leaders, like Matteo Salvini, who belittled the border island as "Europe's refugee camp" (BBC News 2018; Jones 2018). Europe's condescending views of its southern margins have been blunt. But increasing challenges of asylum and the EU's securitization have brought to the fore the geographical and historical significance of Europe's peripheral Mediterranean regions (Herzfeld 1987; Stivas 2021; Léonard and Kaunert 2019; Ferreira 2019).

A notable difference between the two cases lay in ethnic, racial, and religious composition. The historically formed homogeneity of Greece and the diversity of Sicily sharply contrast. "The Greek national myth of differentiation from the 'Other' " (Karyotis 2012, 399) was reinforced in the 1922 population exchange with neighboring Turkey as part of a nationalizing process of people and economies (see Hirschon 2003). Subsequently, Greece became religiously and ethnically the most homogeneous country in Europe (Karyotis, 2012, 399). Then, the 1985 Schengen Agreement on European unification led to the gradual tightening of the EU's external borders, including Greece's border with Turkey and Italy's close neighbors, Libya and Tunisia.[28] In the aftermath of the unification, border checks among EU member countries were abolished at the cost of securitization of external borders.

Long before the refugee flow from Syria, Greece had already declared migrants as "threats" during the Albanian refugee influx in the 1990s (Stivas 2021, 1). The "largest episode of (in)securitization of migration" was performed during the right-wing government by Konstantinos Mitsotakis (1989–93), the father of current prime minister Kyriakos Mitsotakis (2019–present) (Skleparis 2016, 96). The anti-immigrant rule came to a short hold in 2015 during the radical-left Syriza government, which regarded securitization and the related violation of refugees' human rights as threats to European integration (Stivas 2021). As the refugee flow to Greece via Turkey peaked in 2015 in the aftermath of the Syrian civil war, Turkey and the EU signed an agreement in March 2016 to externalize the EU borders to Turkey. Rather than deterring or ending forced displacement, though, the agreement led to increases in migrant deaths, illegal pushbacks, and violations of human rights and international law.[29]

Like Greece, Sicily, Italy's southern border island and an autonomous region, more recently became a hub for irregular migrants and asylum seekers. Although there is a long history of irregular crossings and familiarity between Sicily, Libya, and Tunisia (Ben-Yehoyada 2011, 2017), until recently, the island was predominantly a migrant-sending region. The Schengen Agreement marked the beginning of new security measures, transforming the clandestine travel of migrants from being an exception to the rule (Bigo and Guild 2005; Guild 2009). As the goal after the unification was to protect the security of Europeans at the expense of outsiders' freedom of mobility (Balzacq and Carrera 2016, 18; Bigo 2016, 44), the southern border of Italy was urged to securitize when Italy joined the Schengen area in 1997 (Balzacq and Carrera 2016).[30] Hence, Europe's integration stands as a powerful example of the juxtaposition of freedom and security.

Following increased migrant flows after the Arab Spring, the European Court of Human Rights condemned Italy in 2012 for violating the principle of *non-refoulement* (Palm 2017)—the foundational principle that outlaws sending migrants back to a country where they would face irreparable harm. Since the refugee flow from MENA peaked in the aftermath of the outbreak of the Syrian civil war, the violations of international law and agreements by the EU member states continued to rise.

National Political Landscapes and Municipal Governments

In these border geographies, the municipalities of Athens and Palermo played pivotal roles maneuvering refugee flows from outside Europe. Backed by social democrats and the Green Party, the former mayor of Athens, Georgios Kaminis (2011–19), coped with the impact of flows by creating a vice mayorship specifically focusing on migration issues. Upon the worsening of the situation and human right violations after the 2016 Turkey-EU agreement, the municipality cooperated with a strikingly high number of pro-refugee NGOs, international NGOs, and human right activists in Athens (Komporozos-Athanasiou and Papachristou 2018) and won the Innovation of Politics Award in 2017.[31]

During the peak of the migrant flow, Palermo's Mayor Orlando was serving his fourth and fifth successive terms (2012–17 and 2017–22). Upon the 2013 shipwreck of a migrant boat near Lampedusa, Sicily's southernmost border island, the Italian government launched an emergency search and rescue operation called Mare Nostrum, carried out by the Italian military (BBC News 2013). The shipwreck marked Orlando's urge to begin pro-migrant politics for the city and to defend migrant lives against the EU's border management. When Mare Nostrum was discontinued after a year and replaced in 2014 by a collective European effort, Operation Triton, migrant deaths in the Mediterranean increased dramatically (Merelli and Rosi 2017).[32] Most of my pro-migrant interlocutors underlined the transition in authority from the Italian military to the EU as a turning point in the deterioration of search and rescue activities.

In 2017, the Italy-Libya Memorandum of Understanding was signed to slow, and eventually stop, the migrant flow in the central Mediterranean (fora critical analysis, see Cusumano and Riddervold 2023). However, instead the externalization of borders to Libya fueled the inhumane treatment of and racial violence against migrants (Ferreira 2019). Even though the memo of understanding was signed soon after the 2016 EU-Turkey agreement, which it tried to mimic, the political instability in Libya made a similar agreement impossible for the central Mediterranean (Landau 2019). Major differences between the so-called third safe neighbor countries—mainly Turkey, Libya, and Tunisia—explain the pervasiveness of human smuggling between Turkey and Greece versus human trafficking between Libya and Italy (for the difference between trafficking and smuggling, see Ferreira 2019, 43–46).[33] Despite multiple differences in implications and outcomes, the agreements signed with Turkey and Libya, and with Tunisia in 2023, have been flagged as the source of menace of Europe's brutal border regime (*The Guardian* 2024).

Italy's repressive migration and border policies climaxed when Minister of the Interior Matteo Salvini passed two decree laws in quick succession in 2018 and 2019. Referred to as "the Salvini laws," the decrees closed Italy's ports banning entrance to irregular migrants and rescue ships. Violating both international law and human rights, the decree laws criminalized search and rescue and humanitarian aid by accusing them of "facilitating human trafficking" (Osborne 2019). Infamous for his anti-immigrant and anti-South politics, Salvini despised Sicily as a major receiver of migrants from North Africa and engaged in a personal fight with Mayor Orlando and his pro-migrant allies. Chapter 3 analyzes the period of confrontation by Palermitan solidarity of Minister of the Interior Salvini's decree laws, particularly the so-called "closed port policy," which was implemented between March 2018 and August 2019 and culminated in a series of judicial allegations against him (Aru 2023).[34]

Similarly, in Greece negative feelings about the EU's imposition of austerity measures and rising nationalism contributed to the landslide victory of the conservative New Democracy party in 2019. Having promised to stop the refugee influx, to fix the economic crisis, and to bring back security, Prime Minister Mitsotakis vowed in his first week in office "to deport ten thousand people by the end of 2020" (Crabapple 2020). The New Democracy's war on asylum is discussed in Chapter 2, which explores the disobedient Exarcheia neighborhood of Athens. I analyze the new government's "fixation" on Exarcheia, and its "flagship policy" of "normalising Exarcheia" (Vradis 2020, 554).

As anti-immigrant policies and rampant nativism, Islamophobia, and racism escalate in Europe, Greece and Italy have continued voting for right-wing anti-immigrant political leaders in national elections. Even though the far-right Salvini was brought down and replaced by a coalition of the center-left and right-wing populists in 2019, he has served as deputy prime minister, and minister of infrastructure and transportation, since 2022—this time under the far-right Prime Minister Giorgia Meloni. Similarly, Greece's center-right New Democracy was reelected in national elections in 2023.

Overall, the ideological makeup and the political landscape of Greece and Italy vary tremendously. Greece has multiple leftist parties, including the radical leftist party Syriza, and a strong leftist activist legacy in major cities, particularly Athens (Vradis 2020; Skleparis 2018). In contrast, Italy is a land of right-wing populist parties, which have mushroomed and come to dominate the political landscape since the 1960s (Tarchi 2015; Biancalana 2020). Despite different types of nation-states, political party systems, and ideological landscape, the Greek and Italian governments both externalize their borders and engage in border violence and routine pushbacks. Investigative journalists and human rights organizations have continued documenting not only the pushbacks by Greece and Italy and pullbacks by Libya and delayed or unperformed rescue operations, but also the violence by the EU-funded forces in Libya and Tunisia.[35] Whether pushbacks of migrants were denied or justified by the anti-migrant officials that I talked to, crimes against humanity became the norm of securitization in the Mediterranean Sea. The Pact on Migration and Asylum adopted by the European parliament in April 2024 presented the most severe blow to asylum by establishing the most repressive border and migration governance so far. In response, pro-migrant forces selectively confronted the national government and the EU, as they engaged and relied on other state institutions, such as the courts, the constitution, international law, and city police forces. In this respect it is important to note that former pro-migrant mayors, Athens's Georgios Kaminis (2011–19) and Palermo's Leoluca Orlando (2012–22), were previously professors of constitutional law. The former deputy mayor of Athens, Lefteris Papagiannakis, later the director of the NGO Greek Council for Refugees, was a lawyer practicing international law and a human rights activist. The pro-migrant former mayor of Naples, Luigi de Magistris, a close ally of Orlando, was a prosecutor. This similar legal background of pro-migrant mayors is revealing of the violation of laws, including human rights laws, in Europe's governance of borders and migration.

A Processual Approach

Rather than focusing on discrete events, or isolated incidents, this book presents a processual approach (for a similar approach, see Yuval-Davis et al. 2019), tracing continuities and shifts for a period of seven years, and situating the changing nature of resistance to the larger racial border regime. Instead of providing a straightforward model or a universal formula for policy, the ethnography presents a deeper understanding of the struggle between native-migrant solidarity and the racial security regime by way of a contextual and processual ethnographic inquiry. Concretely, Chapters 1 and 3 demonstrate that, in both Athens and Palermo, municipal governments and mayors mattered tremendously, empowering local resistance against securitization and making a difference in the everyday experiences of irregular migrants.[36] Chapters 1 and 3 illustrate collaboration between municipal governments, NGOs, (non)activist natives and migrants, and migrant associations against the EU's border regime. The ethnography follows the process through which these pro-migrant governments at both *local and national* levels were replaced by anti-immigrant governments in Athens and Greece in 2019 and in Palermo and Italy in 2022. Chapters 2 and 4 document and analyze both the shifts and continuities of everyday life and local politics after the electoral victories of anti-migrant governments. By tracing these transitions, my processual ethnography has shown a clear pattern since 2017 in both cases: Activists and the solidarity rely on and express trust mainly in local networks and reach out to transnational activist circles by largely bypassing (referred also as *scale-skipping*) the securitizing anti-immigrant nation-state.

My emphasis on the geopolitics of emotions does not mean I underestimate the role of the ballot box or the repercussions of the electoral victories of the anti-immigrant, right-wing parties. On the contrary, I highlight the arbitrary treatment of migrants, injustices towards them, and the violation of their rights through the electoral victories of *all* anti-immigrant governments—both right and left. Importantly, however, my findings also illustrate that native-migrant solidarities have persisted beyond electoral shifts, largely because of the central role of the geopolitics of emotion, which neither elections nor security forces can reduce, mute, or erase. Hence, instead of the policies, protests, and party politics that are largely prone to electoral outcomes, my focus remains on everyday sense and sensibilities, which elections cannot destroy. My processual approach allows me to situate my interlocutors' responses, actions, and emotions in the larger geopolitics of securitization.

Competing Notions of Solidarity

A clarification of terminology is needed here. Different meanings have been attached to *solidarity*, and different agendas associated with it in everyday life and scholarship (Bauder 2021; Bauder and Juffs 2020). Scholarly approaches differ depending on their focus on policy versus on the everyday reality on the ground. Similarly, views on solidarity diverge between studies that prioritize a national scale and those focused on a local urban scale. From a policy-centered perspective, Fischer and Jørgensen (2021) compare Athens—the poor arrival city—with Hamburg— a destination city of Germany—and argue that both cities failed in their solidarity efforts because they fell short on engaging with and impacting national policies, even though they "symbolically" declared themselves a "safe harbour" or a "solidarity city" (Fischer and Jørgensen 2021, 1063). This approach does not take into account the geopolitical difference between the arrival and destination states, and thereby the contextuality—the different geographies, migration histories, collective memories, socioeconomic statuses, and geopolitical emotions that shape solidarity in them. The study also dismissed the different roles of ports in arrival and destination cities. This policy-centered approach to solidarity overlooks the importance of historically and geographically situated everyday politics. A deeply situated ethnographic analysis reveals that all these factors make big differences in migrants' daily lives and in their participation, activism, and leadership in local and transnational solidarity (as opposed to engagements in national policies). Different from this policy-centered approach, my perspective of *solidarity* includes everyday practices, responses, and reactions affected by geopolitical emotions.

Moreover, during the peak of migrant flow, the majority of frontliners in borderlands had little or no time or energy left to engage policy circles in urban centers of the First World. Most of the leading activists, migrant and native, whom I met in the borderlands were struggling diligently and around the clock, performing several low-pay jobs, getting minimal sleep, and living under the constant risk of criminalization, which was intensified by their proximity and frequent visits to the landing sites or entry points, like Lampedusa or Lesvos. While these frontliners made the difference between death and life, violence, insecurity, and safety, only very few of them were also actively working in national governance structures or formal political institutions.

I am also interested in how cities that host solidarity carve out places that migrant and native actors perceive as relatively safe. My findings show that pro-migrant circles in gateway cities were wary of declaring their city a safe harbor, mainly because the arrival ports were closed by the EU border regime, which continues to lead to the death of many migrants. My interlocutors knew (and consistently expressed in interviews) that nothing, no act of solidarity, could make the journey of irregular migrants entirely safe. In this border geography, fighting against the tide of criminalization in everyday life in alliance with migrants appears to be the main characteristic of solidarity against the proximity of danger, i.e. the racial borders, and against the background of unlawful ambiguous reception procedures of the EU's security regime.

An in-depth inquiry of migration inevitably requires multiscalar analysis. The local solidarity movements and actors I studied in two cities and on several border islands were involved in cross-border and transnational activist networks. In Athens, a high number of local and international NGOs linked the city's resistance transnational networks until 2019. In contrast, in Palermo (and Sicily), NGOs did not abruptly emerge and disappear with the same density and speed. Rather, cross-border and transnational activism in Palermo was pioneered by local activists in cooperation with the municipality until 2022. The processual approach showed that, later, under anti-migrant governments, solidarity had different trajectories in the two cities. In Athens, the high number of local and international NGOs (along with accommodation and housing capacities for migrants) decreased and spaces of solidarity shrank and withdrew to pro-migrant sites and parts of the city. In Palermo, the numbers of migrant-led associations increased, and a larger space and louder voice emerged for a dynamic Black activism.

One of the important defining qualities of the solidarity analyzed in this book is that (pro)migrant resistance went above and beyond humanitarian aid and provisional services. Leading migrant and native activists whose words and lives have shaped this book were allies, standing together with migrants. While solidarity was not immune to inner conflict and power issues, the general trend I observed was that my interlocutors' worldviews and emotions were in alignment with their actions. That is, solidarity work was at its best when honoring the agency and dignity of racialized migrants, not when winning awards presented by political authorities in major capitals of Europe.

Multisited Ethnography of the Everyday

Since 2017, I have lived and conducted participant observation for prolonged periods in Athens and Palermo, and I have frequently visited Greece's border islands and Sicily's southernmost border island, Lampedusa. In addition to my one-year sabbatical supported by a Fulbright research chair scholarship in 2021–22, I spent long summers (mid-April–September) and winter breaks in the Mediterranean, and each year I carried out many shorter visits in between. Although I lived in many different neighborhoods of Athens and Palermo, I often rented and spent most of my time in migrant neighborhoods: Exarcheia and Victoria Square in Athens, and Ballarò, Vucciria, and Capo, where historic markets of Palermo are located. I conducted fieldwork and interviews in city governments as well as in local pro-migrant, and migrant-led associations. I undertook participant observation in outdoor markets, squares, cafés, restaurants, shops, kiosks, and art events, and I attended public events, protests, and private gatherings in people's homes. I also traveled to Geneva in 2019 to interview officials of the UN High Commissioner for Refugees and to Florence in 2023. To gain a broader comparative perspective of transitory and destination sites in European cities, I conducted pilot interviews in Trento, during my visiting professorship at University of Trento in 2019, and in Berlin during my fellowship at the Max Planck Institute for Multidisciplinary Sciences in Göttingen in 2018.

Using snowball sampling to expand my circles, I conducted 164 in-depth, semi-structured interviews with open-ended questions. These interviews ranged from one-and-a-half to four hours and were recorded and transcribed. In addition to more than forty-five ethnographic interviews, I also collected life stories. My interviewees were prominent politicians and officials of local and national governments and the European parliament, NGO representatives, frontline humanitarian workers, members of rescue teams, activist and nonactivist natives and migrants, local artists, journalists, and academics.[37] I use pseudonyms here for all respondents who were not public figures or spokespeople to protect their confidentiality and privacy.

A considerable portion of the insubordinate practices in peripheral borderlands often remains out-of-sight and beyond the reach of the security regime and EU policies. Parallel to this, the bulk of everyday pro-migrant resistance at the border remains off the radar of formal news venues, unless a distinct or isolated event is brought to the attention of investigative journalists. All these factors render in-depth qualitative research, particularly long-term multisited ethnographies, an imperative for gaining a deeper understanding of native-migrant solidarity in the border zones.

Borrowing from urban ethnographies of (in)security (e.g., Monroe 2016; Glück and Low 2017; Glück 2017; Low and Maguire 2019), this book bridges border and urban ethnography (Duneier et al. 2014) with the goal of decentering the security regime, security professionals, and their policies. My ethnography of everyday life also borrows from Migdal's (2001) "state-in-society" approach, which helped me capture the manifestations of the security regime in daily life at the periphery. This approach enabled me to contextualize the everyday interactions between local dissidents and security forces. Inspired also by Bayat's (2013) "life as politics," Lipsky's (1980) "street-level bureaucracy," and Ellenmann's (2006) "street-level democracy," I interviewed mayors (of border cities and border islands), municipal officials, and several city council members and followed up with them through elections and changing governments.

Finally, unlike the conventional comparative studies in political science that start with comparative hypotheses to be confirmed, my comparative insights emerged from the multisited ethnography that unfolded as I traced resistance in the borderlands. In-depth ethnographic data helped me to note and analyze similarities and differences between the two cases as I moved between sites, neighborhoods, cities, and regions. By spotlighting resistance in Athens and Palermo, my ethnographic findings invite "a larger rethinking of the political [as] not merely what takes place in the realm of formal politics but as an ongoing set of struggles in everyday life" (Morgan and Orloff 2017, 7). These cities offered me a toolbox for explicating the processes through which the securitization of migration was resisted at the local scale, where safe places were carved out of violent border zones; where fear was refused and local trust was embraced in pro-migrant neighborhoods of the border city; where native-migrant solidarity was achieved in the city center and a dynamic Black activism gradually became vocal in downtown Palermo. None of these could be hypostasized or predicted prescriptively, but only experienced as they unfolded in time thanks to processual multisited ethnography.

Chapter 1 examines the cooperation between the pro-migrant municipality of Athens (2011–19), NGOs, and local activists in the aftermath of the 2016 EU-Turkey agreement. While the inventive maneuvering capacities of Athens did not solve "Europe's refugee crisis," the chapter elucidates how safe places of the gateway city were built from the bottom up in everyday life. I argue that securitized spaces were proliferated by the fear of the Muslim refugee, while safe places were generated by the inclusion of them.

PART ONE

Athens, the Eastern Mediterranean

ONE

Safe Places Versus Securitization

During my field visit, in December 2017, Athens looked quite different from how it used to, before the flow of Syrian refugees through Turkey. Since the peak of flow in 2015, the city had been transformed sociospatially and politically. Alexa, a Greek citizen, a lifelong Athens resident, and a project manager in a pivotal NGO dealing with refugee issues, pointed to the rapid transformation of ethnically diverse immigrant neighborhoods. Contrary to the predominant association in Europe between Muslim refugees and in-security, Alexa argued that the migrant neighborhoods were "safer" places in Athens. Referring specifically to Victoria Square, Omonoia Square, and Kypseli, she refuted the stigma attached to these neighborhoods:

> There is some misperception that Athens has become very dangerous [owing to the refugee flow]. . . . This is what the media, the racist, and the intolerant say. . . . But I think Athens is one of the safest cities. . . . Safety is not just about the lack of physical violence or threat; it also has everything to do with the refusal of exclusion. When you take your child to school and see people demonstrating and denying education to him or her, you do not feel safe . . . The mixed immigrant neighborhoods of Athens welcome and include refugees instead of making them feel out of place, unwanted.

My conversation with Alexa left me thinking about how safety and fear were experienced in the daily life of refugee-receiving border cities. Most of my interlocutors made similar connections between safety and inclusion. Yet both the policies of the EU and the bulk of scholarship on refugees and irregular migrants have largely dismissed this important link.

———

At the peak of the refugee flow in 2015, Greece was already worn out by austerity measures (Arampatzi 2017a, 2017b). When the geopolitics of borders, austerity, and the EU's repressive refugee politics rubbed up against each other, the border situation became increasingly complicated. Athens found itself squeezed between the EU and Turkey, both of which have treated refugees as pawns in negotiating power politics. Turkey continues to be the world's largest refugee-hosting country with 3.6 million refugees, which constitute about 10 percent of refugees in the world under UNHCR mandate.[1] According to UNHCR statistics, the number of irregular sea and land border-crossers from Turkey to Greece amounted to 850,000 in the peak flow in 2015.[2]

This chapter reveals and analyzes how Athens coped with the flow under the leadership of the center-left municipality during the leftist national government of Syriza. Against the background of the securitization of migration, a growing number of border cities took on a new role. At Europe's southern borders, several port cities—Palermo, Naples, Barcelona, Marseilles—opened their doors to refugees at the expense of confronting the EU's anti-immigrant policies.[3] Focusing on the period of the pro-migrant municipal governance until 2019, this chapter shows that the struggle in the cities was not just with the security regime but also with anti-immigrant locals and ultranationalist forces who feared and invoked others to fear refugees.

Cities that claim an openness to migrants and that display welcoming attitudes and practices, such as passing pro-migrant policies, are known as cities of refuge or sanctuary cities (e.g., Bauder 2017; Darling and Bauder 2019; Collingwood and O'Brien 2019; Mancina 2013; Ridgley 2008, 2013; Delgado 2018). Although such efforts "humanize what it means to be a city" (Delgado 2018, 14), my findings contradict the public image of sanctuary cities as peaceful, conflict-free places. In fact, this book views gateway sanctuary cities as urban spaces of high sociopolitical contestation. In Athens, pro-refugee actors cooperated against anti-immigrant forces by generating inclusive safe places for refugees and asylum seekers. Accordingly, I modify the term *city of refuge* to analyze the politicized nature of making safe places for refugees and the highly contested nature of their inclusion in Athens. Unlike the apolitical principle of "neutrality" in dealing with refugee and human rights issues that is central to international organizations, such as the UN High Commissioner for Refugees, my research exposes the ways in which refugee accommodation is enmeshed with political conflict at multiple levels—local, national, regional, and international. As my findings show, there is no smooth accommodation to be romanticized in the city of refuge, especially after EU member states closed their doors to forcibly displaced people.

Clearly, not every port city in the securitized border zones takes on this politically loaded commitment at the cost of standing up to the EU's border regime. What makes Athens the perfect laboratory for studying refugee reception and the making of safe places for the arriving refugees? During the peak of the migrant flow, Athens was also in the middle of an intense political struggle with the ultranationalist, neofascist party Golden Dawn. The party's racist and anti-immigrant political agenda added to the challenges posed by the austerity and the refugee flow. This chapter demonstrates that the key to Athens's pro-refugee resistance was its strong alliances based on local trust between the municipal government and pro-refugee actors. During the period 2016–19, Athens displayed a close engagement and cooperation between the municipality's strong center-left leadership, a rooted local activist tradition, and the large number of NGOs flooding the refugee sector. Admittedly, the sector became a major source of income for many natives, given the concurrent financial crisis during this rather short period.

Unsurprisingly, the bulk of refugee-related local efforts in the border city were focused on reception, accommodation, and safety rather than integration. Due to austerity measures and large-scale unemployment in Greece (Arampatzi 2017a, 2017b), the long-term or permanent settlement of most refugees was difficult, if not impossible. In Athens, the largest city of Greece with more than three million inhabitants, the refugee population was transitory. During peak flow, migrants often passed through with the intention of settling in northwestern Europe.[4] Different from integration and long-term policies of settling immigrants in destination locations (e.g., Bloemraad 2006; De Graauw 2016; Hinze 2013), accommodation in this period in Athens was spatial and temporary. Hence, I use *inclusion* in a narrow sense here to refer to the sociospatial practice of generating temporary places conducive to the feeling of safety for refugees.

The case of Athens raises further questions: How was it possible in Athens to generate safe places for refugees, given that the country maintained some of the world's most insecure and inhumane refugee camps, in the Greek border islands (Ferreira 2019, 3–4; Mamo and Tondo, 2018; Kingsley, 2018)? Why and how was Athens able to rise to the challenge of providing sanctuary to refugees at a time when EU member states had banned and criminalized rescue operations? Why and how was Athens able to carve out safe havens for refugees while the followers of the neofascist Golden Dawn party were fueling fear of refugees and committing violent attacks against them? The proximity between the EU's highly securitized and deadly borders and the safe spaces created for refugees was puzzling. The disparate lived experiences of fear and safety in such proximity and in the same geography presented a curious situation.

While spatializing fear and safety, this chapter situates the border city in the larger context of Islamophobia and the racialization of Muslims in Europe that intensified after the terrorist attacks of September 11 and was reinforced further by the Syrian civil war. Although the history of harsh treatment and border brutality against refugees and immigrants predated September 11,[5] the result intensified the securitization of Muslim immigrants and refugees (Sajed 2012, 23–26; Dikeç 2007; Cesari 2012). Under these circumstances, Athens received and accommodated refugees from many Muslim-majority states, including Syria, Iraq, Pakistan, Afghanistan, Somalia, Morocco, and Bangladesh.

This chapter reveals and analyzes the ways pro-refugee actors in the city resist the security regime by generating safe spaces through a sound collaboration between the municipal officials, local activists, and NGOs. Complicating the debates on sanctuary cities, I argue that the power of the receiving border city comes not from reducing conflict about forced displacement but from its ability to produce new bonds of trust and pro-refugee alliances out of high contestation in securitized borderlands. This argument is largely based on my interlocutors' testimonies: My interlocutors juxtaposed their trust in strong municipality to their deep distrust of the Greek state and national governments. By spatializing fear and (in)security (see, e.g., Boyce 2018; Glück and Low 2017; Monroe 2016), this chapter empirically and conceptually distinguishes safe places sustained by trust and inclusion from securitized spaces sustained by fear and intimidation. My ethnographic fieldwork in Victoria Square, a migrant neighborhood in the city center of Athens, provides an in-depth look into how safe places for refugees are built from the bottom up despite gloomy conditions. This bottom-up urban process, I claim, is a strikingly effective force for countering the top-down securitization of borders and migration.

Spatializing Fear and Situating Safety

The power of daily experiences in shaping local refugee politics particularly struck me during a talk at a reception at the Greek embassy in Boston in September 2019. The founder and CEO of one of the largest NGOs offering shelter to unaccompanied minors in Athens told us a remarkable story of a right-wing anti-immigrant Athenian. The woman feared Muslims as terrorists and felt threatened by them. She stormed into the center and demanded to know why the NGO sheltered the children of ISIS. After a few days the staff had managed to calm down her anxiety and insecurity, and she was invited to interact with the children in the safe environment of the center. Soon, she became one of their reliable benefactors.

The CEO's story supported a key finding of my field research, that fear was the backbone of anti-immigrant politics, and that it was fought and subverted most efficiently in daily urban life. Fear of migrants affected multiple groups in the city in different ways. On the one hand, Athenians, like the residents of other gateway cities of Europe, were bombarded by news, media, and propaganda outlets that tried to justify widespread fear because of the alleged threat of terror and crime posed by Muslim refugees. On the other hand, refugees were frustrated upon their arrival in Greece by the realization that the uncertainties, insecurity, violence, and danger they encountered during their journey would not end until they were granted asylum and could settle in a final destination.

Unlike the fear propagated for the natives in Athens, refugees' fear was formally delimited in the accepted definition of *refugee*. According to article 1 of the 1951 Geneva Convention (as amended by the 1967 Protocol Relating to the Status of Refugees), a refugee is "a person, who owing to a *well-founded fear* of being persecuted for reasons of race, religion, nationality, membership of a particular social group or political opinion" is unable to reside or seek protection in the home country of origin. Despite the centrality of fear even in the formal UN-definition of a refugee, neither the global politics of fear nor the local urban ways of coping with fear have received sufficient scholarly attention in refugee and asylum studies (Delgado 2018, 33–34).

The so-called refugee crisis may seem to be fueled by the fear of the racialized migrant, but the crisis is primarily political, resulting from the politicization of fear. Unlike emotions, which are often triggered by psychological factors and impulses, the politicization of fear is a "conservative choice" (Body-Gendrot 2012, 10). Shaped by political agendas and worldviews, the choice is made and propagated primarily by nativist, right-wing populist, far-right, and racist political forces.

The politicization of fear sheds light on an irony of our time: We feel less safe and more fearful in an increasingly securitized world. "Fortress-like, that is, walled, gated and guarded communities encode fear—materially, not just metaphorically—producing a literal landscape of fear" (Low 1997, 53). But it is a two-way political process between the emotion of fear and space: Not only do highly securitized spaces generate fear, but the persistent fear of the "undesirable" targeted racialized Other sustains the security regime (Goldstein 2010; Besteman and Gusterson 2010; Caldeira 2000). The governance of the EU's southern borders exemplifies this cyclical relationship between the politicization of fear and the persistence of the security regime. Jones (2012) rightly picked on border securitization as the most severe and lasting consequences of the global war on terror.

The fear of the Muslim refugee in Greece was reinforced by the negative perceptions of the Muslim neighboring country, Turkey, where the refugees were arriving from. The feelings and discourses about Athens as a major entry point, or a place of refuge, were rooted in the bitter geopolitics and collective memory of the Turkey-Greece border. Up until 2017, Athens presented a sharp contrast to the heated debates over sanctuary cities in the United States.[6] Early in my research, none of my Athenian interlocutors in the refugee sector, except for Vice Mayor on Migrant and Refugee Affairs

Lefteris Papagiannakis, knew of or had heard about the terms *city of refuge* and *sanctuary city*. Evi, who worked with a nonprofit organization and was responsible for the well-being and housing of refugees, was puzzled by the terminology. When I offered a definition and examples, Evi said:

> All the so-called sanctuary cities in the US are very far away from the coast of Turkey, aren't they? Moreover, they are not used by the EU like Athens is used as a gatekeeper of European borders. When I am in France or Germany, I hear them say, "We welcome the refugees." It must be easier to welcome them when refugees do not arrive at your doorsteps in rubber boats in miserable conditions and with dead and dying humans. When they are stranded there for an unlimited time after fighting to stay alive during the transport by smugglers, our response in Athens does not qualify as welcoming. It is simply about coping, emergency, rescue, and sheer survival.

Evi's irritable reaction speaks to the difficulties of living in a major gateway to Europe and working in the refugee sector at Europe's securitized periphery. The defensive emotionality about refugee reception, rescue, and safety is embedded in the geopolitics of the Eastern Mediterranean.

Trust in a Municipality Versus Distrust in the State

Migration is as old as human history, and for centuries, the eastern Mediterranean has been accustomed to continual human mobility and forced migration (Betts and Collier 2017; Işın 2018; Kasaba 2009). But before the arrival of ethnically Greek refugees from Turkey in the aftermath of the Greco-Turkish War of 1922 and the population exchange between Turkey and Greece in 1923, immigration to Greece was relatively rare, and it remained unsystematic until the 1980s.[7] The flow intensified after 1991 with the arrival of migrants from former communist countries and refugees escaping war in the Middle East and Africa. However, the refugee influx from Syria in 2015 was unprecedented in its intensity and had a massive impact on reshaping the sociopolitical landscape of Athens. Unlike major European destination cities, Athens bore the bulk of the burden of the EU's externalized borders in the eastern Mediterranean, mainly because of the EU's flawed Dublin Regulation, which assigns asylum processing to arrival countries. Most Athenians were frustrated by the unfair nature of this regulation, as it enabled destination states to avoid sharing equal responsibility for migration with arrival states (Ferreira 2019; Karageorgiou 2016).

Even though migration and refugee policies were the responsibility of the nation-state, "it falls to local and regional jurisdictions to frame the *living experience*" of migrants (Mollenkopf and Pastor 2016, 2). Accordingly, then Mayor of Athens Georgios Kaminis decided that "Athens itself needed to respond to the crisis" (Komporozos-Athanasiou and Papachristou 2018, 127). He abruptly created a new position in the municipal government, the first of its kind in Greece: vice mayor of migrants, refugees, and municipal decentralization. Ironically, the appointment of Lefteris Papagiannakis to the office preceded the creation of the position in municipal government. Papagiannakis came to this position with substantial experience in European and international law and with expertise on Muslim migrants. He held a law degree, a postgraduate degree in European law earned in France, and solid work experience both in the European Parliament in Brussels and with Muslim minorities in Greece. I met Papagiannakis when he was working around the clock to cope with refugee-related emergencies. A Greek diplomat in the United States observed to me: "He is not one of those soft, fancy leftists we have in Greece. Lefteris is the real deal." The comment drew my attention because in the European context, where the far right was on the rise, anti-migrant sentiments were shared by a wide range of the political spectrum from the Left to the Right. I wondered whether Athens stood out among other European capitals regarding the role of ideology and party politics in pro-migrant resistance and local migration governance.

How do we explain that certain cities in the same country engage in pro-migrant practices and activism—some even pass municipal sanctuary ordinances, like the sanctuary cities of the United States—while others do not (see Bazurli et al. 2022; Delgado 2018; Mollenkopf and Pastor 2016)? Among alternative explanations of geopolitical, economic, and demographic conditions, local political partisanship is a major factor, shaped by political culture and the historical legacy of activism (Steil and Vasi 2014; Ramakrishnan and Wong 2010). In analyzing local partisanship, Steil and Vasi drew attention primarily to the proportion of people who vote for parties on the Left and the Right. While important, the explanation of local political partisanship in municipal elections provided limited insights into the case of Athens, because the outcomes of local elections typically fluctuate, and often, between the Left and Right parties. Also, along with ongoing clash between the Left and the Right, ultranationalist forces persisted in Greece.[8]

Hence, rather than party politics, the findings of my research point to a historical contextuality of leftist activism in the border city. Chapter 2 unpacks how the fear-ridden securitization of migration was confronted by the legacy of leftist urban activism in Athens. In 2019, when Turkey's President Erdoğan openly threatened Europe with releasing refugees, in order to leverage his power in the region, the flow of refugees from Turkey to the Greek islands peaked again (Fallon and Boersma 2020; McKernan and Boffey 2020; BBC News 2020). In response, Athens did not remain silent to the human miseries caused by the border governance. Thousands of Athenians marched to protest the inhumane border politics that turned refugees into tokens in power politics between Turkey and Greece. Despite the city's pro-migrant protests, the following years witnessed the eventual normalization of Greece's pushbacks. After 2022, Greek authorities and unidentified local groups regularized violence against refugees at the sea and land borders between Greece and Turkey.

Considering the conflictual nature of relations between Turkey and Greece (*New York Times* 2020), Papagiannakis concluded: "If you give the key to your main problem to Turkey, you can no longer make independent decisions about your internal affairs." Taking a different perspective, Gina, an NGO representative, said: "The EU sold refugees to Turkey. Europe should not have paid anyone to get rid of our problem, especially to President Erdoğan. But who pays the price of this unethical deal? Athens! We do!"

This complaint was expressed often in my interviews. Rather than acknowledging the flow of money from the EU to Greece and the formation of a whole new transnational refugee sector as a new source of income, most referred to and disapproved of the money paid to Turkey by the EU for refugee accommodation. Many observed to me that the EU-Turkey deal was a blunt violation of human rights. "Migration cannot be stopped by obstructions," I was told by local activists. "People on the move will always find ways to pass through them." Without exception, my interviews with the natives were inundated with frustration about the EU's top-down management of borders and migration. Only a few respondents, who had substantial previous experience in European institutions such as the European Parliament, admitted that the EU was the key to tackling the refugee problem.

I also probed Athenians about their trust in the Greek state to deal with and solve refugee issues. All my interlocutors stated openly that they trusted neither their own nation-state nor the Syriza government. The collectively shared distrust in the state and political institutions were explained by corruption, economic crisis, unaccountability, incompetence, lack of good leadership, and weak institutions. Athenians I talked to also expressed distrust in the EU, owing to the severe austerity measures. The perception of a double crisis—financial and migration (Arampatzi 2017a, 2017b; Rozakou 2017, 2024)—made not only nonstate actors but also state actors distrustful of their political system.[9]

When in the Contested Victoria Square . . .

At the heart of the politics of fear and safety in Athens lies the story of a place called Victoria Square. Over the past couple of decades, this neighborhood became a hub for migrants and refugees and their social lives, informal networks, shops, and exchanges. I spent a lot of time in Victoria's shelters and associations and also frequented small ethnic shops, where I enjoyed shopping and interacting with diverse migrant populations. As I hung out in and around the square, I did some of my work in coffee shops, took photos and notes, and met with friends and interlocutors who worked in the refugee sector.

Previously, migration flows had transformed Victoria Square from an affluent downtown neighborhood into an ethnically and racially mixed, transitional migrant neighborhood. Historically, notable influxes took place when Filipinos arrived in the late 1980s and Albanians in 1991. After the fall of the Berlin Wall, many Eastern Europeans settled in the neighborhood. As upper-middle-class Greeks began moving out of the downtown neighborhood to new suburban housing, buildings gradually were vacated. Migrants moved in and rented relatively cheap apartments in the city center, allowing them to form ethnically concentrated pockets.

Eleni, who lived and worked in Victoria for many decades, witnessed this slow and steady transformation. As we were having coffee in the square, she brought up one of the many challenges of the neighborhood:

The Golden Dawn, the fascist party of Greece . . . [she stopped to cor-
rect herself]—well, the neofascist party of Greece—started establishing
itself here. The Golden Dawn formed its strongholds in Victoria in order
to spread and capitalize on fear. The fear justified their presence. They
appeared as saviors of the local population from the newcomers. Using
their populist strategies, for example, they escorted elderly ladies to the
ATM, you know, to "protect" them [she made quotation marks with her
hands] from potential migrant thieves.

Eleni's recollections were similar to those I heard from other locals. Cyn-
thia, a young activist who worked for a shelter of unaccompanied refugee
children close to Victoria, also told me how Golden Dawn had taken advantage of economic crisis by manipulating people's economic frustrations
and spreading fear of refugees.

I met Mimi, another experienced frontliner, in Victoria. She worked
for an organization focused on pre- and postnatal care for refugee women.
When the organization opened its center in a spacious first-floor apartment
in Victoria Square in 2016, neighbors were terrified and infuriated. The
center was next-door to another UNICEF-funded NGO, which crowded
the entire block with refugees waiting in line for services. Mimi remem-
bers locals pouring water on refugees from their windows to make them
go away. "But, in a short time," she continued, "these negative responses
stopped, when they got to know us and the vulnerable refugee women."
Among many services, the center was offering midwife appointments to
some three hundred women per month. According to Mimi, physical proximity on that street and face-to-face interactions humanized the interactions between locals and migrants and ended up dismantling preestablished
stereotypes and fear of the stranger: "When locals see at their doorsteps a
woman's water break with three other little children crying at her skirts,
they forget about their fear and run to help." I heard similar stories about
the impact of proximity in urban space with the newcomers. The interactions in Victoria had a humanizing effect by undoing fear and encouraging
people to lower their barriers.

At the same time, however, Victoria Square was a microcosm of in-
termittent tension between a wide range of leftist activists and locals and
a much smaller group of anti-immigrant ultranationalists who visited the
neighborhood randomly. The Golden Dawn's fear-invoking efforts were not

limited to Victoria. They culminated in violent events such as the murder of the antifascist Greek rapper Pavlos Fyssas on September 18, 2013. The murderer, a Golden Dawn supporter, was associated with the party's leadership (Smith 2013; Charlton, 2013). Fyssas's murder was followed by Communists' attacks on the Golden Dawn's headquarters in another instance of the ongoing right-left clash in Athens. This murder and the ensuing trial were followed by subsequent criminal acts of the far-right party members, who eventually were convicted in 2020. The persistence of this tension showcases what Steil and Vasi (2014) refer to as the "new immigrant contestation."

Few studies went beyond temporal unfolding of collective action to explain the spatial aspects of the interplay between social forces and their opposition.[10] Taking spatiality into account, Steil and Vasi (2014, 1107) examined "the impact of movement protests not only on the intended outcome but also on the social construction of threat by a countermovement in nearby locations."[11] Victoria Square was the perfect laboratory to capture and analyze the salience of spatiality in two major ways. First, it was the hub of ongoing conflict between left and far-right politics in urban life. Even while the trial of Fyssas's murderers was going on, the ultranationalists continued mobilizing locals and maintaining their hold on Victoria. Second, Victoria Square was the place where the politics of fear met with the resilience and resistance drawing refugees together and providing them with a sense of safety.

Despite high levels of contestation in urban space, most refugees prefer to live in cities rather than refugee camps. To understand the attraction of city centers for refugees, it is crucial to consider that the refugee camp and the city of refuge are pitted against each other along the continuum of safe-unsafe places. The city of refuge is perceived as a "place-based" effort of inclusion and protection (Bagelman 2013), whereas the refugee camp is constructed as a sterile, isolating, and hostile place that violates human rights and strips people of their identities, feelings and personal histories (Diken 2004). Nevertheless, research shows that major safety threats and risks exist in both places; they simply manifest differently.[12] The question then becomes whether local pro-migrant practices and initiatives are helpful at all in ensuring the safety of refugees. How is safety generated sociospatially to render certain sites safe for refugees who have already made a long, violent journey? How are safe places created and sustained in highly contested gateways at racial borders?

Intersecting Gender, Place, and Race

While it is difficult for activists and frontline service providers to reach out to refugees at camps, it is even more difficult for them to have direct access to refugees' private lives once they move into their own dwellings in the city. Hence, activists and frontliners face different challenges in identifying domestic (and other forms of) violence and discrimination and in ensuring the safety of refugees and their families.

Nadina, the founder of the NGO Melissa Network, working with migrant and refugee women, explained how an unintended place-based shift in the organization's strategy made an important difference for the NGO's outreach:

> On International Women's Day in March 2016, we were invited to participate in an event that was taking place at one of the camps. The mayor was there, the UNHCR, the Red Cross, . . . all the big organizations, and the state. There was good intention but not enough dedication to do it properly because they forgot to install a sound system, and people could not hear anything. So, unfortunately, we and the refugee women politely sat through the speeches. . . . And one of our activists, an African woman, was at the same panel. At the end of the speeches, three refugee women went up to our African activists and reported an instance of gender-based violence.

This impromptu incident was a significant learning moment for the organization. Although it was difficult for NGOs and activists (and everyone) to enter the camps, it was easier for refugees to leave the camps to reach pro-migrant centers and associations. Instead of begging for and negotiating access to camps or housing, Nadina and her team decided to attract refugee women to Melissa in Victoria Square. This simple awareness led to important outcomes. First, the inviting space of the association acclimated refugees to a warm, welcoming environment of female solidarity. In bringing refugee women together, Melissa Network presented a unique opportunity for female refugees to meet and connect across ethnic and racial lines. Second, Melissa made entry and inclusion easy for refugee women, so they could build a vibrant social life and improve the quality of their experience in Victoria. Access to Victoria Square changed social dynamics for refugees by bringing them out of the toxic camp atmosphere, by extending their safety networks, and by allowing them to get to know other migrant women in similar situations. As I observed, migrants from various ethnic, racial, and national backgrounds regularly socialized and mingled. Subsequently, the patterns of their interaction extended from Melissa into Victoria Square and beyond.

Victoria Square humanized and increased the quality of refugees' lives by enabling them to get out of inhumane conditions in the camps and participate in the public sphere. In crowded parts of cities where daily life flows at a relatively fast pace, refugees often feel out of place while "doing nothing" or just people watching, and often feel idle. The square, as a safe venue for gathering with other refugees, but not necessarily doing anything, disrupted that feeling of discomfort, the sense of being out of place. The newcomers did not have work permits, permanent jobs, or disposable income. Yet, many of them invented daily routines in the square. I often observed small groups of migrants sitting, talking, and looking around in a leisurely and relaxed manner. Their body language and interactions gave an impression of familiarity with the square as their prime social place in the city. As Mimi told me, "To feel safe, refugees need a community, or at least some friendship bonds." The square was a sociospatial enabler for refugees to build new bonds and experiment safely with their newfound ties. While not a comfort zone, it gave a breathing space to refugees, where they could temporarily and sociospatially avoid the feeling of being perceived and targeted as a threat.

Once Melissa Network managed to draw refugee women out of the camps to their center, the women found comfort in meeting, talking with, and learning from other immigrant women who had similar experiences. Nadina said with pride that "no associational logo can build and no international funding can accomplish the trust" that Melissa Network was able to establish among refugee women over time. Melissa Network's campaigns to entice refugee women to the center soon became well known across the city and beyond. After running a few programs and workshops in the camps, refugee women started coming by word of mouth with many ideas and goals.

I remember the first time I laid eyes on Melissa Network's building.

It was a rainy afternoon in December 2017. After walking through the narrow streets of Victoria searching for the address, I found myself in front of a charming old building. City-run shelters were often run-down, chaotic-looking places, not like Melissa's building. Someone buzzed me in, and I went upstairs, immediately taken in by the warm and welcoming decor. Sun streamed through the flat's large windows. Before we took a coffee break on couches in Nadina's office, she gave me a tour of the sparkling clean, light-filled, and spacious center. It was easy to feel at home there.

Nadina is a Greek Athenian who holds a PhD in anthropology from one of the top-ranking universities in Canada. With her guidance and the grant money that she secured from multiple sources, Melissa Network never stopped creating innovative ways to surpass conventional and inefficient practices of accommodating refugees. The organization aims primarily to achieve migrant women's empowerment and liberation. The center offers a range of programs in literacy, art and creativity, advocacy, psychosocial counseling, information and networking, capacity-building, and individual and community care. Nadina told me that Melissa also offers practical programs, like Greek-language classes. "That's the pull factor!" she explained, the thing that attracts women to the safe place.

What exactly made these vulnerable refugees feel safer at Melissa? How, if ever, were they able to experience safety, especially after having been surrounded by fear, exclusion, and insecurity during their long journey and then in the camps? How could space itself be capable of transforming those risky and dismal experiences at racial borderlands into safe, comforting, and sometimes even enjoyable practices?

I couldn't stop staring at the walls covered with migrant women's art from the stairs in the main entrance into every room. Feminist paintings, drawings, and posters praised refugee women's agency and dignified their emotions, celebrating their skills, potential, and power. In addition to feeding emotions of safety, dignity, and hope for a better future, the place took into account women's practical needs. A nicely organized, colorfully decorated playroom welcomed their children. Kids played while their mothers participated in programs and projects. Melissa even had a small, charming backyard with a large table and chairs for hanging out, mingling, relaxing, and socializing in the fresh air.

In the middle of my long conversation with Nadina, three migrant

FIGURE 1. **Melissa Network offices, Victoria Square, July 2024. Photo by the author.**

women from the Philippines who worked for Melissa Network came by to update her about their activities for the day. They were taking freshly made food to a refugee-inhabited squat, the City Plaza Hotel. As Nadina praised their dishes, she told me that good food was one of the factors that glued migrant women together as a social base for solidarity. I observed that for many women, cooking and sharing food from their home countries became a common way to become visible, recognized, and appreciated and to feel connected. I made similar observations in the downtown migrant neighborhood of Ballarò, in Palermo (Chapter 4).

Throughout the years of my multiple visits, Melissa became famous for its activities and the flavors and aromas wafting from its kitchen, which was run solely by migrant women. Whether through food, art, friendship, or much-needed trust, this renovated home, with its modern furniture and spotless elegant bathrooms, provided the feeling of a collectively owned safe place, a place cocreated by migrant and refugee women. With Nadina's conscious efforts, Melissa delivered the feeling of belonging and a shared sense of dignity to refugee women, which were not comparable to the top-down integrationist policies of northwestern Europe.

A contrasting example is what Esra Özyürek (2023) refers to as "false promises" of inclusion into German society by the Holocaust reeducation of newly arriving Muslims. While such integrationist endeavors are primarily didactive, they are also explicitly emotional, reflecting the guilt of German society. But the difference from what occurred in the context of Melissa is that the German instructions were solemnly centered on the geopolitical emotions of the natives of the host country. Özyürek's in-depth analysis shows meticulously how these practices not only sidestep the emotions and agency of the Muslim newcomers, but also imply Muslim migrants are a hindrance to German appeasement with its fascist violent past. By embracing the agency and emotions of the refugee, Melissa presents a fresh divergence from such Eurocentric integrationist practices that are presented as "rational," but in reality recognize and honor only the historically situated emotions of white natives. Rather than the First World stereotype of wanting to "enlighten" and "civilize" the displaced racialized people of the Third World, Melissa enabled the coconstruction of common meaning and purpose. This approach that prioritizes refugees' emotions breaks down prejudices against the racialized migrants as ignorant, uneducated, and uncivilized (and potentially harmful) that are implicit in most integrationist ideas and policies.

Although Athens did not have the experience northern Europe had had with guest workers since the 1960s, my ethnography illuminates the pockets that achieved anti-racist practices in many ways. Nadina observed:

> In eight municipalities around Athens, we launched a project with forty-five thousand students, which was . . . huge for us because we were just a small initiative. All these students were packing gifts for refugees. . . . I mean it's not just the packing, it's the fact that if you pack a bag with that thought in your mind, you're not going to become a racist. . . . It was a bonding time; it was an outreach time; it was a great opportunity to really seed empathy . . . and plant the roots of hope, and solidarity for a better future.

This effort deserves to be highlighted, as it turns the conventional integration paradigm upside down. In contrast to the resocialization of the migrants into the host countries' presumably "higher" cultural and political values, Melissa worked to transform the nationalist and racist sentiments pervasive in the receiving society. Instead of educating refugees to adapt and melt into the local society, Melissa offered anti-racist education to native children and youth. I asked how these pro-migrant practices then translated into the next step, the production of safe places for creating bonding and coexistence. Solidarity, she explained, was built slowly and through a piecemeal process:

> At the time, when all the international NGOs came in, and the state, and the United Nations . . . and when borders were about to close, a lot of women from the refugee camps . . . were passing by and asking, "Is there anything we can do?" It was high time for us to start seeing them not just as transient rescued refugees heading elsewhere, but at the prospect of the borders closing, to start thinking about their inclusion. And by the winter of 2016, right before the borders closed in March 2016, we shifted focus from *aid*, to living together, to coexistence, and to think of them not just as refugees, but as our new neighbors. (Italics added.)

Nadina's powerful words pointed to the transition from humanitarian logic of aid to acts of solidarity: standing side by side and cohabiting with the refugee.

Nadina received one of ten Child 10 awards in 2019 for developing Melissa Network into a home-like haven for female refugees and migrants. She explained the situation prior to Melissa:

> No matter how amazing female refugees were in organizing overnight about whatever emergency there was, they didn't have strong, solid, and sustainable links to one another. There was no communication. They lived in parallel but disconnected ethnic groups. I would go to the Filipinos on a Sunday morning and see that they were running a microcooperative for women. They have a community school . . . a lot of wonderful initiatives. Then in the afternoon, I would go meet the Georgians for another community meeting, and they were discussing the same issues . . . That's how the idea [of] the community center emerged, where all these [refugee] women could have basic access to shared resources, like computers, Wi-Fi, an office, and to each other. Melissa became their shared venue for coexistence.

Despite these impressive community and refugee networking endeavors, sexist stereotypes about women's organizing abounded. Youly, who worked with international donors in another NGO for many years, sarcastically told me:

> When you seek funding, sympathetic people from the international human rights organizations and from the ministries would often say, "OK, you know, maybe we can give you a grant of 1,000 euros, you can go make a social kitchen . . . or you can organize a fashion show."

Such gender-based stereotypes obscured and downplayed the reality that Athens has hosted strong female migrant leaders who engaged not only in refugee politics but also in world affairs. But as in other arrival sites, forced displacement was generating a strong bias that rendered political skills, experiences, and careers of these refugee women invisible to the host society at large. (I came across similar blind spots, gender discrimination, and stigmatization of female migrants in Palermo, which I discuss in Chapter 4.) These gendered stigmas were being challenged and dissolved spatially in the safe places carved out of the racial border zones.

Over the course of seven years, I kept asking natives and migrants in solidarity—many of whom have lived in and around Victoria Square—whether they considered Victoria a safe place. Activist friends responded sarcastically: "Have you been hanging out too much in Kolonaki?" Kolonaki is a wealthy Athens neighborhood associated with luxurious lifestyles and privilege. As we sipped small glasses of ouzo, they each expressed strong dislike of class inequalities in the city. They talked about how migrants were excluded by "the privileged and the loaded," and about how rich people in Athens would rather fence in their neighborhoods, to keep out not only refugees but also people from other social classes who did not look or live like them. They were referring to the intersection of class and racial privilege that is masked by the discourse of concerns over safety and security. Here, the politics of emotion (fear of the Other) that targets and excludes the stranger is similar to the urban fear and the logic behind gated communities (Low 1997, 2001). My activist friends told me that such fear-ridden classist exclusion targeted them, too, the native leftists and radicals in the solidarity movement, as potential threats.

Fear underlies the commonsense assumption that the city of refuge has higher crime and insecurity. Yet, the reality is different from this stereotypical view. In line with my conversations with NGO workers and service providers, my activist friends assured me that Victoria and Exarcheia were safe and also the most inclusive parts of Athens. In fact, recent works on cities of refuge align with the activists' views about the safety and low crime rates in migrant neighborhoods of Athens (O'Brien et al. 2017; Ridgley 2013). These studies on sanctuary are preceded by a remarkable consensus across disciplines that migration reduces crime (e.g., Lee and Martinez 2009; Lee, Martinez, and Rosenfeld 2001; Kayaoğlu, 2022). As I walked the streets of Exarcheia alone later that evening on my way home, I experienced firsthand how safe I felt as a stranger in this part of the city.

But of course, safety is a complicated proposition and feeling for refugees, and natives working in NGOs are no strangers to threats and acts of violence in refugees' lives. For example, Maria worked for an organization that ran several shelters for unaccompanied children. To my inquiries about safety, she unequivocally commented:

> Let's not kid ourselves. Refugees are not safe. It's not safe travel for anyone, no matter if you're a child or you are an adult. . . . Safety is partly having some sense of control of life, physical integrity, and knowing your direction. The refugee route does not have a certain beginning and a determined ending. Refugees are deprived of the ability to make any plan and even to imagine the next step or a vague direction in this inhumane journey. Most of what we are doing here is creating temporary safe places for vulnerable refugees in passing.

In all my interviews, I asked what makes a space safe for refugees. Depending on the type of refugee work, the emphasis shifted from curfews (for minors) and unisex centers (for teenagers, pregnant women, or sexually and physically abused or assaulted women) to welcoming and helpful staff and volunteers, access to services, friendly reception, safe and reliable connections in the city, and regular psychological counseling. Many frontline workers highlighted the importance of establishing a routine to create a sense of stability against the backdrop of trauma and the never-ending uncertainties of mobility in forced migration. A commonly shared point about safe havens was the need for careful surveillance of who was allowed to enter. Panos worked for one of the shelters for unaccompanied children in Athens for a long time:

> When we tell children, this is your home, your private space, we make sure that strangers will not be allowed in. In arrival cities of Europe, smugglers and traffickers are everywhere to take advantage of young refugees. We do not trust anybody to enter our shelters. Kids may have arrived here by someone they call "uncle," but in reality, that person might be a trafficker. For me, the key to creating a safe place for refugees is hypervigilance.

Except for within the humanitarian corridors that enable safe, legal entry for refugees coming from Lebanon into Italy, most refugees are transported illegally by smugglers or traffickers. The violence of the journey violates their basic human rights, while threatening and often encroaching on their dignity and physical integrity. Even at the long-anticipated finish line, if they reach it, it is unlikely that refugees can easily resolve the feelings of insecurity and fear that they accumulated on the journey. Creating a new and entirely safe life is often illusory for refugees, and with recent EU migration policies, family reunification has become an unlikely dream for many.

In the middle of the multiple layers of fear, uncertainty, and insecurity, arrival border cities try to offer the only thing they can; a safe place for refugees to stay put for a while, and perhaps a little longer. In the context of a perilous journey, the bottom-up making of safe places is the only buffer. In such temporal and spatial circumstances, there is not much beyond that safe place embodied in a community center, a bedroom in a shelter, or a church on a square to provide a transitory sense of sociospatial inclusion.

Proactive Municipality Collaborating with Civil Society

I visited Vice Mayor on Migration and Refugee Affairs Lefteris Papagiannakis and his team in their municipal offices, which were located in a run-down building apart from, and dissimilar in appearance to, the main municipal building. I waited in a room that looked as if it were under construction: There were fickle paintings on the wall and unfinished floors, and the space was crowded with old desks of administrators and other

random furniture. The entire place seemed to be making a blunt statement—a denial of glamor and exclusive focus on management of the refugee flow. Papagiannakis's team occupied several floors, one of which was
reserved as a "safe place" for refugee mothers and their children. The social
worker who worked in the so-called safe room was busy, so busy that she
couldn't find a moment to talk to me for hours. The safe place was created
for mothers and their children to spend time and seek any needed municipal services. For a few hours, I observed the high turnover of refugee
mothers, witnessing the municipality's open doors to refugees and asylum
seekers in search of safety rather than bureaucratic processes. I asked one
of the vice mayor's team members, Vasilis, why a municipal office would
even have a safe room. The aim, he said, was to help refugees develop a
sense of familiarity and get them used to coming to the municipal offices:

> We would like the refugees not to shy away from us and feel free to enter
> municipal buildings. They need to know that Athens municipality does
> not only serve local citizens but everyone who resides here. You can
> think of it as a symbolic way of expressing our inclusivity, but it also
> gives us firsthand contact with them without a need for mediators.

Vasilis added: "As Athens is full of centers and associations that offer safe
places, we are not trying to do the job of civil society organizations or
compete with them." To the contrary, the municipality created a new plat-
form to connect dispersed NGOs and associations under a new umbrella
organization, the Migration and Refugee Coordination Center and Ob-
servatory (MRCC&O). A better-known pillar of this organization is the
Athens Coordination Center for Migrant and Refugee Issues.[13] Established
under Papagiannakis's leadership, MRCC&O brought together numerous
disconnected but like-minded NGOs operating in Athens with the goal of
facilitating communication and cooperation. In this endeavor, the municipality went far beyond the "traditional refugee service provision" that pro-
migrant local governments typically perform.

The center distinguished Athens from other border cities across the
world by providing a model for creating close engagement between the local
government, a strikingly large number of NGOs, INGOs based in Athens
and local activists. These actors preferred working together under this umbrella organization rather than working in parallel or towards different

ends. Most importantly, they were similar in their left-wing resistance to the right-wing, ultranationalist forces and anti-immigrant policies of the EU. Dionysia Lambiri, the project coordinator of MRCC&O, explained that the organization's aim was "the creation of an effective and evidence-based mechanism that can actively prepare for refugee-related emergencies."[14] These services were not offered by former Athens municipalities to refugees. Papagiannakis explained: "People without documents can access municipal services, like healthcare and education, because we have an anti-discrimination policy" (Papagiannakis, quoted in Komporozos-Athanasiou and Papachristou 2018, 128).

The complex spatiality of forced displacement was worsened by temporal complications. The period of "waiting" for processing was left to the discretion of governments and political leaders in power (Bagelman 2016). Such complications of the refugees' journey cannot be grasped or solved with the integration paradigm, which might begin to be helpful only after refugees are settled in the destination country. But this paradigm remains irrelevant when trying to understand or solve refugees' journey in transitory places. As the management of refugees' reception fell on the shoulders of arrival cities, the Athens municipal government played a pivotal role in handling refugee issues in the city. This required workers to develop skills in spontaneity, adjustment, and flexibility. Ironically, these qualities are the opposite of how the locals described their bureaucracy, as not adjustable, inflexible, inefficient, and out of date.

However, as a severe economic crisis had left Greece unable to take care of local problems, such as orphans, the unemployed, the poor and so on, a large segment of the native population felt left behind. Even during such a challenging time, Athens municipality worked hard to include unaccompanied minor refugees and find housing and food for the refugee population. Unlike most NGOs, which have private funding from international donors or the EU, funding for MRCC&O came from ECHO (European Community Humanitarian Office), the EU's humanitarian agency through UNHCR.[15] This atypical funding source safeguarded the center somewhat from the experience of most NGOs, whose funding was inconsistent and unreliable for longer-term commitments. Moreover, nonprofit organizations were supposed to be registered officially, but bureaucratic processes were so inefficient and time-consuming that many were unregistered. This unstable landscape of refugee work in Athens underlies the strikingly high number of NGOs, which seemed to appear and disappear casually on a regular basis. Neither the municipality nor the civil society actors knew from one day to the next exactly how many NGOs were serving, forming, or expiring in the refugee sector.

Despite all these challenges, my interlocutors who worked in NGOs were proud of being part of the good work on behalf of refugees being done in the city. Engaged activists, hands-on service providers, social workers, and others explained to me that they had received support and help from the vice mayor's office. The municipality and the vice mayor were a phone call away any time of day or night. Whether it was about reporting an abusive husband who walked the streets of Victoria bullying and posing a threat to his refugee wife in hiding at the shelter or asking for help to deal with the traumatized teenage boys who had been sexually harassed or violated in the refugee camps or prostituted on the streets of Athens, all stakeholders I met expressed gratitude for the full support from the pro-migrant municipal government.

However, despite the primacy of refugee work in Athens during the pro-migrant local government, I was consistently reminded by the mayor's office and NGOs that refugee issues were the jurisdiction of the state, not the municipality. Consequently, unlike in American sanctuary cities, local police in Greece did not have leeway to refuse to cooperate with national law enforcement on refugee issues.[16] Nevertheless, NGOs in Athens acted much in line with pro-migrant actors in sanctuary cities in the US: Under Kaminis's municipal government, they facilitated refugees' interaction with the police by giving them a choice and voice. Anna, who worked at the main branch of a large NGO that provided health, education, medical, and psychosocial services to refugees in Athens, explained the organization's interaction with the police:

> If the refugee wants to report a crime, then we go along with the person. If the person doesn't want to, we do not go to the police on our own without the person's consent. . . . Unless the police have gotten a prose-cutor's order, they cannot enter our premises. We don't collaborate with the police. If an undocumented person comes here, we are interested in their needs for our services, medical or psychosocial, not their asylum status.

Until the 2019 local elections, I observed multiple interactions of refugee workers with various branches of the state, all providing everyday services to refugees. It was striking to witness how little NGO workers trusted their own state and state officials while fighting for the rights of the racialized Other. The NGO workers expressed trust to refugees and had faith in their testimonies, while the same testimonies of refugees were suspected and distrusted by the state officials during their interviews upon arrival. Who was trusting whom in the refugee sector was ironic and pointed to the primacy of political emotions.

Local Trust and Cocreation of Public Space

Housing and accommodation were the most pressing needs during the peak flow and required engagement between the municipality and NGOs. To discuss these issues, I met with Olivia, lead architectural consultant to the Athens municipal government. We sat at a downtown coffee shop on a sunny day in the winter of 2017. Olivia was an architect and urban planner interested in shaping how Athens evolves. A big fan of interdisciplinary projects, she was keen on bringing together experts from different fields to find fast-track, practical solutions that benefited both refugees and locals. Having worked in Greece, London, and New York, she had international experience in sustainability, city making, and collaborative design "through an architect's point of view or lens," as well as in refugee-related emergency situations in Athens and internationally.

At the time we met, Olivia had just finished a consultancy for a large NGO based in the US that provided emergency relief to refugees around the world, in places like Iraq, Afghanistan, and Turkey. When the NGO arrived in Greece on the heels of the country's initial phases of the refugee influx, Olivia's job was to prepare an unusually high number of housing units in Athens. It seemed like a "mission impossible" to move thousands of refugees from the camps in the border islands to the city in a very short time span. This feat became possible only because downtown Athens had many vacated flats as a result of the country's economic crisis. With funding flowing from ECHO, the UNHCR started working with the Greek asylum office to place refugees in the vacated flats. Luckily, rushed preparations to house refugees were put in place just before the EU-Turkey agreement was signed and Europe's borders were closed.

During this period, refugee housing facilities were scattered throughout downtown Athens, but there was a high concentration in Victoria Square and Omonoia Square. I wondered whether the municipality had strategically placed refugees in existing immigrant neighborhoods. Olivia commented that the municipality offered a lot of housing in immigrant neighborhoods because of high vacancy rates and relatively lower housing prices compared to other downtown neighborhoods, such as Kolonaki. She also noted that the uneven distribution of the flats across the city center created an unplanned, and unintended, advantage. She argued that it was easier to integrate refugees into the city's life when they lived in the diverse city center rather than ethnically segregated places in the periphery.

The debate about whether ethnically concentrated neighborhoods are conducive or not for inclusion has not been settled. Mustafa Dikeç's 2007 book *Badlands* explores Muslim neighborhoods in France, all of which are located at the outskirts, or banlieues, of French cities. Hubs of racial profiling and police brutality, Dikeç's "badlands" became characterized by the politics of fear, discrimination, and insecurity in the aftermath of September 11. These poor neighborhoods of France were much different from the ethnically concentrated "Turkish neighborhood of Berlin," Kreuzberg, in the city's center. At the cost of a high-speed gentrification, Kreuzberg displayed multiple patterns of interaction, and mixing, through interethnic romantic relationships, marriages, business partnerships, and so on between native Germans and Turkish immigrants (Turam 2015).

As Muslim immigrant neighborhoods became an increasingly complicated issue for Europe, I was curious about Olivia's and the municipality's perspective. Were they regarded as dangerous or safe? Olivia responded:

> Do I feel completely safe when I pass by these places . . . ? I mean, completely? Not really. But it's only a perception that I might not be so safe. . . . When something is closed and/or secluded from the rest of the city, you just don't know about it. It might be intimidating only because it is the unknown. When these places become the hubs of actual mixing, then they are really safe. In Athens, I see refugees being really open, especially Syrians, because they are placed in various parts in the city center rather than being clustered.

Olivia's words made me wonder if mixing was undermined or blocked by the presence of ethnically concentrated migrant neighborhoods or by the unwillingness, doubts, xenophobia or racism of the native locals. Reflecting on how the housing strategies of refugees intersected with other cultural and societal factors, Olivia continued:

> For me, integration is important and needs to be achieved without disrespecting their culture. Syrians are very close to Greek culture in the way they talk and work with us. . . . But for example, Afghanistan is very, very different. Especially how women in their society live and so on . . . is quite different, and makes everything challenging.

To what extent did cultural differences of refugees present a challenge to Athens in terms of accommodation or refugees? Wimmer and Soehl's (2014) quantitative study tested and challenged cultural explanations. The authors examined whether "*distant* linguistic or religious origins (including Islam)" were underlying factors of failed acculturation to a host country. Rather than "cultural distance," their findings showed that legal factors or social disadvantages were the main determinant of failed integration. Put differently, rather than a specific ethnic, racial, or Muslim cultural background, failure to acculturate was shaped by the institutional infrastructure—that is, political institutions—and by policies that disadvantaged certain groups.

I wondered how Olivia's refugee-related consulting work fit into the institutional political milieu. I asked whether she trusted the political institutions. She responded with a firm "no." She did not trust the Greek state nor other EU member states. She complained that their policies "inflamed" the political crisis instead of offering solutions to the refugee influx. In sharp contrast to her distrust of the nation-state, she emphasized her commitment to working with the municipality:

> I do trust the people that I work with in the municipality—not the entire structure of the local government. This trust is based on years of collaboration with those dedicated people. . . . When you collaborate in the middle of a crisis under pressure, and when they have your back in panic situations, you know they're really trying to find a solution. The solution is right here in the city and right now. It is not in some slow-motion bureaucratic process of top-down policymaking by the state. We learned to take care of the mess on our own in Athens.

With little faith or trust in the immigration policies of EU member states, most of Olivia's efforts went towards creating a safe local environment.

After finishing her project on housing for refugees, she began working as a project manager to create inclusive public places. Her major effort was to ensure a safe urban environment in which people from different walks of life, ethnicities, races, classes, and genders could come together publicly to interact and cooperate regardless of their migrant or refugee status.

The public sphere has long been applauded as the heart of democratic participation. Scholars put a lot of critical thinking into how public space can melt away artificial walls of unfamiliarity and distrust and ease disagreement between diverse groups, all by way of urban planning, architectural innovations, and public debate and deliberation (Sennett 1998; Calhoun 1993). However, most theories about the public sphere ignore power dynamics between unequal participants in that sphere, such as racialized migrants or nonbinary genders; therefore, the safety of vulnerable or marginalized groups, including newcomers and migrants, has not been the primary concern of these theories of public space, most of which lacked intersectional analysis. Olivia's vision of the public space and the city went beyond Habermasian optimism on communication as a facilitator of agreement in the public sphere.

Public spaces are not self-generating "magic zones" of racial justice and equality. The public sphere is not innately capable of taking care of conflict and coping with power hierarchies, and thereby smoothing away sentiments of fear and the presumed threat of the Other and cultivating trust and safety. Olivia's project on inclusive public space in Athens used quotidian tools for the inclusion of all residents, including racialized migrants and refugees. She achieved this by inviting noncitizens to become active in the cocreation (not just the use) of safe inclusive public places (for a similar idea, see Harvey 2003). Olivia's excitement about collective placemaking was inspiring:

> This is about giving all residents incentives to cocreate the public realm, and thereby urban life. There is small funding—very tiny funding, indeed—that citizens can apply for . . . Think software though, not hardware! So, software would be equipment for streets or squares that are temporary, such as a commonly shared landscaping cart. Basically, right now I am strategizing with the municipality to set up the procedure for having a bottom-up (as opposed to a traditional top-down) mechanism. This means civil groups learn to demand their needs from the city,

but at the same time, the municipality proactively exercises how to take on the responsibility to respond and provide services to all residents, including the refugees and migrants.

The passionate words and ideas of this architect with a vision reflected an uplifting urban spirit blooming in an ascending anti-immigrant regime in Europe. Between 2017 and 2019, I witnessed how the vice mayor on migrant and refugee affairs, his team, and their projects expanded beyond Athens to several other cities in Greece. Like the innovative edge in Olivia's projects, Papagiannakis empowered his team to develop ideas, projects, and networks. Dionysia Lambiri proudly shared that the "vice mayor trusted and gave [his staff] freedom to think critically and act independently," even though this sometimes meant "not going by the book," because the infamous "Greek bureaucracy would have prevented [them] from being spontaneous and acting upon crisis situations promptly." The municipality facilitated and supported the production of inventive ideas for inclusion and safety. In the following years, I witnessed how this open-minded inventive pro-migrant spirit was entirely lacking in heavily bureaucratized national and international institutions that deal with refugee issues.

Lambiri, the then project coordinator of MRCC&O, continued to update and inform me about developments in Athens and the municipality's projects. When the conservative New Democracy party replaced the leftist Syriza in 2019, Kyriakos Mitsotakis, the new prime minister, began introducing major changes to refugee policies. Greece's new deputy defense minister, Alkiviadis Stefanis, declared that the operations of NGOs performing refugee and migrant work would be "subject to new criteria." Athens was already on alert to the impending political shift, when Stefanis announced that "only those [NGOs] that meet the requirements will stay and continue to operate in the country" (*The Guardian* 2019). These interventions signaled additional securitization: The new government interpreted refugee work as an issue of defense and national security. The new government's prioritization of security in refugee issues was the opposite of Kaminis's municipal engagements with the NGOs, whose missions prioritized safety and human rights.

Although Golden Dawn lost its seats and was left out of the parliament with the electoral victory of the New Democracy, the new right-wing national and local government posed new challenges to refugee work in Athens. While the MRCC&O support for NGOs continued to be intact, its leadership was left to junior members. Most NGO representatives and activist friends I was in touch were deeply concerned that the MRCC&O was rapidly losing its power and influence.

Athens's new municipal government, led by New Democracy (2019–24), could not undermine the leftist activist tradition so deeply rooted in the city. I was not surprised when, in a show of the city's commitment and resilience, thousands of Athenians celebrated in the streets on October 7, 2020, after the Greek court's landmark ruling that the Golden Dawn was a criminal organization. That day, Athenians did not shy away from the two thousand riot police who guarded the courthouse with tear gas and water cannons. Locals rejoiced. It was the "first significant trial of a neo-Nazi party in Europe after World War II."[17] The court's verdict sent the important message to the world that individuals, including members of Parliament, who conduct racist, anti-immigrant activity in violation of human rights will not go unpunished.

The case of Athens shows that arrival cities in Europe are not destined to become cities of refuge simply by their geography. In these cities, migrant support is built from the bottom up by strong but shifting cooperation between the municipality, local activists, and NGOs. Up until 2019, Athens coped with the flow by experientially developing political skills that built upon a strong legacy of leftist urban activism. Through the peak of the flow, the city made significant efforts to accommodate refugees through a series of politically responsible and humane choices made by local activists and officials on a daily basis. My findings revealed the primacy of local trust, by pitting it against an overwhelming political distrust of the state and political institutions. This local trust rooted in the city's leftist activist tradition provided the basis of the pro-migrant alliances between the municipality, the NGOs, and human right activists. These trust-based local alliances opened the way for and encouraged the quotidian links formed between migrant communities against the background of the EU's violent and inhumane hot-spot border regime. Under the pressure of heightened global human mobility, multiple urban actors struggled to keep the city a bulwark against the rising tide of right-wing ideologies that exclude, discriminate against, and inflict violence on racialized refugee populations. Until the conservative New Democracy won the local elections in 2019, Athens continued to carry the flag of this mission.

TWO

The Geopolitics of Fear Versus Solidarity

Frustration about the EU's imposition of the austerity memoranda and the rising nationalism culminated in the electoral triumph of the right-wing anti-immigrant New Democracy party in 2019. Having promised to solve the economic crisis, and to restore security, Kyriakos Mitsotakis came to power by assuring the end of the refugee influx and the deportation of refugees (Crabapple 2020). Upon his appointment as prime minister, New Democracy's revised asylum law, effective in January 2020, extended migrants' detention period and transferred asylum-related work to the Greek army and police, while it also banned immigrants from receiving social security numbers and joined the Ministry of Migration with the Ministry of Citizen Protection.

New Democracy's municipal and national victories intensified the multiscale securitization of refugees. While the ballot box and the following local policy changes did not put an end to pro-refugee resistance, they forced it to concentrate in pro-migrant corners of the city. By the time securitization was "on full display" (Fischer and Jorgenson 2021, 1069–70), all my activist interlocutors in the refugee sector were complaining about the government's security practices and human rights violations. Ironically, these Athenians, who had worked so hard through the peak with high spirit for the safety of refugees, were now admitting their own sense of insecurity in their hometown. Securitization in the form of police surveillance and attacks targeted areas that were densely populated with irregular migrants and refugees, places like Exarcheia, a downtown neighborhood identified as the anarchist quarter of Athens.

Against the backdrop of repression of pro-migrant resistance (Della Porta and Steinhilper 2022), historically insurgent Exarcheia (Vradis 2020) provides a perfect laboratory for studying the dynamics of persistent pro-refugee solidarity. Parting ways with the predominant focus on (pro)migrant social movements, this chapter scrutinizes everyday life in a neighborhood that has a distinct historical memory and political purpose. I explore the resistance in this neighborhood, formed through locals' widely shared emotions, including indifference, contempt, frustration, and distrust in the anti-immigrant government. A close look at the resistance reveals coexisting, yet at times contrasting, responses of pro-refugee locals who do not act collectively or in political alliance with each other. The chapter concretely details how humanitarians, anarchists, and (non)activist locals resist securitization alongside one another, despite their different political agendas and ideological allegiances. Zooming in on the daily manifestations of locals' reactions to the security regime, as well as mundane interactions among residents, my research examines the underpinnings of a dissident pro-refugee solidarity in the very center of the border city.

The key to Exarcheia's complex resistance is a shared aversion to government-led fear. The geopolitics of emotion generated by the hypersecuritized border largely shapes the dynamics between security forces and the pro-migrant resistance. The geopolitics of emotion play a major role in empowering the politically diverse solidarity in Exarcheia. Accordingly, parting ways with emotion-blind, state-centered theories of securitization, a focus on geopolitics of emotion helps me center fear and its antidotes—fear aversion, safety, and trust—as catalysts of spatially contained pro-refugee resistance against a violent security regime.

In "Compassion Protocol," Fassin (2011, 87) elaborates on the irony of how the new moral economy has come to value and prioritize emotions over rights. Fassin's (2005) critical analysis of the primacy of emotions, such as compassion, in repressive refugee governance is consistent with the centrality of fear aversion that I encountered in Exarcheia. He rightly problematizes how human rights issues are replaced by the politics of emotions, such as care and compassion. Importantly, however, at a time when security regimes are increasingly violating freedoms and rights, my findings draw attention to another aspect of the nexus of emotions and human rights. Rather than triggering people's compassion for humanitarian aid and care, I uncover the ways in which the native-migrant solidarity is empowered by geopolitical emotions. Hence, against the background of fear-mongering political regimes of Europe, my ethnography illuminates how the geopolitics of emotions inspire, motivate, and bolster the fight for migrants' rights and freedoms.

By shedding light on the importance of local opposition to (presumably) global securitization, the chapter illustrates how Exarcheians unanimously express feeling safe in their neighborhood despite police surveillance and raids. The ethnography also reveals and analyzes how locals react to all-encompassing narratives of "global fear." By subverting government-led fear, the geopolitics of emotions are capable of disrupting and circumventing the securitization of migration at the local level. To gain an in-depth understanding of the "actual reality on the ground" of multiple stakeholders (Triandafyllidou 2022, 812), this chapter goes beyond local and national policy under the New Democracy and spatializes fear, safety, and (in)security in everyday life. I uncover how Exarcheia shelved fear, replacing it with other widely shared emotions, including safety, trust, and belonging, to strengthen a bulwark against securitization of migration.

Geopolitical Emotions in a History of (Cross) Border Relations

One month before Mitsotakis's victory in the 2019 national elections, his nephew Kostas Bakoyannis[1] became mayor of Athens and immediately renamed and reclassified the position of vice mayor of migration created by the previous mayor, Georgios Kaminis. The new position—municipal councilor of migration—entailed less decision-making power. Corporate attorney Melina Daskalakis filled the position while continuing her private law practice. During my interview with Daskalakis in her municipal office, she criticized the former Syriza government for using refugee issues as a bargaining tool. But when I asked about ongoing pushbacks to Turkey and human right abuses, the direction of the conversation changed:

Daskalakis: If Turkey is relatively safe, then Turkey must keep them.

Me: Is Europe dumping its migration problem on the Global South?

Daskalakis: No, it's not Europe's problem more than it is Turkey's. But Europe pays for these countries. . . . If we open Europe's borders . . . there will no longer be a Europe left as we know [it].

The response of Councilor Daskalakis must be understood in the context of two geopolitical particularities of the eastern Mediterranean. Greece's historically troubled border conflicts and political animosities with Turkey have had great impact in shaping the present-day perceptions and emotions about the refugee flow through Turkey. Further, the numerous tensions and conflicts between Turkey and Greece, including the Cyprus war, have shaped geopolitics in the eastern Mediterranean. Turkey—a Muslim neighbor and a large military power in the eastern Mediterranean—has always been a threat, and Erdoğan's aggressive relationship with the EU reinforced that perception.[2] As discussed in the previous chapter, Turkey was considered a major problem even by the actors of the pro-migrant solidarity. This differs from the view of solidarity in Palermo which accuses Italy as a former colonizer of Libya and for its externalization of borders to Libya.

International migration scholarship attributes two conflicting roles to Turkey: the gatekeeper (the protector of "Fortress Europe") and the troublemaker. "Far from being in contradiction with the first role, the Turkey-as-trouble-maker narrative reproduces the Eurocentrism of [international relations] (security) studies regarding non-European states' intentions, calculations, and strategies" (İşleyen 2023, 370). My findings suggest that the Eurocentric double-sided view of Turkey is widely shared across the political spectrum, from the Left to the Right in European context

It is not surprising, then, that even leftist pro-refugee circles perceived Councilor Daskalakis as a relatively cooperative member of the uncooperative New Democracy party. Many activists observed to me that her politics were "fine" despite her membership in New Democracy. Yet Daskalakis's perspective echoed Greek security professionals' view of Turkey as a threat to Greece and Europe. Recent research points to Greek security professionals who problematized having "a neighboring country with which [they] have national sovereignty problems, and which also is a Muslim country" (Skleparis 2016, 99). External actors to EU securitization—including

Turkey—have often been regarded as exploiting securitization to achieve their own geopolitical interests (Leonard and Kaunert 2022). Even so, these pervasive perspectives on Turkey largely overlook the fact that the country is among the top refugee hosts in the world, along with Iran and Germany.

My interviews suggested that the widely shared emotional stance against Turkey appears to dismiss Europe's historical complicity in the forced displacement of racialized people. Daskalakis's discourse represented a dominant perspective, which regarded Europe as a bystander, releasing it from all historical responsibility for colonialism, and Greece as the victim of the refugee crisis. The emotional dimension of cross-border relations between Greece and Turkey was based on the idea that Greece was innocent and did not deserve to be put into the position, on Europe's behalf, of dealing with the flow of migrants from Turkey. This prevailing perspective in Greece was notably different from the anti-racist and anticolonial discourses that circulated in solidarity in Palermo, embraced more consistently by pioneering Black activists (see Chapter 4). Concretely, the geopolitics of emotion about Turkey in Greece interrupted and obscured locals' recognition that most migrants were from former European colonies. Even if Greek historical memory constructed Turkey on the basis of its origins in the Ottoman Imperial power, Syria, the major sending country of refugees, was a French protectorate until 1946. Similarly, Britain invaded and occupied Afghanistan three times before its independence in 1919 (Danewid 2017, 1680). As discussed in the introduction, the geopolitics of Greece's borders continue to evolve around fear, distrust, and historically rooted rage towards the Muslim neighbor

Integration Issues as Cover-Up for "Racial Security"

A prominent official in the New Democracy's municipality observed to me that it would be easier for refugees to integrate into Muslim-majority Turkey. Given that most irregular border crossers to Greece have been Muslim, I asked why religion mattered. The discussion landed on the topic of fear of the Other:

> Official: Religious people have a barrier to integrate to Europe.
> Me: Religious people? You mean Muslim people? Does not Europe look more like a Christian club, where Islamophobia is on the rise?

Official: No, I don't really agree on Islamophobia, no . . . I understand that many people demonize Muslims but . . . behind that fear, there is the reality of difficult integration.

In my interviews with local officials in Athens and in the border islands, the issue of integration came up often as a justification for securitization, but it was not only about national, public, or welfare security. The arguments also indicated what Fassin (2005, 381) refers to as racial security that is protective of the "European, Christian, and white civilization" against Muslim and Black populations. Problematizing the issue of integration further, De Genova (2018b, 1777) argues that the "complacent demand for 'integration' consistently enfolds the Muslim Question within the broader parameters of a cultural politics of 'European' identity." Cultural politics, he claims, are inextricable from the present (migrant) crisis, which manifests as the "historical moment of *racial crisis*" (1769). Underlining the mutually constitutive crisis of European borders and European identity, De Genova asserts that they both are "replete with reanimated reactionary populist nationalisms and racialized nativisms, the routinization of antiterrorist securitization, and pervasive and entrenched Islamophobia" (1768; see also Burrell and Hörschelmann 2019). He uses Islamophobia interchangeably with "anti-Muslim racism."

After September 11, fear of the Islamist terrorist served as justification for anti-Muslim racism, expanding the definition of terrorism and "spreading the tentacles of the security state" (Fekete 2009, 46).[3] Parallel to this, populist parties promoted a politics of fear by championing a "nativist and authoritarian understanding of the social fabric in which states should be inhabited exclusively by natives" (Bazurli and Delclós 2022, 65; see also Blokker and Anselmi 2020; Duyvendak et al. 2023).

In my conversation with her, Councilor Daskalakis continued: "I don't discriminate against Muslims, but I acknowledge why people have become Islamophobic. . . . Every culture has a fear of the alien."

Do cultures really have an inherent fear of the alien? Or is fear of the Other shaped by a political ideology, government mandates, and policies? As already discussed, the main challenge to integration does not originate in major cultural or religious differences, but in the failures of political institutions, and the state in particular, to accommodate migrants (Wimmer and Soehl 2014). In the light of this, it is not surprising that the issue of Muslim integration created a major conflict between civil society and the New Democracy government.

Nadina, founder of Melissa Network, shared with me a different approach to integration:

> Integration should start from the very first moment of arrival at the border. . . . The more welcoming we are in dealing with vulnerabilities at reception, the better the prospects for change and contribution from the refugees. . . . We receive people who never experienced peace. Their history consists only of war terminology, violence, and fear. How do we expect them to integrate into our societies unless we are able to offer them a friendly welcome, a safe place, and a peaceful coexistence?

I asked Nadina if she was referring to integration in Greece, as most refugees preferred to continue on to northern Europe. Nadina's response was insightful:

> Integration should not aim at one-to-one people-country matching! It's not like a vacation plan as if they leave Syria to embark for Greece or Germany. People escape from unsafe places—not only their homeland but also the receiving transit countries—such as Afghans in Iran or Syrians in Turkey. Integration needs to equip refugees with a tool kit that would work *for them* in different settings and countries, and not just a fixed formula to make good Greek or German nationals out of Syrian or Afghan refugees. (Italics added.)

Nadina's idea of a humane and geographically fluid concept of integration sharply contradicts the territorially fixed, Eurocentric national projects of securitization. The contrast between these perspectives brings to the surface the problematic entanglement of integration and national security. Hence, disentangling integration issues from national security agendas would be a big step toward freeing vulnerable refugees from the geopolitics of fear. If detached from racial security, inclusion could become more sensitive to human dimensions and emotions, such as dignity, and would honor the sense and sensibilities of migrants as deserving human beings.

Clearly, integration issues were not the only controversy between the government and solidarity. Even though the resistance had been able to cooperate with the former municipal government, cooperation became impossible between the pro-migrant resistance and the New Democracy government. When pressed about the pushbacks in my interviews, officials in Athens and on the islands offered me the rhetoric that every country had the right to protect its borders against smugglers and traffickers—those who, absent a humane border politics, provided the only transportation available to refugees.[4] As the security rhetoric of self-defense does not apply to vulnerable refugees, who are not attacking but seeking asylum in the arrival country, they and their allies had to be lumped together with traffickers and other criminals.

Athens's Mayor Bakoyannis followed suit. I asked him after a talk at Harvard University in 2020 how he situated Athens within Europe's refugee landscape. After reluctantly admitting that he "did not want to talk about this," he said that "the states in Europe took the initiative and the societies followed their states' lead," whereas in Greece people "went forward and embraced refugees, and the state followed them."[5] Accusing the former leftist government of weakness and failure, his state-centered security proposal was instead to "save" the distressed city by securitizing and fighting the "refugee crisis" and restoring law and order.

Who Is Afraid of the Disobedient Neighborhood?

Exarcheia, a hotbed of radical left activism, has for long been claimed as "a liberated space" by anarchists (Fischer and Jorgenson 2021, 1071). The neighborhood has thereby served as an "effective anger diffuser" in a regime that fails to provide for welfare and material needs (Vradis 2020, 553–54). Historically, the uprisings in 1973, 1985, and 2008 epitomized the neighborhood as the locus of insurgency against the state. Politically, the 1973 student riots that contributed to the overthrow of dictatorial rule in 1974 played a major role in establishing Exarcheia's image as the hub of antiauthority, anticapitalist, and radical intellectual insurrection.

In spatial terms, Exarcheia is in the city center, bordering the upscale neighborhood Kolonaki to the east and the large Omonoia Square, which hosts mixed migrant populations, to the west. The campus of Athens Polytechnic in Exarcheia contributes to the neighborhood's diversity, with its students, alternative youth, academics, intellectuals, artists, the radical left, and anarchists.

FIGURE 2. **Exarcheia's narrow streets,
September 3, 2021. Photo by the author.**

During the 1973 protests, the narrow streets of Exarcheia proved well suited to resistance, providing convenient escapes for protestors from the main demonstration. Following the 2008 protests, Greek officials introduced motorcycle police to overcome the difficult access to these "unruly" parts of the city center (Vradis 2020, 551). After a short break from harsh policing during Syriza's leftist rule (2015–19), the conservative government's "law and order" slogan brought the motorcycled squads back, along with crackdowns on migrant squats.

Between 2015 and 2019, Exarcheia's squats routinely accommodated refugees who could not obtain housing.[6] The squats represented both an "inclusive model of co-existence" (Cappuccini 2018) and a "privileged site for activism" (Arampatzi 2017a, 50). In line with the state's historical tolerance of Exarcheia's contained insurgency (Vradis 2020), former mayor Kaminis had allowed the squats to exist. But this changed rapidly when he left office. Prior to becoming prime minister in 2019, Kyriakos Mitsotakis had called Exarcheia home to a "new generation of terrorists" and promised to "clear the area," if elected.[7] In January 2020, Mayor Bakoyannis was criticized in a *New Yorker* op-ed about his right-wing urban politics and hands-on securitization and encroachment on the squats in Exarcheia. In my meeting with Mayor Bakoyannis in September 2021, he defended the closures: "One cannot illegally occupy someone else's property. In many cases these places were tied with crimes, with drugs . . . and trafficking." Bakoyannis also declared Athens to be much safer as a result of the closures, as well as his police reform, community policing, and a new "coordination center" that facilitated cooperation between the police and the Ministry of Citizen Protection.

Deeply intimidated by the radical left and the dissident nature of the neighborhood,[8] the new municipal government tried to rebrand Exarcheia, by presenting the changes there partly as urban transformation from a "grungy" to a "model" neighborhood. Securitization expanded the role of riot police by pitting them against the anarchists in clashes on the main square, near a new metro station (*National Herald* 2019). A permanent police presence at strategic neighborhood junctures eventually replaced abrupt police attacks on Exarcheia's periphery. In my last visit in 2024, the police presence was a fixture in the Exarcheia square, day and night.

The Clash Between Security and Freedom

Expecting to hear an alternative approach to securitization, I met in Exarcheia with Lefteris Papagiannakis, vice mayor on migrant and refugee affairs from 2016 to 2019. Importantly, however, despite being a committed pro-refugee human rights activist, Papagiannakis did not romanticize the neighborhood's squats, and he warned me against confusing them with "safe havens."

Why, then, had he been an enthusiastic resident of Exarcheia for more than twenty years? "Do you share the fear of the current municipality about Exarcheia?" I asked. He shrugged and said that he was not afraid of anything in his neighborhood. He and several members of his family had a strong sense of belonging and felt safe there. I wondered whether he felt insecure when he served as the vice mayor, walking around occasionally in a business suit in a neighborhood associated with grunge, hipsters and punks, and anarchists. In asserting his belonging to this emotional space, he assured me that his attire did not matter, as locals "knew, respected, and trusted" him. After all, he was a highly trusted figure of solidarity in Athens.

Our conversation made me wonder how Exarcheians felt about their neighborhood. Did they share the New Democracy's concerns and alerts about danger, disorder, and insecurity? Yorgos, a middle-aged, long-time resident and nonactivist, said:

> It is not so much about who is not let in or unwelcome here. It is about who is afraid of Exarcheia and will not put a step in our neighborhood, the racists, the conservatives, the ultranationalists. . . . They will send their police but will stay away from our safe habitat. We don't need more resistance here. Their fear suffices to keep them away from *our* island of freedoms. (Italics added.)

Describing Exarcheia's resistance as primarily spatial and emotional rather than mobilizational, Yorgos linked insecurity with "the organization of fear in [the] spatial sense" (Ahmed 2014, 68) and pitted insecurity and fear against freedom. Only those afraid of what Exarcheia represents tend to enforce its image as the dangerous Other. Yorgos juxtaposed the securitizers' fear to his own sense of belonging and territoriality. He explicated how locals dissociated from the government-constructed fear.

The aversion to fear in the pro-migrant resistance was closely aligned with the primacy of feeling free and defending freedoms. Moreover, in a country with a recent dictatorial past, the defense of freedoms in Exarcheia was an expression of fervent antiauthoritarianism. In this regard, Papagiannakis told me that his early schooling in a politically liberal elementary school seeded his antiauthoritarian and antipatriarchal worldview and his advocacy on behalf of vulnerable groups, including women, LGBTQ, refugees, and asylum seekers. Exarcheia attracted like-minded people like Yorgos and Papagiannakis, who would not consider living anywhere else.

Epitomizing the clash between security and freedom (see Balzacq and Carrera 2016, 15), the neighborhood's political purpose was not just about intellectual and political deliberation. It was written into the built environment, everyday practices, and ways of life. A large banner in Exarcheia's main square bluntly spelled out Exarcheia's political message in English: until all are free.

FIGURE 3. **Banner in Exarchia's square,**
September 3, 2021. Photo by the author.

Who Resists Securitization?

Exarcheians unequivocally stated that they did not trust the Greek state. After the New Democracy came to power in 2019, Exarcheians also expressed deep disappointment in the government, describing feelings of sociopolitical and economic insecurity and mistrust and anger in party leadership. In sharp contrast to these negative emotions, my interlocutors unanimously reported feeling safe in their neighborhood, and no one expressed fear of danger or disorder caused by refugees, the radical left, or anarchists.

Importantly, the shared objection to securitization did not arise from a homogeneous neighborhood community. Concretely, the common rejection of the government-led fear did not originate either in a shared identity politics or a collective political ideology. The glue that united the locals in their resistance against securitization of migration was the widely shared geopolitics of emotion in the neighborhood. Shared distrust of government and an aversion to fear facilitated the cultivation of belonging and local trust (for local trust, see also Bilgiç 2013). Exarcheia's resistance presented a clear case against the notion of receptive audience of security theories.

Everyday life in Exarcheia provided a counterargument to the municipal project of "dispersing" migrants to neighborhoods, including places where they were unwelcome, judged, excluded, and feared. As I was having coffee with activist friends at a street café one Sunday afternoon, a young Syrian refugee woman who was passing by casually greeted my friends. They asked her to join us and introduced her to me. Aysha, an elementary school teacher in her homeland, enjoyed a cup of tea with us. Careful not to turn her leisure time to an interview, I asked: "How is life in Exarcheia? Do you feel safe here despite increased police presence?" She said:

> Were you here when migrant masses were merging in Victory Square? Thank God, we did not stay there or move to unwelcoming places. We avoided a lot of suffering by finding ourselves in this neighborhood. Sure, the police attack. . . . But we are welcome here . . . they are not.

Aysha did not express insecurity despite the police raids and recently cemented doors of the squats. Existing literature associates securitized spaces, with their fences, walls, and guns, with feelings of fear and insecurity. In border cities, however, securitized spaces that are sustained by fear also coexist with safe places that are sustained by trust and inclusion . Hence, in Aysha's life, these distinct spaces and the contrasting emotions they elicit coexist side by side; that is, police attacks and local trust take place in proximity and concurrently in everyday life. Considering that such emotions are "individual, socially circulated and spatially contextual" (Askins 2016, 517), Aysha felt safe in Exarcheia, where locals were assertive about their negative feelings towards the police presence and objected to government-led securitization.

Unsurprisingly, my participation in instances of spontaneous social interactions in Exarcheia did not compare to everyday dynamics in other parts of Athens. In fact, since New Democracy took office, the pro-refugee urban space had shrunk to a few pockets in the city. Exarcheia proactively pushed back against the fear-based repression of solidarity spaces and resistance in the city (Della Porta and Steinhilper 2022; Ahmed 2014, 64).

The avoidance of fear was spatial across nonactivists and noncitizens (who often did not mobilize) and activists and anarchists (who did not mobilize together). Hence, the geopolitics of emotion integral to resisting securitization were neither a resource of collective action nor an asset for political alliance. Instead, the geopolitics of emotion manifested as one quality of the everyday flow of life. This is best captured by Askins's (2016, 516) phrase "meaningful encounter," described as the "interactions that shift entrenched and largely negative versions of the 'other' to reduce social tension." Meaningful encounters, he argues, nurture sociospatial inclusion. Clearly, Exarcheia is not unique in showcasing these encounters. Other dissident (pro)migrant spaces exist across Europe, such as Ballarò in Palermo, Sicily (Chapter 4), and Kreuzberg and Neukölln in Berlin, Germany (Turam 2015). Rather than representing these instances of meaningful encounters as frequent or generalizable, I examine them closely, as they are crucial for a deeper grasp of a pro-migrant urbanity in anti-immigrant security regimes.

The Kallidromiou Farmers Market was another place where meaningful encounters took place. Located on Saturdays in the heart of the anarchist district on a street closed to traffic across several blocks, it is the largest outdoor market for local producers in Athens. Locals from all walks of life mingled, tasted food, and listened to street music. Local activists socialized, distributed leaflets, and promoted their campaigns (see also Arampatzi 2017a, 50). Welcoming all residents, regardless of citizenship or migrant status, the sociability of the space was natural and peaceful, with no signs of insecurity, exclusion, or discrimination.

On one of those Saturday mornings, my friends and I ran into one of the anarchists who had participated in the creation of the squats. As we continued walking and chatting, he told me that nonactivist residents supported their efforts to settle and host refugees. My interviews also revealed that Exarcheians were astutely aware of the difference between a contempt for securitization and the anti-state sentiment central to anarchist's "anti-security" efforts. Put differently, Exarcheians were cognizant of the difference between being against securitization and against security. There was no naivete in pro-refugee resistance: Rather than turning a blind eye to different shades of extralegality, Exarcheians selectively filtered and refused the "false" threats and dangers constructed by the government. Concretely, their objection was not directed toward the fight against an "actual" crime but at the harm done to innocent vulnerable populations, like refugees and asylum seekers. But Exarcheians' sense of safety in their neighborhood was based on the fact that anarchists do not harm civilians and support refugees.

The locals ridiculed and criticized the government's security policies, which focused on fabricated dangers and nonexistent threats, while wandering the market and sipping coffee, and later ouzo, with like-minded neighborhood residents. For Exarcheians, walls and cemented doors of the squats did not create a sense of insecurity (or security); they simply did not feel intimidated or threatened by the securitized sites. Their aversion to fear was a politically sophisticated response, enabling Exarcheians at times to be sarcastic and dismissive of the government's encroachment on their neighborhood.

When the bulk of the literature shows "the racialisation of migration, [and] how marginalised groups are excluded from the public realm," it becomes imperative to explore emotional geographies (Askins 2016, 516), as exemplified here by Exarcheia. My findings suggest that these geographies hold the key to alternative ways of interrupting securitization in violent borderlands. Establishing a strong affinity between political feelings and geopolitics, Gökariksel and Secor (2018, 1250) argue: "Attending to affect—to the production, circulation, and effects of 'political feeling'—is not an exercise of turning globally writ geopolitics on its head. This *is* geopolitics."

Unlike protests, routinely crushed by security forces, the geopolitics of emotions were neither erasable nor suppressible in this refugee-hosting neighborhood. Dimitri, a local architect, explained: "This is not Berlin. . . . We cannot turn squats into legal entities and give the squatters the right of property." When I asked why not, Dimitri responded:

> The squatters in Exarcheia did not have the least intention to interact, negotiate or settle with the government, the state, or any political authority. Anarchists hate the state and want it to wither away. They will neither obey nor cooperate. . . . It does not matter to them whether it was about refugees or whatever.

Indeed, the squats were self-organized solidarity units that refused to collaborate with the state and with NGOs. They exemplified a solidarity in which locals and refugees made independent decisions together (Tsavdaroglou and Kaika 2021, 1138). Michael, a forty-year-old solidarity activist, observed to me that anarchists were "standing close with undocumented migrants as their situation was aligning with anarchists' antagonism to state authority." Many argued that anarchists used migrants as pawns, and some expressed reservation about squats. By safeguarding refugees, the anarchists simultaneously achieved two aims: protecting refugees from the regime that they opposed and confronting the state by disregarding its policies and the law.

To explore locals' sense of (in)security, I asked how they felt about sharing the neighborhood with anarchists. During a brunch with activist friends, Evi explained:

> Look, we all know people in those circles. They would not harm us. . . . We also share similar feelings about the police attacks. But we have different agendas and methods. Hence, we may deliver food for refugees, but we do not develop projects together.

Everybody laughed at her last comment. Elias added:

> We do not undermine or disrespect each other despite our different world views. Everybody minds their own business here. But do not kid yourself! Exarcheia is a real neighborhood based on mutual familiarity—not uniformity! Locals trust locals. We value the choice of living here. We all are proud of our neighborhood.

Elias expressed strong emotion associated with this highly politicized urban space: trust, respect, and pride. He reminded me of my previous experience with anarchists at City Plaza, a hotel squatted by anarchists and refugees. City Plaza had made an international reputation for solidarity with migrants in the aftermath of the 2016 Turkey-EU agreement. During my visit in 2017, anarchists had blocked the hotel entrance at the reception desk to protect refugees from "strangers." Even though I mentioned my close and reliable connections in activist circles and showed my multiple permissions to study refugee issues, they did not let me into the building. I was missing the "Exarcheia passport," the unspoken code of access and spatial familiarity. The squat in City Plaza was disbanded by the squatters themselves a few days after the New Democracy came to power in 2019.

Despite the image of peaceful inclusion and nondiscrimination, sanctuary places are often places of high contestation (e.g., Darling and Bauder 2019; Turam 2021). Unsurprisingly, the downtown neighborhood was rapidly becoming a magnet for freedom- and diversity-seekers, who looked for a haven from the global tide of right-wing populism and the far right. Subsequently, the popularity of Exarcheia was turning the neighborhood into "a controversial city-branding location and investment/development project area" (Tsavdaroglou and Kaika 2021, 1133). I heard locals referring to Exarcheia as the "Airbnb hub of Athens," and I experienced the tension caused by such contradictory trends and rapid gentrification. Similar patterns of gentrification can be observed in other neighborhoods where migrant and pro-migrant residents cohabit, such as Kreuzberg in Berlin, Marseilles in France, Cihangir in Istanbul, and Ballarò in Palermo. Vicino et al. (2011) noted that immigrant neighborhoods may entice gentrification by being seen as "exotic" and "bohemian" places by mainstream society.

These multifaceted transformations raised the question of whether the government's city-branding agenda was successful in "taming" Exarcheia. Has securitization transformed the neighborhood from being a dissident pro-migrant space to an anti-migrant model of securitized space? On the contrary, I observed that the more aggressively the local government encroached on Exarcheia with police attacks, squat closures, and the like, the more emboldened and confident the neighborhood became around its purpose. Instead of killing the neighborhood spirit, such encroachment triggered a dialectic between securitization and anti-securitization. Over the past couple of years, inclusivity and nonconformist politics carried Exarcheia's reputation into international debates, panels, conferences, and publications.

What really mattered in this highly politicized place was that the New Democracy party's securitization did not change residents' political agency, and emotions—their fear aversion, love of freedom, and respect for refugees. Consequently, the neighborhood's political message persisted. For example, although New Democracy had set a punitive agenda of fines for residents who did not obey the new mandate of "cleaning" graffiti from their buildings, graffiti still covers walls throughout the neighborhood. Anarchists and human rights activists continue living in proximity, albeit tangentially. The shared pro-refugee agendas culminate in temporary and spatially framed co-presence and selective temporal assistance between them. But this intricate coexistence is capitalized by securitizers to criminalize pro-refugee circles and efforts.

Frontliners Under Attack

Nothing reflects the spirit of solidarity in Exarcheia better than the words of Pia Klemp, captain of a German NGO rescue ship. On refusing to accept a medal of honor from the mayor of Paris in August of 2019, she stated:

> I'm not a humanitarian. I am not there to "aid." I stand in solidarity. We do not need medals. We do not need authorities deciding about who is a "hero" and who is "illegal." In fact, they are in no position to make this call, because we are all equal. What we need are freedom and rights. . . . Fill the void with social justice. . . . Documents and housing for all! . . . Freedom of movement and residence!

Not only rescue operations but also solidarity with refugees in border zones have largely been criminalized as cooperation with extralegal forces, traffickers and, in the case of Exarcheia, anarchists. Along these lines, EU member states justify the securitization of migration in terms of a battle against "outlaws." This justification carries inherent political and moral inconsistencies. First, in externalizing their borders to third countries that commit human rights violations and crimes against humanity, EU member states not only cooperate but also sponsor those crimes (see El Qadim et al. 2021, 1611). Yet, the ethical and moral aspects of refugee politics and border management remain unstudied (for an exception, see Parekh 2020). Second, with state of emergency and decree laws, arbitrary decisions and "exceptionalism become engrained in ordinary law and the routine work of security professionals at the external borders of the EU" (Skleparis 2016, 93; see also Heyer 2022). Third, under such conditions, asylum seekers, who are bereft of safety and deprived of rights as decreed by the 1951 Refugee Convention, are left with no choice but to seek alternative allies. Closed borders, pushbacks, detentions, and deportations expand the ambiguous zone between legal and illegal—a zone that includes clandestine support mechanisms for refugees and irregular migrants (Feldman 2019). Further, "[t]he performative power of words" helps justify repression and criminalization by shifting the status of the legitimate asylum seeker to "undocumented" or "illegal." "To disqualify asylum seekers . . . [t]he claimants are commonly designated as clandestine, thus justifying official actions against them, such as sending them to detention centers or driving them back to their countries" (Fassin 2005, 375).

Routinized lawlessness has been detrimental to both refugees and their allies—activists, nonactivists, and NGOs. While the former Syriza government had been criticized for institutionalization and NGOization (as opposed to forming solidarity with activists), the conservative New Democracy government targeted pro-refugee NGOs. As NGO workers felt increasingly unsupported, at risk, and attacked by the national and local governments, they found refuge among Exarcheians with similar purposes, pro-migrant agendas, and lifestyles. Similar to the refugees they were trying to assist, their sense of belonging to Exarcheia made them feel safe. Even though frontliners' daily work was emotionally draining and exhausting around the clock, Exarcheia's built environment, decorated with symbols of counterculture and dissidence, such as graffiti and banners, offered workers pockets of sociability with like-minded people struggling against securitization. Designated taverns and bars provided frontliners venues for emotional bonding and social camaraderie to help them cope with their shared frustration about institutional blocks and political obstruction.

After being dragged along by my friends to several of these nighttime social spaces, I quickly understood that sociability among frontliners had a casual flow and spontaneity. Their demanding work life—emotional labor and extended hours of duty—necessitated a social life free of preplanning. Soon, I learned whom I would "run in to" and where, and the rhythms of "hanging out in the hood." In one neighborhood joint, I met for dinner with Electra, then president of one of the largest NGOs for refugees. After many greetings and quick chats with regulars at other tables, Electra was at last ready to sit down and dine with me. I had first met her in 2018, when she was working long days as a frontliner. Not much had changed since then: As president of the same NGO, she was still running back and forth between the border islands and Athens. We were still sharing our observations and experiences in the islands, comparing horrendous situations in each.

When I asked Electra about Bakoyannis's police reforms and green city project, she snapped:

For a few flowers planted in Omonoia Square . . . we lost our safe havens to this municipality. I am not sure what community policing is referred to as, because all I see is violation of human rights around me . . . not only of the refugees anymore, but all of us, the frontliners.

My conversations with frontliners were full of despair and anger about the New Democracy party's attacks on pro-refugee work. Athena, who spent most of her life working for NGOs in the border zones, said:

> Unlike the policymakers in their nice offices, we get our hands dirty. We burn out, we fight depression and need long-term trauma therapy. Yet, we are criticized and attacked from so many fronts. On the one hand, we are at constant risk of being criminalized as facilitators of trafficking, even though all we do is save lives. On the other hand, some researchers reduce our work to complicity with security states. This is our broken lives in a nutshell.

The perception of securitization as an all-encompassing and unavoidable reality often reduced frontliners in securitized borderlands to "docile" actors prone to collusion with the security regime. On the contrary, many humanitarian workers often fell into conflict with security professionals. As "Greek (in)security professionals still insist on traditional solutions and rely on local knowledge and a national security agenda," they "struggle for the exclusion of NGOs from entering the field of (in)security" (Skleparis 2016, 107–8). During my fieldwork in the islands, especially in Samos in 2017–21, I observed similar conservatism among the islands' natives, many of whom perceived pro-refugee work as a betrayal of local and national security and treasonous to national unity.[9] Conflicts in the humanitarian space also increase insecurity for frontliners, as governments enforce exceptional emergency measures and top-ranking international bureaucrats monitor and control frontliners' work (Beerli 2018). The "increasingly hostile political and legal environment" is evident in how "acts of assisting, hosting, aiding, and saving the life of people in desperate and dangerous circumstances have been met with drastic and threatening punishment and sanction" (Dijstelbloem and Walters 2021, 511).

As securitization strategically blended humanitarian logic with crime and anti-security, (Dijstelbloem and Walters 2021, 512), Exarcheia became a shelter for workers in the refugee sector to recharge their emotional reserves and discharge judgments, accusations, and constant risk of criminalization. Dina, a dedicated frontliner, told me in our first meeting many years ago:

> Borders are borders! It is easy to claim sanctuary status and debate "integration," in well-off destination countries, when you do not have to live in austerity, constant agony of survival, and the imminent threat of being criminalized for saving humans.

Dina articulated the intense emotions—pain, anger, and frustration—of frontliners, emotions that are integral to the geopolitics of borders. Researchers have documented that the criminalization of solidarity permeates all spheres of life for frontliners and even affects their intimate relations with friends, family, neighbors, and so on (e.g., Lampredi 2024; Dzenovska 2017). Dina's words also remind us that the distinct border control practices at the EU's southern borders differ from security practices in northwestern Europe (see also Skleparis 2016, 92–93). Without any feasible plans or making provisions for future arrivals, border cities continue to carve out safe places for refugees and their allies at the expense of being in constant struggle with respective security regimes.[10]

The blur between lawful pro-migrant practices and extralegal spheres of activity in the EU's southern borderlands tends to be arbitrary and unjust. Blurring is often used as a weapon of securitization to undermine and attack the solidarity between vulnerable refugees and innocent pro-refugee activists, and to criminalize both as collaborators with "illicit forces." Fear, in these violent geographies, is capitalized on by securitizers as a geopolitical factor that aims to manipulate locals' relations with political authority. But my research reveals a subversive response to the fear-based agendas and acts of securitization, that is, a fear-aversive solidarity in a dissident neighborhood of the border city.

Migrant Neighborhoods Are Still Safe

An increasingly anti-migrant Europe seems to have entirely forgotten the lesson of history: Anyone can become a refugee (Aktar 2021). The comfort zone of citizenship does not save anyone from becoming a refugee or asylum seeker. As an overwhelming majority of people across the world join the fearful fronts of anti-migrant politics, many of them seem to forget or look past the fact that no one leaves their home and country to become a refugee without a reason that forces their displacement (Aktar 2021).

Greece is no exception to the EU's brutal border regime. The New Democracy made it extremely difficult for refugees to stay and settle in Greece in a series of acts, including pushbacks, the closure of most squats and the major refugee camp in Athens, and forcing refugees out of the city and deporting. In August 2022, the government launched evictions from Greece's last camp, Eleonas, where refugees were allowed to leave. All these government-led hindrances added to an already difficult economic and employment situation. In my latest field visit to Athens in July 2024, homelessness was a pressing problem for migrants during the second term of the New Democracy (see also Tsavdaroglou 2024). In the absence of accommodating policies for refugees, including ones who had already passed through the asylum procedures, migrants were being forced out of Athens, unless they were very determined to stay there.

Pro-migrant organizations condemned what Prime Minister Mitsotakis referred to as Greece's "tough but fair" migration policy. As pushback has become "the main tool" in the EU's governance of borders and migration, Greece has become the "shield of the EU." Not only does Greece face hundreds of complaints and court cases, but the number of violations is so extreme that "even Frontex has considered withdrawing from the country for fear of being accused of being complicit in illegal acts" (Papagiannakis 2024).

In response, Germany has informally "shared" some responsibility for the displaced people who entered through Greece, whose migrant status was processed in Greece (in line with the Dublin Regulation) and who, therefore, were permitted to travel within the EU for up to three months. When some of these migrants visiting Germany chose to stay there, violating their three-month permission, Germany did not deport most of them back to Greece. Courts justified this decision with an irony that postulated Greece was "unsafe" for migrants, while the EU identified Turkey, Tunisia, and Libya as the EU's "third safe countries." As usual, the Global North continues to look away from the huge moral and political contradiction of informally "rescuing" migrants from *unsafe* Greece while sponsoring officials in Libya and Tunisia who torture, violate, and rape displaced people.

The nonchalance of the Western world towards these blatant crimes against Muslim and Black populations has become the new normal—the geopolitics of a seeming "nonemotion" presented as the voice of reason in the First World. Who resists this self-indulgent indifference of the West, including the international Left? Who stands up to the catastrophes that the West is directly responsible for, either owing to the colonial past or to its direct involvement in ongoing mass violence in the Third World that generates ever more refugees and migrants?

But the global catastrophe of refugee politics has not deterred the solidarity. Even though Mitsotakis's war against pro-refugee NGOs culminated in the decline of the provisional refugee sector in Athens and although resistance had retreated to migrant neighborhoods under the New Democracy government, the solidarity remained active, reaching out more vocally than before to international organizations and human rights courts. Melissa Network has hosted large numbers of newly arriving refugee women from Afghanistan and Ukraine. Parallel to the global trend of solidarity, Nadina was becoming more active in building transnational ties on behalf of Melissa Network, as the national governments were increasingly unaccommodating to irregular migrants.

During the final stages of this project, several organizations based in Athens were fighting against pushbacks on legal grounds. During lunch in Exarcheia, Papagiannakis, director of the Greek Council of Refugees, shared with me his detailed assessment of how the court cases on pushbacks were unfolding. Overall, the Greek Council was optimistic that it would soon hear about the first ruling on pushbacks from the European Court of Human Rights. "The first ruling matters most, as it will create a precedent for the rest of the numerous cases," said Papagiannakis.

Importantly, persisting through major political shifts in refugee politics, Athens's migrant neighborhoods were still considered safe. The "neighborhood feel" remained the same in both Exarcheia and Victoria Square.[11] At a time when provisions to refugees are in severe decline and attacks on pro-migrant protests continue, geopolitical emotion remains central in everyday life, mundane sociability, and local politics. Contrary to the shrinkage of pro-migrant collective action, geopolitical emotions intensify in the face of rising dehumanization of racialized migrants and violation of human rights. Zooming in on the subtleties of mundane urban encounters, this ethnography dissociates the spatial and geopolitical leverage of pro-refugee resistance from both provisional NGO refugee work and social movements. The geopolitics of emotion persist in motivating and empowering locals with different political agendas in their resistance to securitization of migration.

PART TWO

Palermo, the Central Mediterranean

THREE

On Decriminalization—
Contesting Legality, Memory, or Emotions?

A new destination for my multisited ethnography unfolded during my fieldwork in Athens as I was tracing pro-migrant resistance in Europe's borderlands in the eastern Mediterranean. Even though Sicily has been largely neglected in migration and security studies, its reputation was echoing across pro-migrant activist circles during my research in Athens. As I continued to hear about Palermo's resistance on both sides of the Atlantic, I also witnessed that the Palermo Charter (2015) was becoming a reference document of human and migrant rights across the world. In 2019, I moved my field research to Palermo.

Palermo's five-time mayor Leoluca Orlando received plenty of coverage in international media.[1] The media portrayed his war with the Sicilian mafia in the 1990s as the precedent of what *The Guardian* called a "herculean mission" of defending migrants rights. Orlando's mission to convince the EU to permit the free movement of migrants clashed with the anti-immigrant regimes of Italy and the EU (Van der Zee 2017). Italy's former anti-immigrant minister of interior affairs, Matteo Salvini, asserted with contempt that Sicily would "no longer be Europe's refugee camp" (BBC News 2018; Jones 2018). But after winning local elections for the fifth time in 2017, Orlando's determination was unflinching. He relentlessly advocated for radical reform. In my first interview with him, on July 7, 2019, he spoke openly about his feelings and resolve despite the government's show of power:

> I issue residence permits to migrants. As a reaction, Salvini publicly threatened me with . . . sending his army to Palermo [he smiled with self-confidence)]. . . . They cannot scare someone . . . who fought the Sicilian mafia and won.

The municipal issuance of residence permits to migrants put the mayor and the resistance in a position of confrontation not only with the Italian government but also with the Sicilian mafia. Because the mafia feeds off illegality and crime, the residency permits and legalization of migrants did not align with mafia interests. To the contrary, the persistence of residency requirements benefited local extralegal actors by preparing the groundwork for "illegal" status and for the criminalization of migrants. Hence, the anti-mafia struggle and the pro-migrant resistance were intermingled in their broader agendas of human rights and justice. On the basis of ethnographic evidence, I argue that although the basis of the struggles for decriminalization of migrants may seem exclusively legalistic, the pro-migrant efforts for justice were reinforced by locals' historical memory of a violent mafia legacy and embedded in the geopolitics of emotions.

―――――――

Sharing sea borders with migrant-sending North African countries, Italy responded to the peak migration flow with increasingly repressive migration policies and the closure of its borders. Italy's externalization of its borders to Libya went hand in hand with nationwide anti-immigrant protests and racist responses. Yet, in this hypersecuritized border geography, Sicily's border cities stood out for their absence of anti-immigrant protests. While this absence by no means suggested a lack of anti-immigrant sentiments (see, e.g., Sorge 2021), Sicily was noted as an "unexpected" exception to Italy's overwhelmingly right-wing, racist, populist landscape (Pettrachin 2022; Giglioli 2021; Panebianco 2022).[2] Interrupting the dearth of research on Sicily, a few scholars have noted that the island managed reception and accommodation of migrants better than elsewhere in Italy (Frazzetta and

Piazza 2022; Panebianco 2022). Unlike resistance in the EU's other southern cities, such as Barcelona and Athens, the disobedient pro-migrant municipalities and solidarity of this biggest island in the Mediterranean have remained largely understudied.

When I moved my ethnography to Palermo, the capital city of Sicily, most of my European friends and colleagues, including Italians from the north, did not understand my decision or share my enthusiasm. On many occasions, I invited several of them to visit me or to coteach a course on borders and migration. The disinterest persisted. Many had reservations about safety in a place that they perceived as a "mafialand." A few warned me about political corruption and offered their views on the "fickle" nature of politics. Others wished me a heartfelt good luck, sharing their multiple prejudices about the place. Whether it was the mafia presence or issues related to the unresolved "southern question" (Gramsci [1995] 2009; Schneider 1998b), Sicily appeared rather negligible from the lens of most northerners, but also by the bulk of researchers in migration studies(see for exceptions, Palmas 2020; Frazzetta and Piazza 2022; Giglioli 2017, 2021; Panebianco 2022; Pettrachin 2022)

I beg to differ. Not only was Palermo's international reputation in (pro) migrant solidarity rapidly climbing, but more importantly, a highly visible "Black space" was blossoming in the city's historic center (e.g., BBC News 2020). Considering the dynamism of the place during this period, the exclusive scholarly focus on migration and solidarity in northern cities did not make sense to me. In fact, it is still enigmatic for me that except for a handful of journalists and a few passionate doctoral students, researchers have not shown interest in the incessant flourishing of Black space in the city center.

Against all odds, the peripheral border city defeats commonsense explanations of geographical determinism and economic and historical reductionism. It reveals that neither geography nor history is destiny. Against the backdrop of Palermo's location on Europe's highly securitized and deadly sea border, its deep poverty and high unemployment, and its history of mafia atrocities that ruined the city and public life for decades, the city still generated a striking migrant-native solidarity.

Considering these major geopolitical, socioeconomic, and historical challenges, my research asks: What are the factors that prepare a margin-

FIGURE 4. **Ballarò Market, July 8, 2019. Photo by the author.**

alized gateway city for resistance to the security regime in predominantly anti-immigration Italy? My findings point to a paradox: Rather than undermining capacities of migrant accommodation, or deterring resistance, these taxing conditions galvanize pro-migrant sentiments and provoke a political urge to fight against the injustices and violence caused by border security. In explaining this political inclination, my ethnography points to locals' meaning-making of their complex history and geography.

This deeply contextualized analysis may fall outside the scope of the bulk of security and migration studies: Despite the recent shift in focus from the nation-state to cities, migration studies have primarily been interested in policy-related issues (Mollenkopf and Pastor 2016; Varsanyi 2010; Ridgley 2013). Diverging from this predominant focus on policy, this chapter decenters the so-called European migration crisis in three ways. First, it identifies and centers the human dimension and sentiments in everyday life as the locus of analyzing the resistance to the violent border regime. Second, it situates the pro-migrant agency and geopolitical emotions of solidarity into the EU's racial security regime. Third, it explores how historical memory figures into the contested notions of (il)legality and how collective memory of violence and marginalization is deeply entangled with the geopolitics of emotion. Considering the activists' differentiation between legality and "lawfulness," my analysis shows that their reliance on "everyday constitutionalism" was not a straightforward legalistic matter. Instead, I reveal and analyze how their struggles against lawlessness, such as Salvini's decree laws that violated international law, were not only legal but also highly emotional matters emanating from an aversion to injustices formed by the memories of a violent past.

My findings show that circulating "scripts" of a historical memory of violence put their stamp on a highly emotional geography that has become overly disinclined to violence, injustices, and the violation of human rights. The collective remembering of mafia atrocities just a few decades ago, I argue, has brought emotions, such as safety, human dignity, and trust, to the center of everyday life. These emotions motivate and empower pro-migrant resistance against the violent border regime that racializes both the migrants and their allies, albeit in different ways and intensities for each.

As Italy's left- and right-leaning parties in coalition governments have not made a substantial difference in the predominantly anti-immigrant political landscape, my analysis shifts the focus from ideology and party politics (e.g., Steil and Vasi 2014; Pettrachin 2022; Gattinara 2016) to a contextual analysis of geopolitical emotions and everyday practices of resistance. My research shows that the absence of racist protests in Sicily is neither unexpected nor surprising if we consider the geopolitical emotions situated in history and reenacted through memory. Importantly, however, the absence of racist collective action does not indicate the existence of a shared anti-racist politics across Sicily. As the collective memory shared by many natives proudly traces the island's multicultural heritage to the Middle Ages, I question the implications of substantiating present-day "diversity" in an imagery of a "golden age" at the expense of deprioritizing the central place of migrants in coexistence and activism.

The next section addresses the contested historical background and geopolitical underpinnings of the zealous pro-migrant resistance. The rest of the chapter analyzes how the pro-migrant municipal government and local activists confronted the anti-immigrant policies of Salvini in this highly emotional geography. The period of solid collaboration between the municipality and civil society up until the local elections in 2022 provides a perfect laboratory for exploring the unwavering determination of solidarity to decriminalize migrants in everyday life.

Contested Historical Memory and Geopolitical Emotions

Like Greece, Sicily has been a major migrant sender to northern Italy, other parts of Europe, and North America since its annexation by Italy in the mid-nineteenth century. Other than the high turnover of irregular migrants who were seasonal workers, mainly from Tunisia (Ben-Yehoyada 2011, 2017), Sicily was not a migrant-receiving destination, given its poverty and high rates of unemployment. When the 1985 Schengen Agreement introduced new security measures for Europe's external borders, irregular migration from the Middle East, North Africa, and other parts of the African continent became increasingly clandestine (Bigo and Guild 2005; Guild 2009). Similar to Greece, the southern border of Italy transformed into a security zone after joining the Schengen Area in 1997 (Balzacq and Carrera 2016).

The death of hundreds of migrants in a shipwreck near Lampedusa in 2013, prompted the Italian government to launch the Mare Nostrum search and rescue operation (BBC News 2013). This catastrophic shipwreck also led to Mayor Orlando's disobedience to the EU's brutal border regime. When the collective European effort Operation Triton replaced Mare Nostrum in 2014, migrant deaths in the Mediterranean increased dramatically.[3] In 2017, the Italy-Libya Memorandum of Understanding was signed to slow and eventually stop the flow. Although MoU was signed to imitate the 2016 EU-Turkey deal, the political instability in Libya made it impossible to export the border agreement from the eastern to the central Mediterranean.[4] Instead, a series of aid packages and trade deals were made with several African leaders who were paid to accept deportees and strengthen border security in Libya, Niger, and Sudan, among other countries (Landau

2019). This method of externalizing borders and using third countries for deportation and detention became regularized by First World countries in the following years. Italy's repressive migration policies peaked when Matteo Salvini, known for his anti-immigrant politics and anti-southern sentiments, passed two successive decree laws in 2018 and 2019.[5] These laws closed Italy's ports to rescue ships, criminalizing rescue and humanitarian aid as "facilitating human trafficking" (Osborne 2019).

The border violence and arbitrary criminalization of migrants is salt in the wound of Palermo's unhealed memories of its violent past. My interlocutors shared with me their memories of the absence of safe public spaces and public life in downtown Palermo in the 1980s and 1990s. Some of my respondents in their forties and fifties told me about their "stolen" youth, owing to the fear-ridden life in Palermo. Locals' life stories were inundated with dark, scary streets with no streetlights in the city center that were washed by blood and ruled by violence and unlawfulness. Partly because of these dramatic memories, the defense of safe places and refusal of the arbitrary rule of fear were non-negotiables for my respondents in Palermo.

The arbitrary criminalization of Black migrants and their local allies also pushed another button for locals. The historical memory of Italy's annexation of Sicily in 1861, perceived by Sicilians as Italy's colonization of Sicily, has long generated negative feelings about the island's subordinate status (Antonsich 2022; Schneider 1998b). Salvini's party, Lega, formerly known as the Lega Nord, played an important role in the racialization of Sicily. As Agnew (2000, 307) stated, "Sicily occupies a particularly important place in Northern League's representations of the South," as the party identifies the border island "with everything redolent in an encapsulated form of all that is wrong with the Italian body politic."[6] Although Sicily later gained regional autonomy with the 1946 constitution of Italy, this autonomy was often perceived negatively by Northerners and Europe as a major cause of the rise of mafia supremacy. Reacting against these stigmas, my activist friend Marco said: "Europeans have mistaken our history of conquests by different civilizations for an inability of self-governance." Rather than representing Marco's personal politics, his point reflected a collective defensive response that "Sicily was incapable of self-rule" (see Agnew 2000, 304).

A Human Rights City in a Mafia Hotbed?

After hearing in Athens about Mayor Orlando's international reputation as a politician and as an arduous defender of migrants' rights, I found myself waiting to meet him in a magnificent room at the Villa Niscemi in August 2019. The charming villa that once hosted Sicilian aristocracy was now serving as the municipal headquarters and a museum open for visitors.[7] When Orlando won his second successive mayoral term (2017–22), he was widely trusted and respected for having stood up to Salvini's repressive anti-immigrant regime. However, despite his depictions in international media as a victor over the mafia, locals knew that the mafia continued to exist, in the city and in high-security prisons, albeit in a much lesser capacity and with much less visibility (Kirchgaessner 2015; Van der Zee 2017).

Contrary to perceptions of the city as the hometown of the mafia, my first meeting began with Orlando's compelling description of Palermo as a safe, neighborly place with noticeably low crime. My firsthand experience of renting by the historic outdoor market in Ballarò, run by racially and ethnically diverse migrants, confirmed Orlando's point. Locals I spoke with seconded his view of the city center. When I inquired about how safety was attained, Orlando's response was concise: "Human rights!" It was surprising to hear human rights as the key to achieving safety in hypersecuritized border zone. Orlando differentiated Palermo from other migrant-receiving border cities:

> Other cities might use other methods to obtain security. . . . But Palermitans learned the hard way by paying the cost of living in an insecure environment. History taught us not to risk and not to place our own safety and security in the hands of *others* again. (Italics added.)

After Orlando compellingly othered the security forces of Italy and the EU, he proudly handed me a landmark document, the Palermo Charter (2015), which solidified Palermo's status as a "human rights city." Although human rights are codified internationally by the UN's 1948 Universal Declaration of Human Rights, only certain cities are officially declared "human rights cities" (Van den Berg and Oomen 2014; Grigolo 2011).[8] The Palermo Charter demanded a radical change in the treatment of displaced people, a shift in perceptions, from viewing forced displacement as solely a form of suffering to defending freedom of movement as a fundamental human right.

Indeed, Palermo was quite different from other European and Italian cities in terms of daily interactions with irregular migrants (see Ambrosini 2013; Marchetti 2020). For example, the deployment of identity checks and racial profiling I had witnessed before in Trento presented a stark contrast to Palermo. While Palermo was not immune to occasional attacks on migrants—particularly outside the city center, racial profiling was considered largely intolerable in the city center. Situating Palermo in the context of other Italian and European cities with high migrant-density, Orlando continued:

> We are ahead of Europe on this matter. Even the cities that are associated with good records of human rights have acquired this image owing to major international transformations. Take Berlin, for example. It was prompted by the fall of communism and [the] Berlin Wall, which led to German unification. It is vice versa in Palermo. Our commitment to human rights came from within . . . from our minds, hearts, and our past. . . . These internal drives motivate us to defend human rights against violations from outside.

Orlando's emphasis on the primacy of emotions and historical memory in shaping the defense of human rights and pro-migrant solidarity was telling. These emotionally intense incentives culminated in the creation of an internationally renowned commitment embodied in the Palermo Charter, an important reference point for the international network of solidarity cities and for political debates locally and transnationally (Maffeis 2021). The "diffusion of local human rights policies almost automatically raises the issue of the role of cities in the international human rights system," disrupting the "exclusive interaction between the state and international organizations" (Grigolo 2011, 1752). Accordingly, the charter enabled the municipality of Palermo to invest its efforts in local and transnational human rights activism, while simultaneously refusing cooperation with, and actively opposing Italy's anti-immigrant national government.

Importantly, confrontation between the Left and the Right did not stand out as a definitive characteristic of local politics in Palermo or Italy, as it has in Athens and Greece more broadly. To the contrary, Palermo as border city is a testament to the fact that the defense of migrants' rights requires more than managing ideological conflict and partisan political disagreements. Solidarity has been open to multiple sources of support and took advantage of flexible and shifting alliances. The words of a staff member of the city government revealed these non-ideological alliances: "Even though I am leftist and agnostic, Palermo taught me to cooperate with the religious groups and the church because of our shared pro-migrant goals." Palermo's municipality simultaneously collaborated with secular NGOs and local religious organizations and churches. I had firsthand experience with Lorenzo's point during my visit to the Mission of Hope and Charity (Missione di Speranza e Carità), where I observed the inner workings of a large shelter that hosted more than seven hundred young Black men.[9] Religious organizations and the church financially supported many NGO initiatives, including the rescue NGO Mediterranea Saving Humans, which was routinely fined and had rescue ships confiscated by the Italian government for its activities. Similarly, I met many irregular migrants and refugees whose rents were paid by various religious organizations.

With Pope Francis taking a clear pro-migrant stance and paying his first visit outside Rome to the migrant-receiving border island, Lampedusa, migrants and the solidarity received plenty of support from faith-based associations and the Catholic Church over the years. The most successful of these was the Humanitarian Corridors, which was a private sponsorship project resulting from the collaboration of several Italian faith-based associations and the Italian authorities, the Ministry of Foreign Affairs, and the Ministry of Interior.[10] By offering a safe passage and legal entry to Italy for vulnerable refugees from Syria and Lebanon after the peak of flow in 2015, the project showcased how violent border regimes could be replaced by alternative migration flows coordinated through public and private efforts.

Hence, the solidarity in Palermo that stood above ideological alliances was different from the largely left-leaning pro-migrant resistance in Athens. Even though a clear prerogative of right-wing populist groups and the political landscape of Italy has been the erasure of immigrants' rights and freedoms (Müller 2016; Norris and Inglehart 2019; Altınordu 2021), Palermo's local pro-migrant solidarity cannot be sufficiently understood exclusively by ideological (dis)agreements or party politics.[11] Nor do partisan ideological rifts adequately explain contestations over migration at the local or national level in Italy. Here, it is important to remember that Italy's border agreement with Libya in 2017 (Memorandum of Understanding) was sealed when a leftist party was in government. Similarly, some of Palermo's leading political figures, including Mayor Orlando himself, shifted their former political party affiliation from Christian Democrat to more liberal and leftist politics. In this respect, the words of a member of Orlando's municipal government were revealing:

> Salvini tries to erase civil rights and human rights. But we, border people, cannot choose between saving or not saving a life. . . . Our battle is not with the right-wing—it is with Salvini's laws. Our fight is not strategic but shaped by who we truly are, and where we live and belong to.

Decentering Illegality

As municipalities take on the management of migration, their horizontal commitments may fall into conflict with their vertical relations (and obligations) with the national government. Concretely, "in times of financial austerity and rampant right-wing populism notably at the national level, addressing migration issues is challenging for mayors" (Bazurli et al. 2022, 3). I asked Mayor Orlando how he managed the tensions between local and national politics. Before answering, he stood up from his study chair and walked to his elegant library full of law books, and pulled down a copy of the Italian Constitution. He opened it to article 10 and read aloud:

> The Italian legal system conforms to the generally recognized rules of international law. The legal status of foreigners is regulated by law *in conformity with international provisions and treaties.* A foreigner who is denied the effective exercise of the democratic liberties guaranteed by the Italian Constitution in his or her own country has *the right of asylum* in the territory of the Italian Republic, in accordance with the conditions established by law. Extradition of a foreigner for political offenses is not admitted.[12] (Italics added).

As article 10 of the constitution clearly integrates international law, violation of international law was interpreted as unconstitutional by Orlando and pro-migrant actors in solidarity. Before his political career, Orlando held a position as a professor of law. His expertise in constitutional law strengthened locals' confidence in him, in a geography stigmatized by unlawfulness and criminality. The esteem he shared with his respected family of prominent lawyers fostered his impression of reliability for the native locals. The mayor concluded: "We defend human rights by following the lead of our constitution, which Salvini's decree laws violate." From this angle, Orlando's municipal disobedience may seem to be purely legalistic. But was it?

Although the law is often misperceived as a universally neutral and apolitical concept, tensions between law and politics intensify during times of political crisis, particularly when a state of emergency is declared (Abel 2018; Dezalay 2020, S8).[13] This ethnography points to how securitization fueled by the state of emergency not only politicizes the law, but also weaponizes the violation of law for political ends and power. In the face of intense securitization during the era of War on Terror, for example, Abel (2018) argues that law was rendered more effective as a shield than as a sword. Accordingly, Palermo's insubordinate stance against Italy's migration governance and security decree laws used constitutionalism as a shield. Activists I interviewed raved about the 1948 constitution, praising it as a good outcome of post–World War II political learning. Moreover, constitutionalism was a collectively cherished resource in the city even beyond the solidarity, and I noted the popularity of the constitution beyond activist circles. Normalized as part of everyday local politics under Orlando's leadership, the constitution routinely functioned as a shield against Salvini, his spite for Sicily and southern Italy, and his decree laws that violated migrants' rights (for everyday constitutionalism, see Scheppele 2017, 35–36). It is important to note that *everyday constitutionalism* marks a striking difference between solidarity in Greece and Sicily. Different from collective distrust in the Greek state and its political institutions (discussed in Chapter 1), solidarity in Sicily and Italy more broadly relied on the constitution and opposed governments rather than the Republic. This contrast in terms of the positioning towards the state put a mark on differing strengths and challenges of solidarity in Greece and Sicily. These differences manifest, for example, in the curious place of anarchists in pro-migrant resistance in Athens versus the centrality of the constitution in native-migrant solidarity in Palermo.

Palermo's everyday constitutionalism used as a shield by the resistance should be understood in the broader national context of right-wing populist grievances about the law and constitutions. Italy's right-wing populists called for comprehensive reform of the 1948 constitution (Blokker 2020, 201; Tarchi 2015; Biancalana 2020, 216; Blokker and Anselmi 2020). Controversy over the constitution emerged when the Northern League mobilized opposition to the state by calling for regime change. The populists' demand was nativist (Duyvendak et al. 2023): The rights of natives were to be "immun[iz]ed from the contagion of outside elements (such as immigrants from the Southern regions or from abroad)" (Tarchi 2015, 5). The populist mindset contradicted basic principles of international law on human rights mainly because of its restrictive notions about who is (and is not) entitled to belong to the national community. Right-wing populists objected to the law, presenting it as a liberal "*obstacle* to achieve collective goals . . . to promote the national interest, and to thrive in international competition" (Blokker 2020, 200). With the rise of the far right across the globe, this pervasive political stance complicates the concept of "lawlessness" beyond Italy.

Everyday constitutionalism helps me disclose the emotional component of these legal contestations. The term, coined by Scheppele (2017, 36), views the constitution as "the lived experience of a particular people in a particular place and time." I built on Scheppele's theory that "constitutions . . . manage to create their own social life." From this perspective, successful constitutions broaden "the idea of constitutionalism beyond any constitutional text . . . into a broader social world, in which constitutional ideas shape social expectations and understandings, and come to be taken for granted" (Scheppele 2017, 35). Accordingly, the constitution becomes a sociological phenomenon that "ought to be understood and analyzed in a contextual and situated way" (Blokker and Thornhill 2017, 6). My findings revealed the geopolitics of emotion embedded in the "social life" of the constitution as an enabler of pro-migrant resistance against the security decree laws of Italy. Human rights activism backed up by everyday constitutionalism was partly an outraged reaction to populists' "resentful attitude towards the liberal understanding of the rule of law" (Blokker 2020, 200).

Because Salvini's border and migration politics originated in the Northern League's long-term contempt of southern Italy, and because this contempt manifested with his direct and sometimes personal attacks on Sicily and Mayor Orlando, the emotional content of the legalistic clash was explicit. Geopolitical emotions spearheaded pro-migrant resistance to the legal field of contestation. Relying on and defending the constitution against its violators, Orlando won court cases in favor of migrant rights. Parallel to these achievements, Palermitan activists diligently taught migrants about their legal rights. Alessandra Sciurba, then president of and spokesperson for Mediterranea Saving Humans, coordinated a legal team at the University of Palermo, where she currently serves as a professor of human rights and international law. The Legal Clinic for Human Rights (referred to as CLEDU in Italian) was launched as a project offering free legal counseling for migrants and asylum seekers. In 2015–16, the project brought CLEDU into contact with large numbers of migrants who had arrived in Palermo after passing through the hot spots of Trapani and Lampedusa (Sciurba 2017).

I paid multiple visits to the provisional offices of the law clinic, where lawyers, students, and researchers cooperated in offering free legal services to migrants. Sciurba told me that the clinic also gave students a chance to engage with a legal clinical approach by offering personalized, face-to-face interaction with migrants. In emphasizing "learning by doing," Panebianco (2022, 753) argues that "practices, ideas, and know-how of actors 'on the ground'" are "better apt to react to crises" than aloof top-down EU policies. Her analysis of the frontliner humanitarian work in Siracusa, another border city in southern Sicily, is revealing of the value of practice-based approach. Similarly, the practice-oriented law clinic of Palermo opened the doors of the university for justice and helped many hundreds of migrants since 2015. Sciurba explained:

> Here, students and researchers cooperate with medical doctors, for example, when we need to certify that people have been tortured or when women arrive violated. So, the law is backed up with medical and psychological expertise to strengthen our solidarity.

Over lunch in May 2023, Sciurba shared with me her deep frustration with Italy's mishandling of the Cutro case, concerning the shipwreck in Calabria, which she examined on site with her law students. Thus, CLEDU offered students experiential learning, familiarizing them with the human dimension of legal cases that was missing in the textbooks. In September 2024, Sciurba received the Solidarity City Award for her "commitment in the field of migrations," particularly for her work in the legal clinic.

Sciurba denounced the detainment of eighty survivors, after ninety-four deaths were confirmed in the shipwreck caused by the officials' neglect in harsh weather conditions as well as their violation of the rescue protocols. By using this catastrophic Cutro case as an example, she emphasized that the law was simply an instrument that could be used for oppression or liberation of human beings. Her words resonated with Orlando's take on legality. Orlando keenly differentiated "legality of law" from legality of human rights. He identified his commitment to the legality of rights by condemning the legality of a series of laws applied at the expense of human misery and oppression, such as fascist laws, Nazi laws, Salvini laws, and so on. Infuriated, he added European legislation in violation of human rights to the list of laws that enforced illegality. "When law is against human rights," he said, "we do not need it." In my many meetings with Orlando since 2019, he reminded me each time that the mafia used to reign in every branch of governance in Palermo, the courts, and the law enforcement. His numerous memories of losing and grieving good friends and colleagues were all rooted in that politico-legal background. Against the backdrop of the city's violent legacy, he adamantly refused to apply the asylum law of Italy, which violated human rights and international agreements and hurt vulnerable human beings. Along with several other southern mayors, he was accused by Salvini of disobedience to the state.[14]

Whether it was the municipality's dissent by granting residency permits to irregular migrants or supporting the rescue boats criminalized unfairly by the Salvini laws, Palermo's solidarity was at the center of an explosive battlefield between Italy's security decree laws and the international law embraced by the Italian constitution. It should be noted, however, that even before Salvini's decree laws there had been legal ambiguity regarding the act of rescue, over whether it was a form of human trafficking, and hence a crime, or legal humanitarian aid (see Başaran 2014). Even though the concept of humanitarian rescue was firmly anchored in national and international law, "anti-smuggling legislation [could] be used to sanction [it]" (Başaran 2014, 377). Anti-migrant right-wing regimes took advantage of this contradiction, which led to ongoing contestation in Palermo.

Even though most ordinary Palermitans did not know or care about these technical ambiguities and complexities of (il)legality, they supported Orlando's municipality and its everyday constitutionalism as a regular feature of the human rights city. The case of Palermo showcases how the increasing prominence of local municipalities in migration governance brings to the fore the context-specific and historicized understandings of (il)legality.

Decriminalization of Migration

In alignment with the EU member states' intertwinement of their discourses of crime and immigration (Bazurli and Delclós 2022; Bessant et al. 2022; Fabini 2017), migration governance in Italy came to be primarily managed by the police forces. Ironically, however, law enforcement managed "illegality" rather than punishing or deporting illegal migrants (Fabini 2017, 47). Scholars coined several terms to describe and theorize this migration governance, such as *differential inclusion* (Giglioli 2021, 727; Fabini 2017, 49; Sciurba 2017, 101) and *illegality factory* (D'Angelo 2018). Such a system is based on maintaining illegality by allowing irregular migrants to stay after stripping them of their rights, including to residence, legal work, welfare, and visibility (D'Angelo 2018, 2224).

Migrants' differential inclusion into Italy is intensified by Sicily's subordinate incorporation into Italy and Europe. By spatializing the notion of differential inclusion in the Sicilian context, Giglioli (2021) reveals the paradox of concurrent processes of inclusion and marginalization. My findings add to this paradox the marginalization and stigmatization of Palermo, often referred to as "the city of the Sicilian mafia." Accordingly, this ethnography points to the simultaneous processes of inclusion and a double-layered criminalization—of irregular border crossers to Italy and of irregular migrant residents of a city with a legacy of crime and corruption. This double criminalization illuminates the importance of the municipality's political struggles to lift residency requirements and support decriminalization.

In addition to municipal disobedience regarding residency permits, search and rescue was also at the center of resistance to criminalization in Palermo. The physical border was a "war zone" for Palermitan activists during Salvini's crackdown on migrants in 2018-19. Many activists frequently flew between Palermo and Lampedusa to serve in or lead the rescue ships or to bring assistance to newcomers at the physical border.

When in August 2019 Salvini barred the Spanish rescue boat *Open Arms* from docking, I flew to Lampedusa. The event pitted branches of the state against each other, and the island was overcrowded with journalists, human rights advocates, intelligence, and security forces.[15] Despite the chaotic situation, I managed to spend time with newly arrived migrants because during that period they were still able to escape from the reception center every night to gather in the square by the church. This was before the high-security measures were established at the reception center in the following years. Migrants' stories of their violent journey were powerful testimonies to the catastrophic outcomes of Italy externalizing its borders to Libya. I heard many stories from the newcomer migrants about the traffickers. Paradoxically, the traffickers who had arranged for their transportation were also the violent gatekeepers of the borders, detention centers, and prisons in Libya supported by funding from Italy.

One of my interlocutors was a twenty-three-year-old Syrian man named Omar. He left his home after it was bombed and journeyed with traffickers for several years. Hence, according to European hot-spot policies, he fully "qualified" as a refugee. Meeting with him several times for hours, I recorded a detailed account of his journey through Libya. Omar was a college student and spoke fluent English. During the crossing of the Mediterranean Sea, his technical and communication skills became helpful, and he was relied upon frequently to contact NGO boats for rescue. Unexpectedly, the night before his scheduled transfer from Lampedusa to mainland Italy, he was suddenly taken into custody for human smuggling. He told me on the phone that night that some migrants on the boat were "persuaded" by officials to testify that he was the trafficker. Omar was then transferred to a jail in Palermo the next day, where he spent the following years in prison.

At the time of Omar's arrest, it was not widely known that traffickers were no longer escorting migrants to a European port. Instead, they were assigning the most able-looking migrant to be the leader before shoving the boat off, whether they were competent like Omar or punished by traffickers for being weak. Every boat had migrant drivers who had no other choice, and they were criminalized upon arrival and reproduced as an easy public enemy to be punished for trying to stay alive and save other migrants. While Africans were "pathologized" for their potential move to Europe, the ones who actually did move were used as "justification to strengthen [the] EU's anti-immigrant policies" (Landau 2019, 176).

As I lost track of Omar during his imprisonment, I learned how masses of refugees were accused of human trafficking and fell off the radar and into the EU's brutal machinery of migration governance. The criminalization of the refugee for having "contact" with human traffickers—while leaving them with no other option for mobility—conveniently blurs the categories of "refugee" and "criminal," as well as "legal" and "illegal." The immorality of the situation raises an important question: "What happens to accepted explanations of EU migration governance processes if the interaction between smuggled migrants and smugglers is assumed to be part of the governance process?" (Zardo and Wolff 2022, 688; for moral aspects of refugee politics, see also Parekh 2020).

Jones's (2016) *Violent Borders* elucidates the logic of border securitization that is based on a flawed assumption that migration flows are driven mainly by traffickers, rather than originating in macro-level inequalities that deprive the Global South of access to resources. "The [EU's] response to deaths in the Mediterranean demonstrates [the] logic that the problem can be solved by using military force against human traffickers, destroying their boats, and attacking their camps" (Jones 2016, 5). This response has had catastrophic outcomes. Studies point to a conundrum: Instead of targeting traffickers, the militarization of the EU's borders weaponized human trafficking between Libya and Italy by facilitating a system of detention and forced labor (Pradella and Cillo 2021).

At the time of finalizing this book, the Italian state was still providing training to Libyan border security in a geography where it is impossible to distinguish Libyan coastal guards from traffickers (D'Angelo 2018, 2224). With the memorandum of understanding signed with Tunisia in 2023, Italy now sponsors officials in both Libya and Tunisia who violate, beat, rape, and enslave migrants (*The Guardian* 2024). Against the backdrop of the brutal realities of the central Mediterranean, Palermo's solidarity has persevered and evolved in proximity with firsthand knowledge of border atrocities. In Palermo, I met migrants who had been forced to captain boats and accused of human trafficking, then imprisoned unfairly for many years. Yet when they came out of prison, they were treated with dignity and respect by the native-migrant solidarity. However, even though they were embraced by the activist community, and even when they someday obtain "papers" solidifying their asylum status, their imprisonment restricts their freedom of mobility and ability to travel beyond Italy.

Perceptive of the situation, Palermo-based organizations, activists, and the municipality were on alert and fought against this arbitrary criminalization of refugees and asylum seekers (see Arci Porco Rosso and Alarm Phone 2021; Borderline Sicilia 2022). Palermo's primary response was to decenter the (il)legality of the asylum seeker in everyday life. Problematizing the criminalization of the racialized migrant, Mayor Orlando said:

> In our Western world, an American or a German is never stereotyped as a criminal, even though all nationalities, religions, and races can have criminals. But if you are a Muslim or Black, people think differently. In Palermo, we do things differently! Migrants call me directly or call the police to report a crime. They protect this city by prioritizing it sometimes even above their attachments to their homelands, ethnic groups, or even religion. Why? Because they feel safe and at home here. They are not afraid of the police. This does not happen in Paris, where they are treated as criminals and not as human beings.

In an interview on July 18, 2019, Adham Darawsha, the Palestinian vice mayor in Orlando's municipal government, reflected on the politics of fear and securitization:

> I'm not afraid of people coming from Nigeria risking death in the desert or drowning in the Mediterranean. If I encounter a boat full of poor refugees assaulted in Libya, why should I be fearful of them? If I see troops, missiles, and bombs, I'd be scared. What has security got to do with refugees?

Palermitan solidarity proactively fought the criminalization of innocent migrants. Alessandra Sciurba, of Palermo's law school, juxtaposed Palermo's border activism against the cruel border regime:

> We demonstrate with Mediterranea that our ports are not closed, as we have embarked several times in Lampedusa. Unfortunately, this local reality does not undo the problem at the national level. Decree laws are very repressive and completely contradict with international law. But we

are a large community of activists in Palermo connected to even larger circles transnationally. We will not stop fighting!

An internationally renowned human rights activist with frequent media appearances, Sciurba has participated in many rescue operations. She and other Palermo activists continued to object to the unfair hierarchies of human mobility. Municipal officials, rescue teams, and NGOs had similar views on borders and border practices. During my visit to Vice Mayor Da-rawsha's municipal office, he told me:

> A wall doesn't create a closed safe area; it creates the opposite: the urge to surpass. Walls don't give you security . . . if one wants to get in, he will find a way, climb, jump, or break into. . . . Give me one example of a community, one nation, or group that lived behind high walls for-ever. No one. All walls and all barriers built to hide will eventually be brought down.

Having arrived in Palermo from Palestine as an undocumented migrant several decades earlier, Darawsha understood the plight of Black and Muslim asylum seekers. After studying medicine in Palermo, he stayed on and became a medical doctor. Darawsha's words were aligned with Or-lando's motto: "A closed port is not a port, just as a cemented door is no longer a door." He also publicly stated that Palermo has been "a complete port" throughout history—that is, until Salvini violated international law (Wintour et al. 2018).

Palermo's call for reform was not about deliberation or lip service. Wrapped up in human suffering and interwoven with collective memory and personal histories, solidarity was not strategizing decriminalization, but rather living through it as part of everyday life. Voicing strong support for Orlando's call for the abolition of the residency requirements, several interlocutors also recommended specific reforms to border and reception practices:

1. The migration flow will not be stopped by externalization of borders. Collusion with third countries must end. Palermitan activists echoed Cuttitta (2018, 634): The "most significant political task, in the cur-rent reconfiguration of the Central Mediterranean, [was] opposing the externalization of [search and rescue] to Libya."

2. Humane border management would cost Europe less than paying third countries to stop migrant flows.

3. Only expert committees should conduct interviews at reception centers, replacing decision-making of the European border police Frontex and national coast guards.

4. The small scope and limited experience of humanitarian corridors that proved to be the best and safest way to transport refugees should be expanded and normalized.

5. A representative of Mediterranea Saving Humans told me, "As we know Mare Nostrum and humanitarian corridors had previously worked in Italy, there is no excuse for doing it wrong since then!"

These "alternative scripts of migration governance" (Zardo and Wolff 2022, 688) and ways to decriminalize human mobility have multiplied in years, but in the absence of national- or EU-level cooperation, Palermo continued to serve as the main hub of pro-migrant solidarity in the borderlands of the central Mediterranean.

Trust in Local Police

With a striking participation of frontliner women in rescue operations, including female captains, human rights violations took a blatant gendered turn. Alessandra Sciurba shared her experiences with me:

> They cannot stand us, the women at the sea, the young activist women! There is a lot of sexism about the women of the rescue NGOs, who are challenging the government. Of course, this is not our goal. But because of our defense of migrants many of us, like Carole Rackete and I, have been the target of endless insults, bullying and offenses from the public, ordinary people . . . sometimes anonymous sometimes not . . . Death and rape threats. Threats of locking us up with migrants, specifically with Black men. . . . They say we go to the sea to be with these men. . . . With the help of our lawyers, we report these harassments to the police.[16]

Although Sciurba, a single mother of two children, had come under attack in the right-wing press for her participation in rescue missions, she never felt unsafe in Palermo. Palermo was successfully defeating the politics of fear not only for irregular migrants but also for their allies. The city center was proof that polarization by fear was not the zeitgeist but a politically "conservative choice" (Body-Gendrot 2012, 10). The municipality in cooperation with solidarity made a different political choice—to evade such fear, defend human rights, and decriminalize migrants.

Erasmo Palazzotto, then a member of the parliament, was a pro-migrant Palermitan activist and led several rescue missions. Unsurprisingly, right-wing populists accused him of being a traitor. He received countless insults and death threats. When I met with him at a café in Palermo, he told me about Palermo's ethos:

> One day I was coming home in Palermo, and a stranger was waiting at my doorway. Owing to the threats I receive everywhere, I felt intimidated. How did he know my home address? As I cautiously approached my door, he told me in a friendly manner that he really appreciates my pro-migrant politics and thanked me wholeheartedly. [It is] only in Palermo [that] I receive this kind of warm support and appreciation. . . . We feel safe and supported here.

The local police played an important role in defeating the politics of fear that the security regime was generating. Before Salvini's decree laws and the signing of the memorandum of understanding with Libya in 2017, the ports of Sicily, and even Palermo's port in the Northern part of the island, were still receiving migrant boats. Furthermore, the local police were actively involved in welcoming them. A member of the municipality shared with me: "During the early years of Orlando's previous term, the police were asked to arrive at the port without any weapons. Greeting refugees and migrants with weapons would give the wrong message, as if they were criminals." Standing tall against securitization, the cooperation between the irregular migrant, the city administration, and the police was part of the municipal efforts to decriminalize migrants and to legalize their residency.

Vice Mayor Darawsha at the time concretized the role of the local police in maintaining the city's safety and inclusivity:

> The police must be vigilant here because of the mafia's past ascendency. . . . But policing is for the safety of *all* residents in our city, not for discrimination of vulnerable minorities.[17]

The municipal government was keen on strong cooperation with the local police, not only to keep the mafia under control but also to prevent the mushrooming of other organized crime groups. When five Nigerian criminals were arrested in Palermo, hundreds of Nigerian migrants gathered in front of city hall and protested criminal activity committed by Nigerians. This incident showed migrants' feelings of belonging to the city, as they prioritized safety in the city above their bonds with their homeland or ties to co-nationals. This incident showed the cooperation between migrants and law enforcement in the fight against illegality and criminal activity.

Pro-migrant municipal governments in both cities went above and beyond in different ways. I heard numerous stories from migrants about Mayor Orlando's participation in their cultural rituals and support during difficult moments, for example, when Roma people were evacuated and transferred to another place in Palermo. Orlando and other municipal officials went to the evacuation site to talk with people, to calm them down, and to assure them about the place they were being moved to. As symbolic acts of recognizing migrants' dignity, Orlando's co-presence with migrants contrasted sharply with evacuations and demolitions in other cities of Europe. Vice Mayor Darawsha told me:

> When the Roma asked for a final prayer in their mosque on their last day, Mayor Orlando took his shoes off and prayed with them. Importantly, the policemen stayed out, paid respect to the Roma's ritual, and at the end, they even offered car service to people who needed a transfer.

Such cooperation is rare in Europe, as it may put local police in direct conflict with the central government they serve. Yet Orlando believed that trust in law enforcement was vital to migrants and to the safety of the community. He told me:

> When their rights as humans are not protected, migrants close their eyes, mouth, and ears, and refuse to call the police even when in danger. Last year, eight Bangladeshi shopkeepers called the police to inform them about illegal mafia activity by some Palermitans. Now, you tell me who acts as the real Palermitan here?

My ethnography suggests that anti-immigrant security regimes and their crimmigration strengthen migrants' sense of belonging to cities that carved out safe spaces for native-migrant solidarity. As in Exarcheia, refugees and asylum-seekers prioritized their ties with the pro-migrant locals and officials of Ballarò not only over their relations with hostile host states but sometimes also with violent homelands. These findings contradict arguments that increasingly authoritarian anti-immigrant states repress and diminish the leeway of municipal governments. While the encroachment of the security state on the solidarity and pro-migrant municipalities have become normalized in the Global North, the bulk of the state-centered analyses fail to capture the deep contextuality and politics of emotion that empower these places and their migrant residents.

Zauna, a Nigerian woman, explained to me why trusting local officials was so important for migrants in precarious circumstances:

> We arrive here from Nigeria in the hands of traffickers who want to keep us captive as sex workers. How can we escape these illegal networks when we are also trapped in a limbo of illegality . . . and when the traffickers bully even our family back in our homeland for a ransom? . . . We need to trust authorities for protection. (Interview, August 1, 2019)

Zauna's words point to the multiscalar nature of illegal networks that "stretched across migrants' country of origin and country of settlement, through mobility, networks, and diaspora politics" (Fossum et al. 2023, 6). Her story corroborated Orlando's argument about how migrants' illegal status served the perpetuation of criminal networks. In many other Italian cities, the police targeted female migrants, replicating border activities of criminalization far from the border and paradoxically using migration law to fight prostitution in the streets (Fabini 2017, 53–54). Both migrants and natives in Palermo stated in my interviews that local police behaved differently towards migrants than most other cities in Italy. However, even though I heard many stories from migrants who felt at liberty to contact the local police and report crime and violations, Nigerian sex laborers stayed away from the police. Their intersecting vulnerabilities of gender and race were causing their criminalization to remain unchallenged: In a predominantly Catholic milieu, they were falling through the cracks of illegality and criminalization. I will return to gendering migrant resistance and the challenges that Nigerian migrant women face in the next chapter.

Solidarity Persists Through Elections

By juxtaposing the disobedient pro-migrant municipal activism against the violence of racial borders, this chapter has illuminated the historical and geopolitical leverage of the border city in resisting the security regime of Fortress Europe. Nevertheless, Palermo is not unique: other migrant-hosting cities in southern Europe, such as Barcelona and Athens, also generated pro-migrant practices and solidarity along with high levels of political contestation (Bazurli and Delclós 2022; Arampatzi 2017b; Christopoulou and Leontsini 2017; Tsavdaroglou 2024; Turam 2021; 2024). Yet in-depth ethnography also revealed how Palermo differed from other European cities, including the EU's gateway cities, such as Athens.

By detailing the nature of resistance and civic disobedience, this chapter documented how a local human rights activism took advantage of ambiguity—the defining characteristics of an inhumane border regime. Under the leadership of a pro-migrant municipal government, the pro-migrant resistance turned the weapon of the violent security regime upside down. Ambiguities were used by the solidarity as an asset and by the municipal government as a leeway to side-step anti-immigrant policies of the state. The ethnographic analysis uncovered everyday spaces where "individuals and public authorities meet, and where varying levels of discretion allow public officials . . . to implement policies that often diverge considerably from formal policy goals and rules" (Morgan and Orloff 2017, 10).

In my interviews since Orlando's local government was replaced by an anti-immigrant municipal government in 2022, Palermitan activists looked back and retrospectively referred to the 2018–19 period of battle between Salvini and Orlando as the "golden age" of pro-migrant activism. This may seem ironic, because the 2018 elections in Italy had brought two right-wing parties into coalition, which had devastating effects for solidarity and Black activism across the country. But when the electoral results made Black Italians and migrants feel fearful, anxious, and hopeless (see, e.g., Hawthorne 2022, 185), the solidarity in Palermo was putting out its best fight against Rome and was feeling energized, resilient, and hopeful.

The key to deeply contextualized resistance showcased in Palermo is the geopolitics of emotions rooted in history and geography. Salvini's anti-immigrant encroachment on migrants and Sicilians inspired and galvanized

Palermitan activists to mobilize nationwide support for rescue and other pro-refugee efforts. Erasmo Palazzotto, the Palermitan former member of Parliament, and cofounder of Mediterranea Saving Humans, recalled those days to me with excitement. For example, they ran a successful crowdfunding campaign for Mediterranea. He described people across the country showering the rescue ship project with money in an unprecedentedly short time of a few days. I had the firsthand experience of the passionate support to Mediterranea during my stay in Trento, the Northern border city near the Austria-Italy border. The clash between Orlando and Salvini was remembered as the heyday of Palermo-based pro-migrant activism. An obvious enemy with a blatant and historically rooted racist hatred of Sicily and African migrants worked quite well to fuel opposition and mobilize people across Italy against the government.

Recent works on mayoral leadership caution us against "mayoral triumphalism and mayoral romanticism" (Bazurli et al. 2022). Here, *mayoral triumphalism* refers to the idea that mayors have immense influence and can handle complex social problems with creative solutions while *mayoral romanticism* refers to the notion that mayors actually want change for inclusion of immigrants. Taking a critical stance to these ideas, Bazurli et al. (2022, 300) argue: "Mayors are in fact strategic and will support immigrant exclusion if that advances their own political objectives." Accordingly, by introducing a third category, *mayoral pragmatism*, to evaluate mayors and mayoral politics, they claim that mayors have a tendency to be pragmatic, as opposed to ideological, when it comes to migration issues. No doubt, pragmatism is an undeniable phenomenon of politics at every scale, but of course it also has its limits. Rather than taking these categoric qualities attributed to mayors as written in stone, my findings suggest a contextual approach that considers personal and collective history, agency and emotions. Some mayors, such as Mayor Orlando (former professor of law) and Luigi de Magistris, Mayor of Naples (2011–2021) (former prosecutor), have been prominent actors in local and transnational solidarity. Hence some mayors carry their pro-migrant activism beyond local agendas and power politics to other scales, such as Orlando's and Luigi's service as a member of the EU parliament. These multi-scalar solidarity performances, I view, as neither pragmatic nor ideological—Orlando shifted his party alliances a few times. Like Papagiannakis, Palazzotto, and other bureaucrats wearing two hats as solidarity activists and politicians, some mayors and vice mayors continued prioritizing their commitment to human rights and pro-migrant politics through periods of mayorship and other electoral outcomes—local, national and regional.

As Italy's collusion with Libya continued after Salvini's fall from power in August 2019, several Palermitan activists complained to me that the leftists who had replaced the Lega in the coalition were elusive, making resistance even more challenging for activists.[18] Paradoxically, after this period when the shared enemy Salvini had helped to bond the pro-migrant actors, the fervor and excitement seemed to decrease in the city.

During the last years of Orlando's two successive terms as mayor (2012–22), my interviews revealed that some of his pro-migrant supporters became critical of and estranged from certain aspects of his leadership.[19] Activists from the younger generation expressed their need for more space for their political decision-making. Feminist activists pointed critically to his father-like leadership figure as outdated. In his fight for human mobility as a global right, Orlando was criticized for his deprioritization of local services and failing in basic municipal provisions, such as garbage collection. There was overwhelming consensus in Palermo that Orlando's city government had lost its dynamism toward the end and had failed to handle the COVID-19 crisis.

Yet migrants continued sharing with me their respect, trust, and affection for him. All complained unanimously about the new municipal government's disinterest in and neglect of migrants. Orlando's successor municipality did not recognize migrants or their associations. In fact, despite his former position as president of the University of Palermo, Mayor Lagalla remained distant from activist scholars and researchers, including myself, not even responding to requests for an interview. It was puzzling that the leading solidarity figures who were connected across borders and internationally to activists and politicians were not able to reach Mayor Lagalla. Locals questioned what the municipality was keeping busy with while ignoring its native and migrant residents. Some commented sarcastically that the city government was only interested in finances in the city of deep poverty and meager revenues.

In October 2021, Matteo Salvini appeared in Palermo's court for a hearing about his refusal to permit embarkment of the rescue ship *Open*

Arms. Rejecting accusations of having violated migrants' rights and facing charges of having abused his authority by kidnapping rescued migrants, Salvini referred to the trial as "political." He tweeted: "This is the court-room of the Palermo prison. The trial wanted by the Left and by the *fans of illegal immigration* begins" (Giuffrida 2021; see also Berger 2021). Infuriated but also desensitized to Salvini's routine insults and contempt for Sicily, Palermitan solidarity celebrated the beginning of his trial. The trial in Palermo ended in December 2024, acquitting Salvini of charges (Bubola and Povoledo, 2024; Tondo and Jones, 2024). Salvini continues to serve as infrastructure and transport minister and deputy prime minister in a coalition government with the Prime Minister Giorgia Meloni's far-right Brothers of Italy party. While the rescue ships continued to enter the ports of Italy after long contestations over human rights and international law, new regulations established by the Meloni administration made rescue even more difficult than before. Even though Salvini's security decrees were repealed, Meloni's far-right government declared a new decree law upon the shipwreck near Cutro, Calabria, in 2023. The new decree law, approved by the Parliament, allows only one rescue operation for each rescue ship —after that, it is obliged to turn back and sail to an assigned port. The decree law aims to undermine and hinder rescue operations, since the assigned ports are typically as far as possible from the rescue location.

My conversations with Orlando continued until he was elected a member of the European Parliament for the second time in 2024 and carried his pro-migrant politics to the EU level. As he ran for the elections from the leftist party, many could not foresee his electoral victory. A few weeks after the new local government took office in June 2022, I met Orlando for a causal chat over coffee on July 9. As usual, he arrived with private security in several cars. Even though the coffee appointment turned into a solid four-hour conversation, the private security parked in front of the hotel did not turn off their car engines during our entire meeting. Several activists have had a hard time making sense of this level of private security at a time when the city center is deemed to be safe, but I see the continuing extraordinary caution as a repercussion of a legacy of violence. After all, Orlando had lost friends and colleagues to bloodshed. He also had been bullied, threatened and even designated by the mafia as a target himself.

Toward the end of our long meeting, Orlando suggested that I join the citywide festivities for the LGBTQ parade, a major source of pride for him on his lasting municipal achievements and legacy. The parade had an emotional significance in the context of his human rights struggles. He explained to me that "the mafia hated everything that it could not control, including the LGBTQ [people] and the migrants, because the mafia was homophobic, and like fascists, they believed in the purity of blood" (my interview, July 9, 2022).

When I stepped out and joined the festive crowds marching across the city, I had the memorable experience of how Palermitans were celebrating their shared joy of being free from the rule of fear, oppression, and violence. The parade was just one of many expressions of the healing and energizing effects of human rights activism on the city. Similarly, during the final stages of writing this book, native and migrant activists were pouring into the streets to protest violence against civilians in Gaza, condemning colonialism and calling for freedom for Palestine.

Surpassing electoral outcomes, the prioritization of human rights remains a fundamental part of the city of Palermo's political agency. The unstoppable rise of the far right in Italy and the anti-immigrant security regime of the EU could not erase the geopolitics of emotion deeply en-

FIGURE 5. **Palermo Pride, July 9, 2022. Photo by the author.**

grained in this geography. Globally pervasive authoritarianism changed political landscapes through repression and securitization at every level, from local to international. But most policy-focused work missed an important fact: These regimes could not reach and ban political emotions deeply embedded in history and geography. Palermo's solidarity outlived Orlando and endured through electoral victories of anti-immigrant right-wing governments in power since 2022, locally by Lagalla and nationally by Giorgia Meloni. Notwithstanding the importance of continual electoral victories of the right-wing parties and the rise in racism in Italy and Europe, solidarity continued to evolve in everyday life in Palermo, making it more crucial than ever to pay attention to the rise of Black activism in Palermo's city center.

FOUR

From Local Insecurities to Black Migrant Activism

Ballarò is a highly contested place of several paradoxes. Formerly a hotbed for the mafia, the city center shelters migrants and solidarity today. Unlike scholars' general disinterest, journalists noted the many contradictions of this place: "Nowhere [was] the African presence more visible than in Palermo's Ballarò neighborhood, which was once the rough corner of the city with long-standing mafia associations" (Einashe 2020). Yet beyond this much-celebrated visibility of Black migrants, the place has also become an unstudied breeding ground of a dynamic Black activism. This chapter shows how Black activism has continued to thrive even under the anti-immigrant municipality and Meloni's far-right government since 2022. Delving into the migrant-led historic Ballarò market, the ethnography explores the challenges and strengths of solidarity by intersecting vulnerabilities of race, class, gender, and place. Considering the anti-immigrant racist politics at multiple levels of governance (local, national, and EU), I ask what fuels native-migrant solidarity in Ballarò. Which (f)actors explain the against-all-odds, high-energy Black activism—despite deep poverty and structures of exploitation, particularly in the agricultural sector but also in the urban center?

Even though much has been said and analyzed about mafia violence (e.g., Orlando 2001; Gambetta 1993), we know very little about how past atrocities and lingering crimes have an impact on the Black migrant and native residents who cohabit in the neighborhood. Put differently, there is a lack of research that explores the effects of the city's violent legacy on today's migration and solidarity. Although an overwhelming majority of Black migrants consider Ballarò a safe place, an in-depth inquiry of the neighborhood reveals different discourses of (in)security among migrants and natives. How do these varying insecurities have an impact on cohabitation and solidarity? And in turn, how do solidarity and Black migrant activism shape the production of a highly emotional Black space.

The securitization of the EU's southern borders is deeply entangled with the racial production of the "Black Mediterranean," both historically and geopolitically (Proglio et al. 2021). In alignment with the term *Black Mediterranean* as a racialized and historicized space (Proglio et al. 2021; Hawthorn 2022), I refer to Ballarò as a Black space situated in the European colonial past in Africa. My ethnography explores what roles the relations of safety and (in)security play in the transformations of Black Ballarò. Parallel to this, how do the intersections of safety, (in)security, risk, and danger foster and undermine native-migrant solidarity?

Here, it is important to revisit Orlando's message to the world, when he proudly proclaimed that "Sicilians have an affinity for the Islamic World in their DNA" (Mattozzi 2019). Considering that race is largely a sensitive "blind spot" in Europe (Ponce 2023), particularly in states with a history of fascism, Orlando's message about racial mixing was provocative. He was not alone in drawing an interracial picture of the city, but he spearheaded the narrative that everybody in Palermo was considered Palermitan. Similarly, I heard many native activists identifying as "migrants" as a result of the historical memory of "mixing" owing to successive invasions of Sicily for centuries.[1]

While the political message "Everybody is Palermitan" may seem like an asset for mixing, it has also been questioned for cultivating a color-blind politics. For example, Orlando's response to the attempted murder of a twenty-one-year-old Gambian migrant, Yusupha, in 2016 during his mayoralty did not refer to the attack as racial violence. Instead, in line with his philosophy of welcoming everybody to the city, Orlando shared a message that such violence could happen to any Palermitan regardless of race. However, locals protested the attempted murder, claiming that violence "was taking advantage of the weakest, especially the foreign workers"(*Cronache di Ordinario Razzismo* 2016). While the protestors' discourse pointed to racism as an aggravating force of the mafia, the terminology of race was not incorporated into the pro-migrant resistance. This is what De Genova (2018b) refers to as "anti-racism without race." This may not be surprising, because race has been absent not only in Italian political, public, and academic discourse, but also in other geographies (for a similar absence of race in Latin American discourses, see Wade 2010).[2] This chapter uncovers how race is actively being brought to the fore of resistance by a rapidly flourishing Black migrant activism, which gradually finds its own language, owns its geopolitical emotions, and forms solidarity in the Black space of Ballarò.

Conventional theories of diversity and mixing do not suffice to decenter Eurocentric approaches to migration, whether they are integrationist or diversity oriented. Among these approaches, multiculturalism, the most predominant, prioritizes the type of the state and its policies (e.g., Taylor 1994; Modood 2005, [2007] 2013). While migration and borders clearly remain the jurisdiction of the states, an in-depth understanding of the bottom-up formations of anti-racist activism, migrant solidarity, and their contextual agendas and practices of resistance cannot be achieved by state-centered or policy-oriented paradigms. Interculturalist perspectives, on the other hand, center on local cultural and urban aspects of diversity and celebrate diversity at the expense of structural barriers of security regimes, their racial borders, and anti-immigrant political rule (Fossum et al. 2023). Responding to recent challenges to and failure of multiculturalism and increasing popularity of interculturalism, scholars also pointed to their complementarity (Mansouri and Modood 2020). Finally, theories of superdiversity accentuate the festive tone of diversity even further. These largely microscale and often single-sited urban analyses fail to recognize pervasive injustices of racial security at multiple scales, and thereby dismiss the importance of a contextual understanding of resistance to anti-immigrant regimes and forces.

A related common shortcoming of these approaches is the neglect of the role of geopolitical emotions—the intervening factor in the relationship between securitization and solidarity. The gaps and silences on the intersectionality of emotions, race, and space explain the celebratory tones of theories of multiculturalism, cosmopolitanism, and superdiversity. Powerful emotions originating in migrants' homelands and host lands meet in the gateway city. As the historical memories of the colonized and the colonizer cross in Ballarò, they incite powerful emotions rooted in the violent past—for both migrants and natives in this case. This chapter, though, questions the extent to which this shared sense of marginalization empowers native-migrant solidarity despite different racializations of Sicilians and migrants.

The next section discusses the historical and geopolitical background of Ballarò. I trace its transformation from violent mafia hotbed to dynamic Black space. Bridging a sociospatial approach to security (Glück and Low 2017; Glück 2017; Monroe 2016) and the geopolitics of emotion, the rest of the chapter strategically juxtaposes geopolitics of danger in the present (related to small crimes by natives) to the local trust and sense of safety that migrants expressed. I argue that these emotions have served as local assets helping the transition from past and recent violence to a vibrant Black space of solidarity.

Precursors of Black Palermo

In his book *Fighting the Mafia*, Orlando (2001, 2) narrates Palermo's troubled past: "We needed finally to take up arms against the *one part of us* that seemed most *intrinsic* but was actually the *most foreign* of all: The mafia and its culture of death." It is important to note Orlando's identification of what is foreign (here, the Sicilian mafia and homegrown crime) and whom he qualifies as Palermitan (the migrants and all residents of Palermo). These public statements by a mayor are telling of what a society fears and detests. Home-based violence is condemned in his discourses, and his understanding of the human rights city's idealized practices leaves no space for xenophobia, or fear of the Other.

Palermo's global reputation as "the shooting gallery of the Mafia" peaked in the 1980s and 1990s as the city became a deathscape, when the body count ascended to thousands per year, including security officials, police forces, judges, and so on (Orlando 2001, 1). Palermitans lost their civic life, public space, and collectively cherished sites of cultural life, such as Teatro Massimo, the largest opera house in Italy, to the brutal mafia supremacy until the turn of the millennium.[3] Adding to the damages of World War II, the city was further ruined by mafia violence and left unfixed for decades. Until Orlando's mayorship (1993–2000), which followed the vicious killings in 1992 of two anti-mafia judges, Falcone and Borsellino, who were also his friends, the mafia continued to terrorize the city. Orlando admitted to having spent most of his life deprived of enjoying public life with his family, including mundane activities for most people, such as going for a walk or to the movie theater with his children. He had noted the first signs of Palermo regaining a civic life in 1999, when people started to hang out and socialize in the public space. Along with the anti-mafia movement, reclaiming the city, and recovering people's rights and freedom, a series of local changes had been introduced, including an anti-mafia curriculum and education.

Under these extreme conditions, Palermo's historic downtown neighborhood Ballarò had remained dormant for decades (Di Rosa and Tumminelli 2022, 285). The mafia was not in favor of revitalizing the city center, as it was providing a shady space for its criminal undertakings. The childhood memories of my interlocutors flooded them with emotions of insecurity, which had annulled both public space and night life in the city. Starting in the 1980s, the historic city center started to attract newly arriving migrants, owing to inexpensive buildings and a low cost of living. This was the beginning of Ballarò's gradual transformation into a neighborhood densely populated by migrants. Former Vice Mayor Darawsha was a long-term resident of Ballarò. As an immigrant, he shared with me how migrants worked hard for placemaking: repairing buildings, opening shops in the historic market, and helping to renew an inactive economy.

Ballarò's story is the perfect example of theories of a "right to the city" defined by residency, that is, urban citizenship (Purcell 2003; Harvey 2008). The neighborhood enabled residents to transform the city in their own image (Harvey 2003), which explains the much-emphasized non-European character of Ballarò. As the main revitalizers, Ballarò's migrants did *not integrate* into a poor neighborhood that was already imbued with crime and insecurity. To the contrary, they became the catalysts of transformation, moving from violence into a relatively safer migrant-centered life while they proactively revived and rebuilt the city center. The arrival and presence of migrants were seen by native locals largely as new sources of renewal, revenue, and a vital public life The case of Ballarò reminds us "not to position more settled residents as the giving, empowered actors in the scheme, or refugees and asylum seekers as only passive, without agency or unable to reciprocate" (Askins 2016, 520). The historical centrality and contextual vitality of the Black migrant's agency in transforming a place with a violent legacy precluded these stereotypical assumptions in Ballarò.

Once the neighborhood came to be seen as a safe place, it started attracting natives, including former residents of Ballarò who had deserted the city center due to its insecurity, danger, and crime. Subsequently, a complex pattern of cohabitation emerged in Ballarò, where "foreigners and local people live[d] in conditions of economic, social and cultural fragility, along with aging [real estate] owners from the upper-middle classes" (Di Rosa and Tumminelli 2022, 284). As the depopulation of the 1970s gradually reversed, and natives and migrants repopulated renovated buildings, local urbanists referred to the downtown as the epitome of superdiversity (Di Rosa and Tumminelli 2022, 285). These views were largely in line with Orlando's frequently announced vision of an "open city and open mind." Despite ongoing socioeconomic challenges, the transitions endowed Palermo with an international reputation of "the city in renaissance." Soon, the place was rising on the shoulders of multiple contradictions, such as the coexistence of deep poverty and rapid gentrification, which manifested in an increasingly impressive restaurant and nightlife scene. Despite vocal discontent about tourism and tourists as gentrifiers, Palermo started to attract international attention and gradually became a destination for not only tourists but also digital nomads.

As discussed at length in the first part of the book, the EU's southern borderlands were hypersecuritized in order to protect member states from the presumably dangerous influx of Muslim and Black migrants. Palermo presents a challenging alternative to Europe's incentives of securitization. On the one hand, memories of a violent past remain part of everyday life by way of small crimes, such as a pervasive drug market in Ballarò. On the other hand, being exposed to lingering extralegality in immediate, everyday life nurtures a sense of anti-mafia bonding, camaraderie, and solidarity among native Palermitans and Black migrants.

The distrust of and estrangement from the central government, along with a contentious relationship with the mafia, have left their mark on the striking emotional inventory in the making of the Black Ballarò. As Orlando emphasized to me many times, the mafia did not like migrant populations, especially newcomers, as they were beyond the mafia's reach, influence, and control. Similarly, *The New York Times* concretized the antagonistic terms between migrants and the mafia by exemplifying how the mafia perceived Bangladeshi migrants as "a threat to their traditions" just because these migrants were cultivating pods and selling them in the Ballarò market (Horowitz 2019).

Despite all the challenges and insecurity, Black Palermo stands in sharp contrast to Italy's predominant right-wing view that defines "insiderness" and inclusion by ethnicity and nationality, excluding the racialized migrant Other (Norris and Inglehart 2019, 7). Parting ways with the pervasive political landscape of the country, Ballarò's migrant-run market hosts migrants from about fifteen different communities—including Sub-Saharan Africa (e.g., Ethiopia, Eritrea, Nigeria, Senegal, Gambia, Ivory Coast), North Africa (particularly but not only Tunisia), the Middle East, and Asia (Bangladesh, Sri Lanka, and Pakistan)—who speak approximately twenty-five different languages.

Although the central role of migrants in revitalizing the city center and forming a racially and culturally diverse space is a widely accepted fact in Palermo, there is also a largely shared belief that traces the city's multiculturalism to the medieval history of Sicily. A considerable majority of locals I met, including some people in solidarity, take pride in the historical development of the so-called mosaic of Palermo: the Sicilian dialect, which incorporates many Arabic words; the very eclectic historical urban landscape (referred to also as "patchwork"); the eccentric Sicilian cuisine, with spices and aromas from the Middle East and North Africa; the striking multireligious architecture; and multilingual street signs.[4]

Four ancient languages were engraved on the medieval marble tombstone of Anne, a cleric's mother—ancient Latin, Greek, Hebrew, and Arabic (MacAllan 2019). Unusual even for cities of historical complexity, the artifact puzzles and impresses not only natives but also commentators, researchers, and visitors from all around the world. However, even though the tombstone may seem to convey a clear-cut message about the striking degree of religious and cultural tolerance in medieval Palermo, research shows that "the four inscriptions [were] not, as some scholars have as-

FIGURE 6. Street signs in Ballarò in Italian, Hebrew, and
Arabic, May 16, 2023. Photo by the author.

FIGURE 7. The Tombstone of Anne, sometimes known as the Tombstone
in Four Languages, from Palermo, the capital of Norman Sicily, 1149.
Source: Realy Easy Star / Toni Spagone / Alamy Stock Photo.

sumed, exact translations of the same text." Different content conveyed in different languages was argued to signal tensions and social division, and to insinuate "belief in Christian superiority" (MacAllan 2019, 179–80). Sparking a heated conversation on the sources of contemporary diversity, the tombstone epitomizes an emotionally laden political debate not only about Palermo's history but also about present-day Italy.[5] One camp, associated sometimes also with the pro-migrant actors, proudly substantiates Palermo's current pro-migrant politics in its multicultural past. The other camp, critics of colonialism, attribute today's multiracial diversity primarily to migration flows rather than any particular historical essence of the place. While this camp includes some local intellectuals and academics, its major criticism is directed to Italy rather than Sicily.[6] Nevertheless, local debates continue contesting where the feeling of local pride about diversity needs to be placed—the constructed history of the multiethnic civilization of Sicily or the recent arrival of migrants and their making of the Black Palermo. Many in the solidarity in Palermo meet somewhere in the middle between these polarized arguments, as they do not see a contradiction between the history of successive invasions and the recent flow of migrants as two sources of racial diversity and mixing.

Even as both migrants and natives assertively argue that "Sicily is not Italy," they often compromise, acknowledging the role of both history and geography and the migrants in the making of the Black space in Palermo. Hence, while contested historical facts do not determine an inherent character of the Mediterranean basin or its frontier port cities, the historical memory of different ethnic and racial groups deserves attention because it invokes powerful emotions that shape the challenges and strengths of solidarity.

Familiarity: Home Away from Home

I met twenty-six-year-old Bobo a few years ago in a coffeeshop after one of his migrant friends connected us. He was a bright, hardworking, and passionate Black migrant activist from West Africa. He arrived in Sicily in 2015 at the age of seventeen after having crossed several violent African borders. As a teenager, he was exposed to violence and had risked his life, especially crossing Libya. When we met in 2022, he was diligently studying for his college degree at Palermo University. Bobo called it "luck" when things went well. It was by pure luck that he arrived alive in Sicily from Libya. He was also grateful for his "luck" when a local helped him enroll at Palermo University and switched his undocumented status to a student visa, after his documents had been canceled in 2019 upon Salvini's termination of humanitarian protection. Ever since we met, Bobo discussed graduate school options outside of Italy with me. He was zealous about his education, the motor of change that was his purpose for leaving his country, where schooling was an unaffordable, far-off dream for the vast majority of young people. We started chatting about Ballarò:

> Bobo: When I first came here, I was fascinated with Ballarò. The historic market was exactly like home in Africa. Similar food, spices, music, people, the mood, and even the way people moved and life flowed. . . . It was so easy to identify with. . . .
>
> Me: How so?
>
> Bobo: Hard to explain. When African friends leave Palermo and move to other cities and countries in Europe, it is not unusual that they come back here during their holiday. It becomes a home away from home. Our community is here in Ballarò. . . . Black friends, who are in Milan, Paris, Amsterdam, et cetera, do not have a similar community and public life there. Looking at our social media posts, they get jealous [he laughs].

Bobo's words reminded me of the short film *Storie vere di Palermo* (2018), which was filmed during Salvini's term as minister of interior affairs.[7] The film presented testimonies from migrants who had left Palermo to settle in northern cities, only to find unwelcoming attitudes and discrimination, which drove them to return to Palermo (on migrants' agency and navigation, see also Triandafyllidou 2019). The short film poignantly juxtaposed Palermo to the intensifying xenophobia and racism in economically better-off parts of Italy and Europe. What was so different about Palermo?

Orlando was not the only figure who admitted that the city was not a European city. African residents of Ballarò made similar comments that the energy of the place felt "more like Africa than Europe." One young Black man called it "magnetic" and reminded me that Ballarò's residents were not moving to other parts of the city. Many pointed to the affordability of

FIGURE 8. **Ballarò Market. Photo by Francesco Bellina.**

rents in old buildings and the Ballarò market as their comfort zone, where they could fulfill both their material needs, such as secondhand clothing and goods, and social and emotional needs, such as friendship and social support.

A native activist friend introduced me to Chike, a thirty-year-old African man. Chike met his native Palermitan fiancée upon his arrival to Palermo when he was living in the reception center. "Love saved my life," he said, half joking. At the time I met him, Chike and his fiancée had been together for six or seven years. When I asked Chike what distinguishes Palermo from other cities of Europe, he answered:

> Palermo is a crossroad for all migrants who arrive from Africa. The place brings us together. As we live here, we make friends not only with other migrants from different parts of Africa, but also with Sicilians.

Chike's description of Palermo was exactly why Italy's right-wing political elite despised the city. But beyond being a hub of newcomers, Palermo also witnessed the emergence of numerous migrant associations. Initially, most of these associations were formed along the lines of nationality. I had learned from Bobo that youth associations were part of the culture in his homeland. Hence, the associations in Palermo helped migrants maintain a sense of cultural continuity with their homeland. But even though many

131

were formed along ethnic and national ties (see also Nee and Sanders 2001), the cooperation and solidarity they cultivated expanded beyond the bounds of ethnicity and race. Natives participated in the associations' events and parties, and they co-organized panels and projects together. Sometimes, common activist agendas and goals brought migrants and natives together to protest, such as in pro-Palestinian demonstrations. Palermo's streets displayed that activism by way of street art, graffiti, slogans, and anticolonial protests joined by both natives and Black migrants.

Even though Palermo's city center was one of the most racially mixed urban spaces in all of Europe, most migrants were mindful of the complications of cohabitation in Ballarò. As deep poverty met the neighborhood's drug market, the latter continued to pose a risk for people with overlapping vulnerabilities of class, race, and ethnicity.

Are Security and Fear Privileges of the White?

Unlike the realist view of the state that needs to be secured from identified threats, critical security studies focus on and question "discourses of insecurity" and "representations of danger" (Megoran 2005, 558). From this perspective, security appears as a sociocultural and political construct that is open to perception, interpretation, and contestation rather than a given strategy or "product of calculation" (Megoran 2005, 560). So, how then did the residents of Ballarò perceive, deliberate, and feel about (in)security in their neighborhood?

Overall, the residents of Ballarò stated that they felt safe in their neighborhood. This predominant view contradicted the ways in which the city center was perceived by the natives who lived in Palermo's outskirts. Chike said that Ballarò was relatively safe despite the frequent incidents of small theft. For example, his fiancée's bike had been recently stolen. They knew that a white fourteen-year-old boy who was involved with the mafia had stolen the bike. Chike's fiancée, a native Palermitan, thought that calling the police was not necessary, as they could easily solve the issue. Chike confronted the boy and managed to get back the bike.

During my stay in Ballarò, I also learned from other migrants about their daily encounters with drug dealers. A native activist friend introduced me to Davu, a young man from West Africa who had arrived in 2016 and lived in Ballarò ever since. Davu worked in one of the major social enterprises in Ballarò's migrant sector. As did many migrants, he had several other jobs. He was also interested in photography, advertising, and film. One day, when he was being filmed on the streets of Ballarò for a BBC documentary, a native white man in his mid-thirties interrupted the film by provoking and threatening Davu. Knowing that the man was a drug dealer, Davu maintained his calm attitude without responding or reacting. But why would the drug dealer disrupt the shooting of the film? Familiar with the man's microaggressions, Davu explained to me that he felt territorial and envious when he saw so much attention and cameras being directed at a Black migrant in "his" neighborhood. Jealous of the international interest in a racial migrant, he was trying to show who was "boss" in the neighborhood. But the BBC was interested in Davu because they regarded him as a representative of Black Ballarò, not the white drug dealer.

When I asked Davu how he felt about this street harassment by the drug dealer, he told me: "After the dreadful Libya experience, nothing can provoke my anger." Because his future depended on gaining residency documents and having a clean criminal record, he had to avoid street-level aggression and mind his own business. "We did not survive the brutal journey and come to Europe to get involved in crime, have our documents canceled, and be imprisoned," he added. The Black migrants of Ballarò, then, learned to temper their emotions and put up with microaggressions and insecurity, especially when dealing with the extralegal actors in their daily life.

When I asked Davu if he ever expressed anger at all, the poised young man had to pause to remember a moment of anger. Then, he responded that he had been infuriated when he had visited migration authorities to renew his residency documents, and the officer at the entrance did not allow him to enter the building and explain his situation. Instead, he took Davu's papers and sent him away without even allowing him to discuss his case. Because his documents had expired six months earlier with yet another major policy change, Davu felt helpless, invisible, and angry. The illicit black market of Ballarò seemed to be easier to avoid than the injustices and human rights violations of Italy's migration governance.

In spite of the crackdown on the mafia's supremacy twenty-five years ago, single instances of aggression continued and manifested abruptly in racial violence. When a mafioso shot a twenty-one-year-old Gambian migrant, Yusupha Susso, in the head in 2016, he was walking in the market with his migrant friend. As he was punched by the Mafioso intruder, he and his friend both tried to avoid a fight by telling the aggressor that they wanted peace. Despite their effort to avoid conflict, Yusupha was chased by the attacker out of Ballarò, where he shot him. Yusupha, a singer, came from a migrant musician family. After coming out of a coma, Yusupha moved to Milan. In an interview, he stated that he was shot because the mafia wanted to show that "the area belong[ed] to them; they are only thinking about territory" (Einashe 2016). The city responded vocally, and masses marched in the streets to protest the brutality of the mafia and in support of the migrant population in Palermo.

Migrant solidarity is entwined with the city's historical struggle against the mafia. Bangladeshi migrants, who had been afraid of mafia retaliation, began to resist mafia crimes and refused to be extorted for "protection." I heard from many locals and Orlando how the Bangladeshi migrant resistance was respected and appreciated as testimony to migrant solidarity in the anti-mafia movement. The resistance culminated in the arrest of the shooter and many others, as well as the imprisonment of a leading criminal from an infamous mafia family. Ironically, the shared fury about local violence brought the migrants and natives together. As the contestation in Athens (Chapter 1) showed, pro-migrant municipalities with considerable migrant populations are not immune to violence by anti-immigrant local forces. To the contrary, the carving out of safe places for migrants, as in Exarcheia and Ballarò, was happening at the expense of increased contestation and occasional racial violence.

These incidents raise the question of whether Palermo continued to be a dangerous city, and if Ballarò was doomed to racial insecurity? I asked this question in my interviews with both migrants and native activists. Most migrants, even the ones who knew Yusupha, refused to believe Ballarò was unsafe for them. There were always two sides to the stories about Ballarò. If we insist on emphasizing safety, we can easily miss the lingering racism hidden in dark corners. I met Fausto Melluso, a prominent pro-migrant activist of Palermo, in the summer of 2019, when he was a member of the city council. He later became president of the Palermo branch of ARCI, a leftist, anti-racist, pro-migrant nongovernmental organization based in

Ballarò. Melluso, also a longtime Ballarò resident, had a nuanced take that complicated the issue of safety there:

> Every city has crime. The indicator of safety is not the small crimes, which are pervasive across Italy and beyond. It is also not the single rare incident of homicide. It is about statistics. . . . Numbers show that Palermo is safer than most other cities in Italy.

Unlike the solidarity's insistence on the safety of the neighborhood, the outcries of native locals about small crimes had increased in Ballarò since COVID-19. Even though Palermo was by far safer than it had been in the 1980s and 1990s, Ballarò's streets have long been a breeding ground for drug dealers. The COVID-19 pandemic expanded the criminal economy and led to increases in drug use and mental health problems. Because most migrants were not able to implement social distancing during the pandemic (given their challenging accommodations and work situations), COVID-19 posed a real threat to migrants' poverty-ridden life in Palermo (Picone and Giubilaro 2022).

The multiple discourses of (in)security and danger reveal differing experiences and emotions for migrants and natives. The most critical voices on responses to insecurity came from activist leaders who were natives. In my meeting with Melluso, he discussed how the persistence of the black market in Ballarò had resulted from the system's failure to provide social welfare. He eloquently tied the persistence of the criminal economy to the deep poverty that defined the historic market of Ballarò. While Melluso was still in the city council in 2022, he worked hard to convince Lagalla's new municipal government to dig into the roots of the problem of small crimes. Like some other pro-migrant activists, he has been a pioneering voice in the anti-mafia movement. Under Orlando's leadership, many stages of the fight against the mafia had been accomplished, such as arrests and the confiscation of mafia-owned goods and property. Nevertheless, without the achievement of an alternative economy for the poor, Melluso continued, the criminal economy could not be defeated.

When Melluso posted a long harsh critique on Facebook of natives' alarming complaints about the drug problem in Ballarò (December 17, 2023), I wrote to schedule a meeting with him. He was critical of the negative reactions and complaints of Ballarò's middle-class natives, who were mostly his friends and neighbors. He dismissed their concerns as conservative outcry. He also criticized their lack of consideration for the poor, who had been pushed into the criminal market for the lack of other avenues of subsistence. Concretely, he rebuffed the natives' inability to see what were systemic socioeconomic failures: "The anti-mafia movement must not turn to a war against the poor people, who are the victims of the black-market economy," he told me. Respected by his friends as a committed fighter for justice, he also refused to hand over the social responsibility of solving the problem of small crimes to the penal system. He objected to criminalization and the imprisonment of poor people victimized by the mafia for small crimes.

In line with Melluso's comments, I heard from other activists that the neighborhood associations were focused too narrowly on their own middle-class interests and had become self-centered. Instead, Melluso called for efforts that were directed to confronting the failing system, including food insecurity in the outskirts of the city, such as in the neighborhood Zen.

A native professor I met sarcastically described tourists' attraction to Ballarò as a "poverty safari." By this, she was referring to the tourists gazing at the broken and stolen goods sold in the worn-out streets of the historic market.[8] The professor criticized the tourists' fascination with deep poverty and damaged buildings that prevailed in the city center. Critical of the commodification of poverty in the city, she argued that Ballarò was attracting tourists who were coming there to escape luxury tourism, but ending up conflating deep poverty with authenticity. The dislike of tourists, who were gentrifying the city center by buying property or renting expensive Airbnbs, was widely shared by the migrants and natives.

Another leftist activist member of the city council during Lagalla's municipal government shared with me her day-to-day exposure to and struggles against deep poverty in the city. Like Melluso, instead of criminalizing the poor, she complained about the structural inability to *prevent* poverty. Importantly, I noticed the persistent absence of race in conversations about class inequalities and poverty among native activism. When I probed, the council member responded that the former city government of Orlando had directed all its efforts towards the migrants, neglecting the deep poverty and hunger of the natives. Considering migrants' huge disadvantage of being

FIGURE 9. **Albergheria Market, May 14, 2024. Photo by the author.**

racialized and criminalized by the security regime, I wondered whether pitting the economic vulnerabilities of natives and migrants against each other was a productive way of approaching justice in the city.

My ongoing conversation with native activists on safety and security pointed to the elephant in the room. I found two related issues in pro-migrant attitudes. First, the terminology of race was sometimes absent in pro-migrant native activism. Second, in line with Melluso's critical points, the nonactivist natives' calls for security as part of their complaints about the drug market were actually weaponizing the privilege of white middle-class residents. Even though these native residents were pro-migrant, and admittedly anti-racist, their safety concerns were overlooking the multiple vulnerabilities of African migrants. This meant that even when claims for security were not racial (i.e., *not* targeting racial minorities as threats), they often overlooked how extralegality in town and criminalization of migrants had left Black residents in even more complicated situations. Unaware of the white privilege embedded in their security complaints, the anti-racism of some white middle-class residents of Ballarò failed to recognize the inter-sectionality of race, class, and place. Ironically, the Black Ballarò was not immune to "anti-racism without race" (De Genova 2018b).

While earlier works in sociology and criminology have clearly identified the role of privilege in shaping perceptions of (in)security (for example, on gated communities, see Low 2001, 2003), the recent geopolitics of security have evolved around notions of globalized fear, leaving out the human dimension and interactional complexities (Pain and Smith 2008; Pain 2009). Hence, a clear distinction is needed between the carving out of safe places for migrants, valued by *all* residents, and claims for security by *some* natives that dismissed the vulnerabilities of racialized migrants.

Even though it is often unspoken, the persistence of the criminal economy in Ballarò renders Black migrants more vulnerable to small crimes than Ballarò's middle- and upper-class natives. Yet in contrast to the natives' security claims, the large majority of Ballarò's migrants avoided complaining about insecurity and small crimes. The juxtaposition of natives' perceived insecurity and migrants' sense of safety in the same neighborhood presented a curious case.

Only one Black activist whom I met, Samba, was living outside Ballarò by choice—he worked several jobs and could afford to live in a nearby neighborhood. I wondered about his choice because all his friends and activist circles were based in Ballarò. He responded: "Ballarò market feels like home, and I go to Ballarò to play football on Saturdays." But Samba's attachment to the market did not change his choice to live outside the chaotic Ballarò. He needed peace of mind, he explained. Samba's migrant friends did not understand his choice.

When Samba first came to Palermo, he lived in the reception center like other migrants. Even though migrants were given the right to receive a small amount of pocket money and basics like clothing, in reality they were provided none of these things. Despite his dire conditions, Samba never begged. He worked in gas stations and washed and parked cars. While rural Sicily was often characterized by structural patterns of exploitation of Black migrants, urban practices were not devoid of exploitative labor conditions. Despite robust pro-migrant solidarity in Palermo, Italy's repressive and restrictive immigration system, which "produces subjects with limited rights or illegal status," is largely pervasive across the country (Giglioli 2021, 727; see also Fabini 2017; Mezzadra and Neilson 2013). Reacting to this system of injustices, Samba continued:

> We [migrants] are not inherently poor people who need help. The problem is political. If you vote for these governments, the Italian political system continues to be the source of the problem of poverty, criminality, and insecurity. . . . What the migrants want is not help, but equal treatment . . . rights and freedoms.

All Black migrants I spoke with were expressive about the volatility of their life conditions and their migration status, whether they lived in Ballarò or elsewhere. But when asked about their fears, Black migrants consistently kept quiet. After much silence and confusion in conversations, I started wondering whether they had never been asked before about their fears. I learned that, similar to race being absent or silenced from discourses of anti-racism in Italy, fear was not part of conversation about the violent journey of migrants, dangerous border crossings, and their volatile circumstances as asylum seekers in Italy. (How) could violence be resisted without the recognition and deliberation of fear? Importantly, presence, absence, or implications of fear were not integrated into the language of migrant resistance and solidarity. When migrants were interviewed by journalists and researchers, the question of fear was largely ignored. That was why when I asked about fear, they did not expect it and paused in confusion. It was an unexpectedly ambiguous subject to reflect on. As I probed, I learned that they did not talk about fear even among their friend circles. I wondered whether the silence about fear was shaped by their masculinity intersecting with their young age. Was it part of an effort to avoid showing weakness or admitting vulnerability?

Pain (2009, 473) elaborates on the paradox of "the unspoken privilege of fear." She argues that "fear is always named, known, privileged and spatialized in certain ways by the powerful," even though its impact on the poorest and the marginalized people is the biggest. "The poor are routinely written out of fear," she continues. That is why the fear of the feared, the Muslim or Black migrant may easily be perceived as an oxymoron: (How) could the feared target of securitization also have fears themselves? The absence of fear from Black migrants' discourse revealed a contrast with the increasingly loud complaints of Ballarò's middle-class native residents about the drug market. In her critique of the geopolitics of "global fear," Pain (2009, 473) points to white privilege, arguing: "Global discourses of 'global' fear are also centrally about whiteness . . . they often do little to challenge the assumption that fear is the prerogative of the privileged." Like security, fear was just another entitlement that came with white privilege. The association of fear and white privilege explains the "passive audience" of securitization. The residents of upscale Athens neighborhoods and rich sea villages at the outskirts of Palermo who were fearful of Muslim and Black migrants, and entitled for more security, welcomed the securitization of migration. Similarly, in world politics, we only hear about the fear and security issues of powerful states and people of the First World, while security of Afghanistan, Palestine, or Sudan and the fear of the people in these unsafe countries remain non-issues.

Even though previous sociological and feminist works on class- and race-based violence had established strong relationships between vulnerability or marginality and fear (Pain 2001; Valentine 1989), since the War on Terror, mundane everyday fear has been disconnected from the notion of globalized fear. Subsequently, the importance of geopolitics has risen to the extent that it "submerged the everyday," thereby rendering people's emotions and responses unnoticed (Pain and Smith 2008, 5). The in-depth inquiry into Ballarò fills this gap by explicating how safety and (in)security are lived out and felt every day, albeit differently by natives and Black migrants.

When Samba told me that "migrants [were] not victims," I noted a subtlety in his language. Even though he did not live in Ballarò, he refused to specify the risk or danger that the criminal economy posed for Black migrants. As our friendship developed, I came to understand that his defensiveness was originating from his refusal to accept victimhood and give in to the inhumane migration regime. Being identified as fearful could potentially be a disservice to vulnerable groups, especially if fearfulness and insecurity were to become regarded as fixed attributes of certain people (Pain 2008, 10–11) rather than geopolitical emotions and responses to the governance of migration and borders. Hence, Samba criticized systemic injustices and demanded equal rights and freedom of mobility. Even though he was not choosing to live in Ballarò, he carefully avoided any disempowering discourses of fear and insecurity associated with the Black space. In time, I realized that the seeming nuance of the language was indicative of a characteristic of Black migrant resistance: Young black migrants refused to admit fear as part of their struggle to reject disempowerment. This partly strategic and partly emotional response is the opposite of repression or denial of a geopolitical emotion. To the contrary, these young male activists were regulating the geopolitics of fear in their immediate lives, which shaped their activism.

Black Activism and Migrant Associations

It took me three long interviews with Bobo, several phone conversations, and a lot of texting between May and December 2023 to gain a deeper understanding of his activist leadership, which was receiving international attention. After observing his political resistance and interacting with him on several occasions in different contexts, I noted a contrast between his calm poise and his passionate, loud, high-energy activism. Wondering how these aspects of his personality merged, I asked him about what would agitate him or make him angry. He smiled and told me that he *never* becomes agitated. Noticing my bewilderment, the twenty-six-year-old man backed up his self-confident claim and assured me that I was not going to see him angry. When I probed further, he loosened up a little and explained:

> I am only angry when I protest, and when I am holding the microphone in a demonstration. When I am out there in a demonstration in the streets, I may seem like a different person. I talk with a *strong* voice, because then, my goal is to transform my anger into *powerful* action. Anger that remains as a loud impulsive voice does not serve any purpose. The protest is the only exception for me, because then my feelings about injustices are well directed, and serve a purpose. (Italics added.)

Knowing how often he holds the mic and how frequently he marches in protests, I asked, "Which purpose?"

> The fight against racism, discrimination, colonialism, Frontex, the EU border regime. . . . It is a long list of injustices, you know. The EU borders are not only physical, but also exist in minds, and turn people against each other. We must challenge all aspects and dimensions of racial injustices.

Cross-border human mobility has transformed Ballarò in multiple mundane ways. The high turnover of migrants and the vibrant change they instigate challenge and even turn mainstream theories, policies, and practices of integration upside down. The peripheral border geography renders the top-down policies and Eurocentric notions of integration irrelevant. While one of the main goals of integration policies is language acquisition of the host country, the young Black migrants with whom I interacted in Palermo already spoke, on average, more than four languages: In addition to Italian and the Sicilian dialect, because they were instructed and educated in Sicily, they all spoke either English or French (or sometimes both), depending on their home country's colonial history, as well as at least two African languages. The multilingual migrant who survived in multiple countries under excruciating conditions presents a new reality and a contradiction in this geography, where most Sicilians speak only Sicilian (and Italian), and many have never traveled off their island or even very far outside their own village. Hence, the integration of the multilingual Black migrants, who crossed many borders irregularly, into a largely provincial peripheral geography may seem like an oxymoron.

Over the years, I also observed increasing fluency of English language among natives working in solidarity. The increasing multilingual skills of solidarity in Palermo was the result of the frequent daily interaction between natives and migrants. But these skills also developed through consistent engagement and cooperation with transnational activist networks and organizations. No doubt, language was not the only indicator of a large-scale transformation in solidarity that had been jump-started in the arrival city. The migrants had arrived with a large skill set, including resilience and the willpower to grow and do better, in addition to the meaningful experiences they gained while moving across borders. The combination of these powerful skills renders Eurocentric ideas about migrant integration shallow and out of date.

The Politicization of Migrant Lives

My findings on dynamic Black activism brought two widely shared opinions about Generation Z migrants into question: their presumed apolitical inclination, including a disinterest in and withdrawal from politics and activism, and the reductive and exclusive association of them with the primary need and interest in earning money. Zooming in on Ballarò's everyday life, I expose Black activism, which extends far beyond limiting stereotypes of African "economic migrants" who work underpaid jobs for minimal levels of subsistence.

Bobo was a respected and valued member and spokesperson of a migrant association who played a leading role in expanding migrant associational life from the cultural to the political realm. Bobo preferred to keep cultural events and celebrations separate from political action. "We should stop thinking that our problems can be solved by other people, and not by us," he told me. His words and his cooperation with his friends planted the seeds of Black youth activism in Palermo. Without denying that culture is important, Bobo criticized the pervasive cultural reductionism that diminished African associational life to dancing and food.

With these ideas in mind, Bobo's co-nationals formed their association in 2018, one year after Bobo had arrived at the age of seventeen. The members of Bobo's originally ethnic association rapidly increased from about 30 migrants to more than 130 in 2025. Members typically contributed five dollars per month to be used for bureaucratic processes or to be used as an emergency fund for members in need.

After witnessing the inner conflicts about taking on leadership positions, Bobo and his close friend proposed to replace these minor power struggles with long-term agendas that would serve them and future generations of migrants. With Bobo's encouragement, the bickering calmed down, and the association started electing executive members democratically. Even though Bobo was nominated for the position of president, he became the spokesperson because he was a good speaker and an enthusiastic representative of the organization.

"The majority of the migrant community may not be very politically aware upon their arrival," he admitted. At the beginning, it was difficult for the members to engage in, and even talk about, politics. Bobo explained to me that migrants who had had no interest in politics in Africa had gradually become part of the resistance. Bobo and his activist friends felt responsible for informing migrants about unjust conditions and convincing them about the importance of political engagement. While native activists and local organizations helped newly arriving migrants by orienting them to the city and teaching Italian and other skills, Bobo and his friends were busy making space and time for political engagement. As their association evolved, it gradually attracted international attention and developed links with other associations of co-nationals in Palermo and other major Italian cities as well as across Europe. Bobo and his friends continued pursuing recruitment while also reaching out to wider (inter)national activist networks.

Why did Bobo's association politicize migrant associational life? Different members of the association explained to me how "everything in their life was about politics." Deep levels of disappointment and distrust in migration governance in Italy and Europe politicized ordinary migrants' lives. Constantly changing and worsening migration policies, chronically arbitrary bureaucratic procedures, and the unreliable, hostile, and violent governance of borders and migration were the main impetus for their activism. Ade shared with me that back at home, he did not listen to or care about politicians' speeches. This changed quickly after his arrival in Sicily. In Europe, migrants were pawns for political gain, he explained to me. He became interested in politics when he realized that migrants' lives explicitly served as tokens for politicians to acquire power and popularity in Italy.

Yet young African men were also aware that they had a generational advantage, which endowed their political engagement and associational life with enormous energy. Political differences were divisive in migrant communities, which had been formed by the now elderly migrants who had arrived earlier. While Bobo's association itself was not polarized by generational conflicts, decision-making was not always easy. Members often disagreed on issues such as whether they should be involved in a particular event or participate in a protest. But Bobo was content with the debates. He preferred democratic disagreement to the unproductive, deep conflict of some other associations, in which older generations of migrants blocked decisions and undermined any change.

Instead, Bobo described his association as "future oriented," and that vision helped migrants in three major ways. First, it provided a motive to overcome the traumatic recent past of "the journey," by opening up and encouraging migrants to take new directions with meaning and purpose. I was told that the members refused to talk even among themselves about some parts of their pasts, particularly the "hell" of Libya, as it was too painful, dehumanizing, and humiliating to revisit. Even though most conversations with Black migrants involved their personal lives while crossing borders, there was a notable silence about crossing Libya. Davu confirmed my understanding of the sensitive subject: "Even between us, we never talk about Libya. It is too painful to revisit." Lamine complained to me that journalists would reach out from different countries to ask exclusively about their past pain, torture, and humiliation without showing any interest in who they are as human beings, their growth and potentials.[9] A similar bias is also prevalent in refugee studies with a narrow emphasis in trauma rather than wide-ranging responses, emotions, and practices that impact the formation of solidarity.

The second positive outcome of future-oriented motivation in the association was agreement that the association's goals were to serve not only the current community of co-nationals but also the larger migrant population, across nationalities, as well as the future newcomers and generations of migrants. Bobo's association had recently started recruiting and inviting migrants from other nationalities to its activities. It also encouraged and invited members of other associations to join the protests. These strategic decisions enlarged their sphere of public lives and political activities while nourishing a broadening sense of community. Third, this future-oriented perspective also motivated the association to expand its activities and participate in demonstrations across Italy in collaboration with other associations in other cities, such as Naples and Rome. This expanded reach created an interest in connecting with cross-border and transnational activist networks. In turn, the association was invited to international conferences and meetings. International broadcast networks became interested in Bobo's association, as it gradually made a reputation for itself in transnational migrant activism.

Along with the democratizing principles of governance, the association also maintained certain taboos from home countries. For example, LGBTQ issues were not discussed, as LGBTQ identities were not accepted in the Muslim culture of the home country. Bobo admitted to me: "I am a defender of gay rights, but if we include gay activism, the association will have to split." As studies on European nativism show (see especially Duyvendak et al. 2023), Europeans from all political allegiances, including the Left, problematize the conservative political orientation of Muslim migrants, particularly around gender politics. Especially in countries such as the Netherlands, where pride in national identity is closely associated with freedom and emancipation from traditional norms of sex and gender, migrants who do not share "progressive" norms are looked down upon, othered, and utilized by some as tokens to achieve anti-immigrant political ends. Progressive sex and gender norms as a source of anti-immigrant sentiment brought together many Europeans from various political fronts. But of course, this "progressive exclusion" is a contradiction in terms, mainly because it contains a major paradox: Sexually emancipated white Europeans continue reinforcing racial hierarchies and exclusion by weaponizing their sexual "liberation" against racialized Muslim and Black migrants. As conveyed in the terminology of "pinkwashing," the sexual emancipation of the white European is not a compelling progressive political stance if it reinforces racial discrimination against Muslim minorities and migrants.[10]

Europeans' prejudices toward Muslim and Black migrants miss the larger picture of a dynamic and powerful transformation taking place in the border zones. A faithful and practicing Muslim, Bobo conceded to me that he would no longer fit in the political culture in his homeland, as he was not able to tolerate discrimination and harassment against any minority, including LGBTQ individuals. Upon hearing Bobo's comment, I asked about the absence of women in the association, which was made up of young Black men. The migrants coming from Bobo's homeland (and other African countries) were predominantly young men, given the dangers of the journey. He told me that, a few years earlier, two young women had arrived from his country; they were welcomed and respected in the association. But they moved to Rome soon after their arrival. A few months after our conversation, Bobo's association invited new migrant members from other nationalities, some of whom were women.

Bobo had five African business partners from different countries, with whom he co-owned a social enterprise in the migrant service sector. They rented the kitchen of a migrant-hosting NGO. Taking turns, the partners cooked and served various dishes from African cuisines for lunch and dinner. When Bobo was not in school or in the kitchen, he worked several other jobs. He performed cultural mediation in the court of Palermo and translations at police headquarters. He had a part-time job managing the social media platforms of a major pro-migrant NGO. And still, he was pouring all his remaining energy into activism. Learning about the details of Bobo's daily routines, I could not help but wonder about the self-discipline such multitasking takes. When I asked Bobo how he managed to fit all his work into a twenty-four-hour day, he told me that he woke up very early every day and did not drink or smoke. His friends advised Bobo to slow down. He felt obliged to explain to me:

> I do most of this because of passion. I feel grateful and privileged for all I have. This feeling pushes me to work more and to contribute more to others' well-being, who may need help and support. . . . I also skip classes to go to protests sometimes [he smiles].

In addition to discipline, passion, and motivation, Bobo felt deeply responsible for many people in his life. He did not spend his earnings only on himself and his education. He sent most of them home to pay for the education of his brother and nephews, and to take care of his family of nine people whom he left behind. Importantly, however, Bobo was not prioritizing money when he made plans for graduate studies. Even though his college education was not in social sciences, he wanted a career in the field of justice, public policy, or international politics. His purpose was to work toward making the world a better place for the marginalized and vulnerable.

I inquired about the roots of Bobo's calling to political activism and human rights. Was his decision shaped by his education back home in Africa? No, he said. Even public education was very expensive there. He had to stop schooling after the first seven years and did not continue it until he was in Palermo. That was one of the reasons he migrated. Was his political passion shaped by his family, then, I wondered. Was he born into an activist family? He laughed at my question and said that his parents were "illiterate" and "traditional."

Bobo's parents did not know about his college education in Palermo or his plans for graduate school in London. They never heard anything about his political activism. Bobo told me that they would not understand or approve any of his undertakings. They also did not know that he was migrating when he told them he was going to "travel." I heard similar stories from other African migrants about their parents. No matter how I inquired about Bobo's passion for politics, his explanations were about his own values and commitment to fight against colonialism, racism, and injustice.

Chapter Four

From Cultural to Racial Politics in Associations

For many years, Moltivolti was seen as the symbol of multiracial "mixed" Palermo. Founded in 2014 by eight (pro)migrant human rights activists from Senegal, Zambia, Afghanistan, Bangladesh, France, Spain, Gambia, and Italy, Moltivolti (Many Faces) is a social enterprise, a gastronomic initiative, and a coworking space for multiple solidarity projects and activism. The space reserved for coworking is utilized mainly for pro-migrant projects and anti-mafia activism, and as a meeting venue by migrant associations, local organizations, and activists.[11] Adjacent to coworking is a café that employed thirty-eight migrants and five chefs from different countries.

I met Claudio Arestivo, one of the founders and a former manager, in 2019, when he was running the Moltivolti café. After answering my question about Moltivolti's international ties with activists in big cities like Bologna and Milan, he changed the subject to food. Like Melissa Network in Athens, Moltivolti emphasized food in shaping migrant-native relations: "Appreciation of good food," he said, "gives dignity to people," by honoring their roots, senses, and even childhood memories. Hearing compliments about dishes of their homelands makes people proud, he continued. Moltivolti was quite purposeful in showcasing migrants' cuisines to try to disrupt "the problematic giver/receiver power relations" and cultivate "shared senses and experiences" (Askins 2016, 523).

When we were chatting in the summer of 2022, Claudio was questioning why Moltivolti, which served dishes from sixteen countries, was referred to as an "ethnic" restaurant. African and Arab dishes were so ingrained into Sicilian cuisine that labeling some of them "ethnic" did not align with locals' sense of Sicilian identity and cuisine. Claudio also asked why Moltivolti was not considered an international restaurant, like American or French restaurants are. His point reminded me of the Tunisians who I asked why they did not have a migrant association in Ballarò. They answered: "The same reason why Palermitans do not have an association: This is home for us."

In May 2023, Claudio reminded me of something that I had long noticed in Ballarò: "We do not talk about integration here," he said. "Instead, we coexist in Ballarò." According to Claudio, cohabitation was simply not a theory or deliberation in everyday Ballarò life. It was a lived experience. As long as integration is not perceived as a "bilateral" process" between natives and migrants, he explained, it is an incomplete concept. "Not just migrants but [also] my Sicilian mom has to adjust to the new normal of cohabitation," he added. This mutual process was not easy for some, particularly the elderly. But when Moltivolti burned in a fire in 2022, it was reopened with efficient crowdfunding by locals from all walks of life. Claudio's family members, who were not pro-migrant activists, contributed as well.

Pointing to the racially mixed group of youngsters at the café's bar, he proudly continued: "It is our lives—the new normal." Claudio continued managing Moltivolti until 2024, when he moved on to work at an interfaith project. Moltivolti echoed across countries and continents as the epitome of what multiculturalists and interculturalists celebrate about mixed places. But further ethnographic inquiry into these mixed places reveals differential treatment of Black migrant workers, reflecting patterns of labor exploitation similar to ones found on the national scale. Even though migrants did everything—opening and closing, cooking, serving, cleaning, bartending, and cleaning—their wages were outstandingly low. Although Moltivolti was originally created by a racially mixed group of migrants, "the new normal" was not immune to structured inequalities among races.

With respect to the "hospitality" culture arguably associated with the city's presumed multicultural origins, some researchers singled out Moltivolti for promoting Orlando's city-branding agenda (Neil 2024). While Moltivolti did promote hospitality and the ideal image of the mixed city, that criticism dismissed the historical and geopolitical contextuality of geopolitical emotions. First, not withholding the contested nature of the concept of hospitality, the celebration of hospitality in Palermo manifests much more widely than just in one social enterprise, whether in the homes and kitchens of older Sicilian mothers or older migrants. Hence, rather than being merely the result of neoliberal tactics to market the city to the tourists, Moltivolti was yet another expression of how historically constructed memory forms geopolitical emotions—in this case, pride in Sicilian history and tradition. Second, the narrow focus of studies that criticize the city's tourist campaign have largely ignored migrants' perceptions and feelings, such as trust, about Orlando's city government. Everyone agreed that tourists' dollars were welcome, but the critiques still dismissed two important points: Moltivolti's considerable support to solidarity over the years, including the formation of Mediterranea Saving Humans, and the migrants' perceptions of Orlando and his pro-migrant vision and agendas. Hence, while the critiques of hospitality make good points about the power dynamics between "the guest" and "the host," the lines of separation between migrant advocacy and hospitality may not always be as clear as existing works assume (for a constructive critique of the guest-host relations, see Squire and Darling 2013).

Over the past couple of years, I have witnessed that the biggest step made by the solidarity movement was to go beyond the self-celebratory culture of mixed places to an emerging appreciation of Black space. New migrant associations started to blossom in Ballarò, creating bonds between migrants across ethnic and national divides. My visits with two of these associations, Right2Be and Maldusa, were particularly revealing. Rather than celebrating the multicultural historical heritage of mixed city life or hospitality, these associations raised a series of critiques of injustice by bringing race into anti-racism discourse. Unlike critiques that focused narrowly on neoliberalism or that reduced racial injustice to economics, these migrant organizations complicated Europe's colonialism by their approaches that integrate intersectionality between race, class, and emotions of safety, security, and dignity. Right2B brought Africa to the fore in discussions of borders and migration by leading debates about how the continent has been exploited for centuries, historically, economically, (geo) politically, and socioculturally. The agendas that Right2Be pursued were critical, vocally anti-racist and anticolonial, and deeply emotional.

My visits to Maldusa's center were eye-opening. Maldusa's agendas focused on freedom of movement, (cross-)border migrant solidarity, and overseeing rescue. Maldusa's Lampedusa branch documented sea crossings from Libya and Tunisia mainly to Malta and to Italy. The association also acquired a boat, not to join NGOs' rescue operations, but to support migrants on the move and to document violations during their journey. The doors of the association were open to anybody who participated in anti-racist, anticolonialist, transnational resistance to securitization. The social events, concerts, and street parties brought together natives and migrants from various nationalities. Unlike Moltivolti, which had previously been the pinnacle of pro-migrant activism, with its support for Mediterranea Saving Humans, the new migrant-led associations did not celebrate mul-

FIGURE 10. **Maldusa offices, December 18, 2023. Photo by the author.**

ticulturalism, interculturalism, or mixing. By way of shared stories and migrants' voices, they cultivated support, trust, and hope to enable freedom of mobility and defend rights and justice for racialized migrants.

The changing landscape of migrant associations reveals how Black space has been unfolding in Ballarò, from celebratory multiculturalist projects driven by historical pride to pro-migrant, native-led rescue initiatives, and finally to migrant-pioneered anticolonialist activism that brought race to the center of the resistance. Importantly, because Black Ballarò was not the outcome of a particular local municipal policy, the solidarity not only persevered but even thrived under the right-wing local government that entirely ignored migrants' existence, politics, and associations. Even though the leap from Orlando's pro-migrant leadership to Lagalla's neglect was drastic, everyday life and politics in Black Ballarò continued on their usual course.

Bobo invited me and a group of my students visiting from Boston to the Mediterraneo Antirazzista, an annual cultural and anti-racist event. The two-day event on May 10 and 11, 2024, consisted of sports, a soccer tournament, music, dancing, and mingling. Although the activities were cultural and brought together natives and migrants from all walks of life, the political message was overtly anticolonial and anti-racist.

While people in solidarity identified strongly with anti-racist politics, migrants observed to me the numerous ways that racism permeated their lives and other parts of the city. For example, despite racially mixed classrooms in Palermo's high schools and university, Bobo experienced racism-infused teaching.[12] When he objected to the way slavery was taught in high school, his teacher had argued that Black people did not resist and were submissive to slave traders. Bobo corrected the teacher: "This is my history. Your teachings of colonial history are incorrect." Bobo was very clear on the role of ideology. He consistently argued that his politics was not about the Left or the Right, because ideological differences did not make much

FIGURE 11. A football game at the annual anti-racism event Mediterraneo Antirazzista, in Piazza Magione, May 11, 2024. Photo by the author.

FIGURE 12. People attending the annual anti-racism event Mediterraneo Antirazzista, in Piazza Magione, May 11, 2024. Photo by the author.

difference in the racial injustice done to migrants. "I am not interested in ideological debates, but only in action for justice!" he concluded.

Bobo's interest in activism started with experiencing injustice in his home country, where his initial goal was to become a lawyer and fight for justice. When socioeconomic conditions did not permit him this goal, he decided to leave the country with one of his good friends. The situation he experienced in Libya, where he was stuck for over a year, sharpened his sense of injustice and his will to fight against violations of human rights and violence. His arrival in Italy and his experiences as an irregular Black migrant only deepened his agendas for justice and equal rights.

Like all African migrants whom I met in Palermo, Bobo objected to his siblings' migration across the Mediterranean. Black migrants in Palermo unanimously agree that nobody should go through what they experienced. For Bobo, the only way to help any of his siblings move to Europe would be after he fully establishes himself, with stable income and reliable immigrant status. Dignity was nonnegotiable for bringing any family members onto European soil.

Even though most migrants were involved in everyday politics in some capacity and were aware of the politicization of their lives, their feelings toward politics differed. Although Bobo and Davu migrated from the same home country and were members of the same migrant association, Davu was skeptical about politics. When I asked him if he was participating in protests, he responded sarcastically, "I don't like politics, but politics likes me too much." He explained how he felt like a puppet in Italian and European politics, where outcomes of the electoral ballot box were largely determined by how politicians "played the migration card." He complained that the rules of the game were constantly changing. So, he channeled his frustration and negative feelings about politics into photography and film, which opened new horizons in his life.

Politics of Art: From Despair to Hope

Osas Egbon, a Nigerian woman, was brave and remarkably outspoken about the experiences of her female co-nationals, victims of human trafficking. I had my first meeting with Osas in July 2019 in a run-down space in Ballarò used by the Nigerian women's association, Women of Benin City (Donne di Benin City) formed by Osas in 2015. Osas told me her life story, how she met her husband in Palermo and had children, and how, with her husband's support, she became a vocal advocate of Nigerian women. Her stories conveyed how most Nigerian women had no choice other than sex labor. She talked at length about violence and inhumane treatment of these migrant women by both extralegal Nigerian forces and racist natives.

The largest female migrant population in Palermo and Italy was from Nigeria, trafficked through Libya and forced into sex labor in Italy. Osas was sad and angry, but also very assertive. An outspoken fearless women, Osas presented a compelling critique of many pro-refugee NGOs to me pointing to their hypocrisy and the intentional neglect by politicians who were turning a blind eye to the situation of Nigerian women. She continued complaining that nobody was offering a hand to their association, Women of Benin City. During my first visit to Palermo in 2019, the subject was so sensitive that even some local feminist activists avoided discussing the issue with me. Most were uneasy to label vulnerable women "victims" and to allude to their criminalization as sex workers. Many natives in solidarity looked the other way, as they were not sure how to help these women who were entrapped in clandestine structures of crime and drawn into systemic abuse, discrimination, and violence. Unlike other male-dominated migrant groups, Women of Benin City was marginalized because of the stigma of prostitution in a Catholic country, but it also was challenging to convince these women to break out of the cycle when they were caught up in fear. I was told by some of these migrant women that even Mayor Orlando, internationally known as a leading migrant ally, kept his distance from Women of Benin City. (Yet I did receive Osas's contact information from Orlando's staff at a time when native solidarity was reluctant about connecting me to Nigerian women.)

Female migrants from Nigeria were kept in captivity in dark, windowless rooms of brothels controlled by "madams." Their fear was multilayered, geographically mobile, and multisited: It originated partly from superstitious Vodou beliefs from their homeland and partly from their material dependency on and threats from people who enslaved and trafficked them across borders. Contemplating both morality and the materiality of fear, Pain and Smith (2008, 12) argue that "fear has a creeping materiality that pervades, constitutes, and binds together the ostensibly separate spheres of geopolitical and everyday life." Both remote (homeland) and in place (in Palermo), fear gained momentum and materialized in every corner of life for women who were trafficked from Nigeria via Libya to Sicily.

Despite a shared experience of racial exploitation, the complexity of the Nigerian women's situation disconnected them from pro-migrant resistance and migrant solidarity. Osas shared with me how some local NGOs used these women's victimhood to secure funds from international organizations, but then never gave them voice or cooperated with Benin City. She was hired temporarily by a few of these local NGOs, but she felt taken advantage of and never received help or support for the association. But the extent of the disconnect between solidarity and Nigerian women became clearer to me when migrant associations began to merge their agendas and came together in events and protests and pulled resources together in solidarity. Nigerian women were not part of any of these increasingly visible venues and sites of Black activism. Interestingly, it seemed that the core group of activists did not even notice the chronic absence of these women from solidarity, even Osas, who was a committed spokesperson. There were multiple, intersecting hierarchies of gender, race, and religion for why these women were left out.

First, Nigerian women constituted a gender minority among the newcomers, who were mostly young Black males. Second, these women were left out of solidarity not only because their lives were confiscated by traffickers, but also because of social stigma and moral sanctions. Feelings of shame and guilt kept them away from the Catholic majority local community and Muslim majority migrant groups. Moreover, I learned that, in addition to being controlled by traffickers, these women were also controlled by "boyfriends," who prevented them from "coming out," or disclosing forced sex labor in public life. Third, these women made decisions on the basis of their fear of sex traffickers who used the Vodou tradition to control them. Even though these women did not have many alternatives, they still made some decisions that determined their paths. For example, many left the reception centers when traffickers reached and pulled them out. Their decisions were shaped by fear of threats by traffickers, of racial violence, and of deep poverty, as well as the fear of breaking Vodou tradition.

In retaliation, Osas courageously engaged in a legal war, disclosed the extralegal actors to the courts, and got several madams jailed. But it was hard to fight alone against a full-fledged, cross-border human trafficking network. In my discussions with native activists, I was told another side of the story: The majority of trafficked women did not trust or cooperate with pro-migrant activists, so they remained in or returned to captivity. As in all cases of violent abuse, breaking the cycle requires multifaceted support and trust. Exceptions existed: Dola, a young Nigerian woman, was enslaved in her hometown in Nigeria after she was sold by her family as a domestic servant when she was a child. When she escaped from her hometown and arrived in Palermo, she connected with Arci Porco Rosso there. After breaking a lifelong cycle of sexual abuse and racial violence, she trusted in local activists and their support. In our conversation, she opened up about her bonds and the trust built over many years, referring to Arci Porco Rosso as "family." When I asked Melluso, the organization's president, about Dola, he smiled and told me, "Of course, she has been a cherished member of our family." But Melluso admitted that they could help very few cases, and Dola was an exception in reaching out to and cooperating with them.

I met a few native activists who had formed friendships and trust bonds with trafficked Black migrant women. Francesco Bellina, an internationally acclaimed Palermo-based documentary photographer and activist, surfaced the experiences and emotions of these women's entrapment. Born and raised in the fishing town of Trapani in 1989, Bellina channeled his intense emotions into his photography, emotions rooted in the mafia violence and poverty that reigned during his childhood in his hometown. Traveling frequently between Africa and Sicily, his research and documentary photography on migration captured how the criminalization of human mobility and the trafficking of Black women migrants were mutually reinforcing processes.

Among many important themes on human mobility from Africa, Bellina's work displays the Vodou tradition and rituals that have kept Nigerian women in awe and captivity.

FIGURE 13. A woman embraces children after being rescued by Mediterranea's ship. Many migrant women who passed through Libya were victims of sexual abuse during their detention there. Photo by Francesco Bellina.

FIGURE 14. **A group of people perform a Vodou ritual in honor of the ocean, honoring Mami Wata, the deity of water. Oidah, Republic of Benin, 2018. Photo by Francesco Bellina.**

Refusing to fulfill mainstream media demands for graphic images of victimhood, violence, and suffering, Bellina prioritized the emotions of migrants and highlighted their dignity by honoring their traditions. As he went through his photos with me, he explained the story of each photo, emphasizing: "These are not some random people from Africa that I use as models. These are friends whom I respect and maintain my relations with long after these shots." Indeed, I had already met some of the subjects of his photographs in Ballarò. Many were his neighbors, his immediate community, the place where his creativity and inspiration were embedded. They were also collaborators in his emotionally laden political art. Moving around the Mediterranean basin and Africa, Bellina's photographic research sought truth, "not the truth in facts, but in the spirit of the places and the people who live there, telling their realities and stories"[13]

Oriri, his collection of scenes, people, and rituals from Africa to Palermo, is not only an artistic revelation but also a blunt political statement.[14] In his work, geopolitics meet everyday life in modest yet fascinating ways, in African ways of lives, senses, and sensibilities. His photographic research projects geopolitical emotion, zooming in on the ties of intimacy that are formed through human mobility between Sicily and Africa. While presenting these deeply emotional photographs in exhibitions and talks across countries and continents, some of which I attended, he contextualizes the photos with narratives about the actual lives of migrants.

Since I met Bellina in 2019, he has gained an international reputation and also received some criticism about his extensive work on Black female migrants. His critics questioned the ethical implications of the representations of Black women by a white Sicilian man. In responding to the critics, he reflected on his own positionality, highlighting the liminality of race, gender, and place. He shared with me in May 2023 this response:

> I never thought of myself as white, as I was mixed through centuries of invasions; I am not quite European, as I was raised and lived with the fact that Sicily was colonized by Italy. . . . My identity as an artist integrated feminine characteristics rather than displaying a stereotypical Sicilian masculinity. . . . Even the language barrier is not dramatic for us Sicilians in Africa, as the Sicilian dialect consists of a lot of Arabic words. . . . I easily get by in Africa. And then, there is the proximity between Sicily and Africa. . . . My critics do not understand this border geography.[15]

Bellina's words go beyond racial liminality to add those such as space, gender, and language, situating him as a Sicilian anti-racist activist artist in solidarity with migrants. Owing to the long-list of "in-betweenness" that he situates in history, culture, and geography, his relationality with African migrants comprised intimacy, deep empathy, trust, and true, lasting friendships.

Several native activists talked to me about their shared sensibilities with migrants and being marginalized by Europeans. Many were aware that their marginalization was different from the racialization and securitization of Black migrants. A few emphasized the importance of having a European passport, which was the key to their freedom of mobility—a freedom that sharply differentiated theirs from African lives. In general, citizenship was a faraway dream for irregular migrants owing to the ethnic basis of Italian citizenship. Other activists highlighted other privileges denied to asylum seekers, such as work permits, residency, equal pay, and the stability of a regular salary. But at the same time, both natives and migrants were largely cognizant of their aligned and allied resistance against the EU regime and its injustices. Accordingly, I argue that the ambiguous and emotionally laden distance of the native activists from Rome and northern Italy emboldens their resistance to Europe's racial borders while facilitating their bonding and solidarity with Black migrants.

Having participated in Francesco Bellina's immediate lifeworld, the center of Black Ballarò, where he lived, I also had the chance to observe his interactions and his camaraderie with migrants. Among the leading native activists in Palermo, Bellina was also one of the most expressive, verbally, visually and artistically, through his photography of race, racism, trafficking, and Europe's past and current complicity in racial injustices. His photography was a fight against what Thompson (2013) calls "racial aphasia," the calculated forgetting, a strategic obstruction of discourse and language regarding the colonial past. Since I met Bellina, he has spent a lot of time traveling and living part-time in Africa and Sicily, building archives of photos and stories that reflect the entanglement of the two geographies.

A politics of art, I figured, was an essential channel for transforming despair to hope. Artistic expression had transformational leverage. I met with Osas again in December 2023, only three years after I first met her, and it opened to me an entirely different window of hope, one filled with opportunities. She invited me to the labor union in an old building in Marina Piazza, where she had worked for a few years. The entrance was crowded with many residents waiting in line. When I asked for Osas, somebody called her name for me. As we sat down and chatted in a busy hallway in her workplace, I had the opportunity of observing how she was appreciated, loved, and respected by her colleagues passing by. As soon as we sat down, Osas shared with me news that made her eyes shine: "I just got back from Turin, where my film won an award in the Turin film festival," she said excitedly. It was an emotional moment for me as well, as I had carried her painful stories with me for several years. I was thrilled to hear that Osas was featured in a documentary, *Osas e le donne di Benin City*, by Gabriele

Gravagna.[16] Finally, stories like hers were being told to the whole world. Osas continued joyfully:

> Things have changed! You know that I was not going to stay silent. Nobody was helping us, but I never stopped talking. My husband supported me to tell the world what was happening. After I came out, Nigerian women realized that they had a choice and that they did not have to be fearful or ashamed. Some started making their own decisions to build their future.

When I first met her, Osas had named some local NGOs that were not cooperating with Women of Benin City and were actively discriminating against Nigerian women. But this time, she was raving about her transnational allies. Osas's story disrupted the fear-ridden enslavement of Nigerian women and encouraged several of them out of cycles of oppression. Fascinated by her shifting story, I asked whether Nigerian sex workers were still being murdered in Palermo. Osas told me that the violence and homicides, which took three of her co-nationals several years ago, had not been repeated.

Like young Black male migrants, Osas refused fear—whether of Vodou, the trafficker, the madam, local society—which has kept many Nigerian women in servitude. She maintained her bravery in situations that made my blood run cold just listening to her stories. As did Bobo and many others, she relentlessly directed her frustrations and anger into activism. She also turned her religious faith into motivation for political action and liberation. However, that day she was not only fearless and motivated but also joyful and full of hope. Her sense of liberation and empowerment was radiant. In sharp contrast to how I had felt after my first interview with her, I felt elated—we went out with migrant friends to celebrate her story of emancipation.

The politics of art brought to the center the agency of Black migrants in Palermo. Chike and Bobo were business partners. When Chike arrived in Palermo, he was staying in the reception center and taking language classes. A migrant from a former French colony, he was fluent in five languages. During a lunch at Moltivolti, he told me that he used to act in plays back at home, and he had continued acting in Palermo and was passionately planning to go on stage in other European cities, particularly Paris, where his sibling lived. But his biggest dream was to bring back the experience of and knowledge about stage acting to his home country. His goals included shooting movies, producing a show, and scouting new talent in his hometown.

Similarly, Davu was receiving attention from broadcasters in London and Poland, who came to Ballarò to shoot him as a model. While his main job was working in a social enterprise, his favorite activity was photography, and modeling in advertising and documentaries. Even though I had known him for a couple of years, I only learned about his excitement about photography after befriending him on social media and seeing his photos.

Between 2019 and 2022, my most interesting everyday encounters have been with migrant artists. Among many, I met Azizi, a poet who signed and sold his poetry book in Moltivolti. Azizi's small book was written in two languages, English and Italian. Although he did not work in Moltivolti, people knew him there. He received local support to print his book and generate some income. I also met many other talented migrants in Ballarò's graffiti- and art-covered streets. Some of the migrants sold artisanry, handmade jewelry, bags, scarves, or accessories in small shops or market stalls. Some tailored traditional clothing inspired by African styles or repaired outfits in the market. Others played African tunes in popular local bars, such as Ciwara, an African bar and restaurant. Ciwara was the epicenter of nightlife in La Vucciria market, intertwining ethnic music, cuisine, street dancing and fun. Overall, the city center showcased a blend of migrant art, artisanship, and political activism, all of which were mediated by and thriving on intense geopolitical emotions.

Local (Dis)trust

An important part of my conversations with migrants in Palermo was the challenge of how to build trusting relationships and whom to trust when in need of help and support. Forming trusting relationships was challenging for migrants not only because of their traumatizing journey but also because of its aftermath: the brutal asylum regime that greeted them at the sea borders. In addition to their distrust of politicians, all the migrants I spoke with had terrible memories and experiences of inhumane treatment by officials. They unanimously shared their low regard for the EU. Assane told me: "The EU is all about hypocrisy. They may give money to pro-migrant sector, but then they also pay Libya that tortures and kills innocent migrants."

Deprived of any institutional trust, interpersonal trust relationships were the only reliable alternative support mechanism for migrants. As they had left their families and friends behind at a very young age, trustworthiness was a key issue (see Bacharach and Gambetta 2001). Keeping away from bureaucrats and formal politics, many found comfort in investing in communal and associational life in Ballarò. Associations provided the main venue for socializing and building trust; there, they cultivated civic skills and learned how to watch each other's back when needed. But even when migrant associations connected migrants from different nationalities and ethnicities, associational commitment and cooperation were not transforming into a generalized trust (for a critical approach to social capital, see Stolle 2001). When I asked whom they considered most trustworthy, migrants unanimously pointed to their closest migrant friends, and some also pointed to native activists in solidarity.

Was this local trust simply a deliberation or did it also manifest in everyday practices? When I probed, I learned that even migrants who brag about self-reliance have put their trust in local solidarity in one way or the other. The outer limits of their "expanded" trust even crossed borders and led to transnational networks. Anything that fell outside of the limits of solidarity was dubious and avoided.

Palermo's reputation as a human rights city and a hub of migrants rendered it a magnet for international journalism and broadcasting. Journalists from elsewhere in Europe visited Palermo to document or report on migrants' lives or to interview them about the city and Ballarò. I talked to migrants who had talked with international media outlets about their media exposure. For example, Samba refused to talk to journalists because of their disrespect and undignified treatment of Black migrants. Like others, Samba had several jobs and went to school. When a BBC journalist called Samba thirty minutes before they started a live broadcast, he refused to be interviewed without a proper appointment:

When journalists talk to white people, they schedule appointments and respect their time and stories. Journalists take us and our time for granted. I also do not trust them because some people manipulate our words. . . . I wish I could tell my story on my own, but I am obliged to trust my words to people that are not always trustworthy.

The distrust in journalists made me contemplate their trust in me as a researcher. As an ethnographer who has conducted fieldwork for five years in Palermo, I received different degrees of trust from locals. My reception in the former pro-migrant municipality and the activist community was friendly, and the solidarity was consistently cooperative. But it took me a longer time to gain the trust of migrants. Time flexibility was an important asset for achieving cooperation with them because their schedules were overloaded with multiple jobs and responsibilities.[17]

The more they observed my effort, time commitment, and prioritization of their lives, and the more they became familiar with my ties with solidarity, the more trusting and available they became. Because, contrary to the primary Western image of Black migrants as economically deprived, time and trust are major scarcities in most migrants' lives.

But of course, these were not the only criteria for gaining their trust. Bobo and his friends were hardworking young men who valued honesty and dignity. The solidarities they built with local activists rested on mutual respect. Bellina shared with me how he built trust relationships with African migrants: "My photography honors migrants' dignity and emotions with the goal of empowering them." Indeed, although he participated at rescue ships, border spectacles, and other brutal sites, his photography excluded the flashy representations of suffering, violence, and dehumanization. Dignity was a key geopolitical emotion for building trusting relationships with migrants in Ballarò.

Common experiences of racialization mattered in bonding with native and migrant activists. Locals' first impressions of me were shaped by their limited information that I was a researcher visiting from the United States. From the nature of reception to the development of cooperation and friendship, the quality of my interactions changed explicitly after they learned that I was from Turkey and now lived as a migrant in America. The positive shift in my treatment and the warm welcome because of my migrant experience and nationality came as a surprise to me; it was quite different from my previous experiences in Europe, where Turkish minorities were treated as the underclass of northern Europe. This gave me an opportunity to experience personally how a sense of shared marginalization affected interactions, despite our different racializations, migrant status, experiences, and challenges.

Another important factor in building trust was different perceptions and historical constructions of racial hierarchies. Because of frequent exchange and interactions with Libyans and Tunisians, Sicilians had developed a familiarity with North African migrants throughout history. Yet most native activists and migrants in solidarity had much less daily interaction with Arab migrants in the city. Occasionally, I came across feelings of distrust and power hierarchies between Arab migrants and newcomer Black migrants.[18] This is due partly to the construction of racial hierarchies between Arab and Black migrants and partly to the presence of the Tunisian community in Sicilian society for a much longer time. Giglioli (2021) notes that Tunisians do not perceive their difficulty in accessing jobs as an outcome of racism but as because of their own "foreignness" to Italy. This is an important observation that differentiates Tunisians from Black migrants, and it may explain their absence from the solidarity, including Black migrant activism, which is centered on anti-racist and anticolonial discourse.

Even though Palermitans would typically know people from local Arab communities, overall, North Africans were largely absent from solidarity networks. When we invited an NGO steered by North African leadership to give a talk at Palermo's youth center, the organization with a professional corporate image sent a young Black migrant as a representative. They delegated the Black migrant a routine job of sharing some generic PowerPoints that presented a hierarchical corporate-like culture with ranks of CEOs and a trustee board. When I inquired, I learned that the Muslim Arabs occupying these "fancy" positions in the organization were highly educated—some held PhDs—and were frequently traveling for business. As they were busy, none were available for interviews or to give a talk. The image and presentation of the organization was the opposite of the activist spirit and horizontal ideals of the Black migrant associations in solidarity. In this case, the young presenter sent to the youth center had limited knowledge about the organization and felt embarrassed to not know how to answer our questions about the NGO. Owing to varying racializations of Maghrebi Muslim Arab and African Black migrants in different contexts and times, the power dynamics between these groups are complicated and need to be explored in future research.[19]

In contrast to the absence of Tunisian migrants in solidarity networks, I had long and rich conversations with West African migrants. When I asked about trust, Bobo observed to me:

> Bobo: If there is a crime, a migrant can go to or call the police in Palermo. Italians respect their constitution, and Palermo's residents trust the law enforcement. But as a Black migrant, I cannot fully trust anybody because racism is everywhere for black people. The only place I can place my trust is *us*.
>
> Me: Who is "us"?
>
> Bobo: The people that I know here personally, people who cooperate with me on a daily basis. Migrants and locals who mobilize together.

This trust in local solidarity was also the base of Bobo's transnational activism. His reliance on local solidarity reminded me of Olivia, the internationally connected architect and urban planner in Athens (Chapter 1). Like Olivia, Bobo learned the hard way whom to trust amid a "crisis and under pressure . . . [and] in panic situations." Bobo's solutions were located neither in host country institutions nor in his parents or hometown friends. He was investing his time, effort, and hope in a better future through the solidarity in Ballarò.

The Coexistence of Racial Mixing and Racism

Ballarò shelters a wide array of interracial practices and relationships: social life, dating, marriage, music, arts, sports, parties, and fun. What do these patterns of interracial practices in Black Ballarò convey about racial hierarchies, racial borders and racism? "Racial mixture," a commonly used term in Latin American contexts, held that "blacks, Indians, and whites socialize, reside together, and biologically mix to the point that racial distinctions become unimportant" (Telles 2004, 5). Among many others, Hernández (2013, 2) traces the denial of racism to the problematic myth of "racial democracy," referring to the assumption "that the racial mixture (*mestizaje/mestiçagem*) in a population [was] emblematic of racial harmony and insulated from racial discord and inequality."

Ethnographic evidence refutes that "racially mixed" places provide channels and venues to put an end to racism. This explains the coexistence of racial exploitation and abrupt racial violence with ample snapshots of racial mixing in Ballarò's everyday life. Despite being home to migrants and solidarity, the Black space of Ballarò presents different challenges to Africans than to natives. The chapter revealed and analyzed these differences manifest in varying experiences and emotions, such as safety and insecurity. Further, even though mixing is claimed to be part of the city's history and heritage, it does not automatically culminate in equality between races and in racial justice. Despite the explicit distinction of Black space from other space in the city, the mixed city center also reflects the failed logic that a racially mixed person or place can't be racist. "While it is becoming increasingly clear that racism is a universal phenomenon, it is less accepted that its manifestations may vary widely" (Telles 2004, 2) within and between white and black spaces.

As this chapter has elaborated, migrants played a major role in transforming an insular, fear-ridden Ballarò run by the mafia into a safer, transnational, pioneering activism hub. Shifting from macro, top-down theories of global fear to more grounded and nuanced analysis of fear and (in)securities (see also Pain and Smith 2008, 13), the analysis has featured Black migrant activists like Bobo and Osas who embraced, confronted, and navigated their fear and refused victimhood despite their striking proximity to local extralegal forces. I have argued that Black activism is empowered by managing geopolitical emotions, tempering some in everyday life and conveying others through the politics of art. Ballarò showcases how fear is countered and decentered by "defiant practice[s] of hope" that are generated out of the repressive border zones of racial security. In this geography of racial borders, the channeling of fear into a hopeful future is "the most radical response" (for hope as a racial response, see Wright 2008, 223). For me, this radical response qualifies the Black space in the frontier city as a transformative border geography.

Although Palermo is not a unique breeding ground of (pro)migrant resistance in Europe (Bazurli 2019; Della Porta 2018; De Genova 2017; Turam 2023), Black Ballarò differentiates the city from many other gateway cities.

Border spectacle is all about creating "shows" of criminalized racialized images of migrants (De Genova 2013), but Black Palermo represents a liminal world beyond and above the binary of Europe's racial security versus multicultural diversity. Different from romanticized notions of mixing, Ballarò boldly faces structural limitations, sociopolitical challenges, and the "growing pains" of solidarity.

Black activism is particularly essential in the shifting practices and discourses of resistance from festive multiculturalism to critical anticolonialism and antiracism that centers race. However, the recent flourishing of Black activism raises a pressing question: Do different marginalizations and racializations of natives and migrants relieve the natives from their responsibility to be aware of racial hierarchies and the intersectionality of race, class, and gender? How does historically rooted pride in mixing affect the empowerment of native-migrant solidarity? If the pride in historical diversity culminates in the omission of "analytical tools to engage with the historically sedimented racisms" (Hawthorne 2022, 120), what is the impact of this omission on Black migrants' willingness to trust and cooperate with native Sicilians against the security regime? Delving into these differing geopolitical sensibilities between racial migrants and natives, the chapter explored their impact on the efficacy of solidarity standing up against securitization.

An important test about the future of solidarity is whether native activists will be capable of deprioritizing and revising their agendas in relation to Black activists' priorities and needs. While native activist leaders have displayed leadership skills in cooperation with migrant activists, a major challenge will be making and holding space for migrant leadership in solidarity. Looking forward, how will the decentering race-blind politics and centering race in solidarity affect the resistance considering the different senses of fear, safety, (in)security, dignity, pride, and other geopolitical emotions of migrants and natives?

Conclusions

On March 5, 2024, a twenty-five-year-old Gambian migrant, Kitim Cessay, was stabbed and then run over in Ballarò. Fifteen days later, a press release signed by multiple migrant organizations and solidarity actors broke the silence, announcing his death while in the hospital. The murderer was unknown, even though the word circulated widely that he was a white man. Kitim's murder was not the first incident of racial violence in the city, but it brought to surface a significant shift that had slowly been brewing in Palermo. Upon Kitim's death, migrants took an unprecedented lead in organizing demonstrations in the city. His death brought together various migrant associations and groups to protest racial violence and mourn together. A leading Black activist, one of my interlocutors, called for united action: "Let's break the silence around Kitim's death to demand the truth about what happened with a loud and united voice." Unfortunately, the murderer remained unidentified.

Skeptical of the fact that no surveillance camera had caught the murderer in the middle of the city center, solidarity kept asking in despair, "Who killed Kitim?" Solidarity criticized the indifference of municipal authorities to the tragedy. Was the murder "without a trace" in the city center an alert to the omission of municipal services, such as surveillance cameras, in Ballarò and/or to the local governments' complicity in the dismissal of race and racial violence? In the aftermath, I causally chatted with ordinary residents of Palermo. Many of them had not even heard about this event, as the city government "did not want to make a deal about it" (from my interviews with migrants in 2024).

On March 26, the local migrant community in solidarity with native activists organized a demonstration demanding justice. After the demonstration, people gathered in front of Arci Porco Rosso in Ballarò. The president of Porco Rosso, Melluso, took the microphone and demanded justice and equal treatment for Kitim. Consistent with his activism, Melluso asserted that security was the privilege of the wealthy, whereas the poor and marginalized were left to live with risk. The large group, which consisted of mostly but not only migrants, chanted slogans and supported his motivating speech. With this heightened emotionality, Melluso emphasized the prevalent emotions of "deep sadness and pain, but no feelings of revenge" in the city center. He condemned the violence committed in the victim's own neighborhood where acts of revenge and territoriality could have easily escalated to counterviolence. Yet the response remained strictly peaceful. Even in the face of such a cruel act of brutality, migrants gave a clear message of denouncing violence. This was a remarkably strong statement conveying migrants' commitment to and prioritization of safety and peace in Black Ballarò.

Ballarò's grief over and resistance to racial violence deserve to be highlighted on the increasingly racist continent of Europe. The world's lack of attention to Ballarò—and Palermo more broadly—is telling of what Gramsci ([1995] 2009) referred to as the "southern question." Southern borderlands close to the Middle East and North Africa are not only neglected but also "distanced," peripheralized and disowned. Palermo is indeed physically closer to Tunisia than it is to Naples. But beyond geographical distance, Palermo's intersecting racialization and peripheralization is a political manifestation of the securitization and dehumanization of racialized migrants. The EU is complicit in unleashing racial violence by having flattened the difference between peaceful pro-migrant resistance and actual local criminal activity.

Peripheralization continued in Athens too, albeit in different ways. In 2022, during the second term of the staunchly anti-immigrant New Democracy government, Melissa Network in Athens opened its doors wide to Afghan refugee women. Melissa's feminist space rapidly turned into a hub for the female members of the Afghan Parliament. When Melissa prepared a list of 150 prominent female Afghan leaders, the anti-refugee Greek government accepted them. The group, which eventually amounted to some eight hundred Afghan refugees, included twenty-five of the sixty-nine female representatives and senators of Afghanistan in Athens (Kuntz 2022). Melissa provided them space to perform their political activism, hold meetings, organize, and join in solidarity under a safe roof. As the media coverage in *Der Spiegel International* clearly displayed, Nadina at Melissa Network prioritized the refugee women's voices, needs, and agendas while withdrawing herself to a position of a feminist enabler ally. For the Afghan women, the experience was unforgettable, fueled by ideas, passion, excitement, unstoppable motivation, and hope. Having run from violence, war, and persecution, these politically prominent Afghan women were adamantly radiant.

Interestingly, feminist solidarity with Muslim women in Athens was interrupted by female benefactors in the Global North. The Afghan women's expressions of gratefulness and feminist bonding with Melissa discomforted the funders of rescue in the First World. When the Afghan women in the political elite thanked and acknowledged Melissa Network publicly, white benefactors objected. Indifferent to the thriving female migrant leadership in Athens, which *Der Spiegel International* referred to as "the Parliament of Exiled Afghan Women in Athens" (Kuntz 2022), funders claimed that they should be acknowledged and thanked, taking credit for female Afghan diasporic affairs. The incident illustrates the sharp contrast between native-migrant solidarity based on trust and camaraderie and a "white savior" approach driven by pity and perhaps compassion, the central motives of humanitarian logic of aid. Even though aid has been the easy response of the West to global inequalities, its actual intentions, aims, and scope of efficacy have been a contentious issue. Historically, aid has fallen short of changing power differentials and race, and class and gender-based injustices. Instead, like hospitality for migrants, compassion-driven aid to the Third World has maintained global structural and racial inequalities rather than remedying them.

In the face of ongoing racial violence, Danewid (2017) pointed to emotions such as pity, compassion and hospitality as repercussions of European colonial need to prove "goodness." This need is associated with an urge not only to mask past atrocities, but also present-day racism and ongoing extractions from Africa. In this context, the aid, like hospitality, serves to the white privilege, by helping the feeling of relief of any guilt, shame, or complicity originating in colonialism (see Danewid 2017, 1676).[1] As the white privilege rooted in colonial history reinforces the securitization of racial migrants and weaponizes borders, any analysis blind to race and Europe's ongoing complicity would fail to do justice to today's resistance against racial security. Instead, a historically and geographically contextualized analysis distinguishes the emotions of pity, compassion, and hospitality that motivated humanitarian aid from the geopolitical emotions that shape and empower native-migrant solidarity.

Clearly, Melissa Network is neither a humanitarian nor a provisional organization, and it does not offer services, funds, flights, or pay for health and legal expenses. As discussed in Chapter 1, it is a safe place for connecting and empowering female refugees. Rather than competing about who "rescued and liberated" the women there, Melissa's goal was to support, enable, and encourage them to continue their political career and activism. Nadina told me: "It is very hard to continue performing your political agendas when you go through the traumatic journey of refugeehood, in which the suffering and insecurity take over and cut women off from their political purposes and careers." Rather than aid, Melissa gave the women a safe space to experience feelings of motivation, inspiration, trust, and hope. But as with general global disinterest in solidarity in Palermo, the world remained indifferent to these striking formations of native-migrant solidarity in Athens, a poor city at the periphery of Europe with minimal material or financial capacities. Eventually, some of the Afghan female activists left for better-off destination countries in the North. Many settled in Canada and a few stayed in Athens a little longer despite challenges of the border geography.

In Athens and Palermo, migrants became the catalyst for the transformation from insecurity to solidarity. On the one hand, they played a major role in the transition from the legacy of homegrown crimes to native-migrant alliances. On the other hand, against the backdrop of their violent journey through brutal borders, the migrants spearheaded anti-racist, anticolonial peaceful resistance in Palermo and a decolonial feminist activism in Athens. Importantly, these Muslim and Black activist voices and demands were not in alignment with the promises of the First World, which never solidified—that is, the conventional solutions of economic restructuring and monetary "aid" to "fix" the Third World while exploiting it to sustain the privileges of the First World. Black and Muslim refugees, many of whom escaped from proxy wars or invasions of Western powers in their homeland, were consistently demanding voice, rights, freedom of movement, and justice rather than aid or hospitality. These imperative political shifts in newcomer migrant activist discourse and agenda were unfolding parallel to concurrent transitions from security to solidarity in everyday life at securitized borderlands. These transitions from insecurity to solidarity were fueled by the geopolitics of emotion in the most impoverished peripheries of Europe.

Conventional thought on center-periphery (Shils 1975) is still largely blind and resistant to the idea that the shifts in the periphery would affect and change "the center." But everyday experiences in migrant-receiving borderlands are presenting new challenges to the traditional center-periphery binaries in explaining transformations. Black activism manifested in the Black spaces of the arrival border city raises questions about how and when Europe will break down its ethnocentric and Eurocentric paradigms, awaken to the potentials of migration, and recognize the transformation that has already been started by racialized migrants in the border geographies. Looking from the bottom-up in these peripheral geographies, the dynamic activism by racial migrants appears unstoppable and renders Europe's demand to remain an impenetrable white Christian Fortress pointless, and probably futile in the long-run.

Emotions Versus Rights? A Wrong Dichotomy

Complicating "humanitarian reason," Fassin (2005, 2012) critically pointed to the shifting moral economy of migration policies from a rights-based approach to one led by emotions such as compassion and care (Fassin 2005, 2012). His argument is helpful for addressing the heart of the issue: Is the First World becoming moved by compassion to help refugees and asylum seekers after having deprived them of their freedoms and rights agreed upon by international law? If Europeans were genuinely mourning for dead border crossers, why do Western countries continue supporting policies that push the migrants back over the borders or that lead to their detention or deportation? Clearly, emotions cannot be contracted like binding agreements on rights and freedoms. But how binding are the international agreements signed by Western countries? How committed has the West been to maintaining the responsibilities it assumed for refugees after the atrocities of World War II? When the refugee flow from the Global South hit Europe, Western commitments for racialized refugees quickly crumbled. As the world witnessed the EU and the United States violating human rights and international law, the presumed influence of nonbinding international agreements and law has become less and less compelling.

On April 10, 2024, the European Parliament voted in favor of the new Pact on Migration and Asylum. The pact became officially adopted by the EU Council on May 14, 2024. The EU presented the pact as a *reform* in migration governance in order to guarantee that "the Union has strong and *secure external borders*, that people's rights are guaranteed, and that no EU country is left alone under pressure."[2] In reality, the pact clarified and materialized which people had rights and which did not. Although the pact exemplified the most severe repression of asylum rights after long negotiations since the peak flow in 2015, the BBC referred to it as "major reform" (Gozzi 2024). But rather than reforming policies of migration, the pact deformed the notion of asylum. Indeed, it was the biggest blow to asylum. Concealed in misleading language of "faster and efficient procedures," the actual goal was to speed up the process of asylum rejections and deportations. Humanitarian organizations, human rights activists, and solidarity condemned the new regulations that took the securitization of migration to new heights.[3] While the EU's increasingly brutal border politics continue to fall short of stopping the flow of migrants into the region (Andersson 2016), the hypersecuritization takes its toll in human lives.

In the age of hypersecuritization, international law and organizations have become increasingly disempowered, unable to cope with crimes against humanity, racial violence, and genocide. In fact, one of the main motivations for writing this book was my observations of the disconnect between international organizations, their regulations, and mundane everyday life in violent border geographies. At a time when states, governments, and right-wing conservative forces collide in nativist and racist politics and collaborate in border security, and when electoral and reform efforts to reverse anti-migrant policies have been largely futile, my research shifted its focus from formal politics and policies to solidarity in everyday life.

In light of recent world affairs, this book points to the various roles that geopolitical emotions play in everyday life. I have argued that geopolitical emotions have an enormous—albeit neglected or denied—impact on relations of (in)security and dynamics of (in)justice, (de)criminalization, and resistance. Even though they are largely dismissed by conventional scholarship, politics, and policy, the ethnographic analysis of geopolitical emotions allows for gaining a deeper grasp of the link between fear and securitization as well as safety and solidarity. When fear is understood as the basis of securitization, fear aversion becomes the leading response of resistance and empowers solidarity across ideological and party allegiances. Similarly, I have argued that shared feelings of marginalization between differently racialized people propel solidarity, especially if the natives express awareness of and responsibility for colonial pasts and Europe's complicity in the racial crisis. These geopolitical emotions carry substantial power and become catalysts of solidarity, empowering migrants, in contrast to violated rights and freedoms found in international agreements. Facing Western states' increasing disregard for international law, and their rising use of politics of fear to violate rights and freedoms, the deeply contextual emotions and responses to securitization emerge as the potential game changers.

As discussed across the chapters, most of these human factors, such as agency, subjectivity, migrants' sense and sensibilities, have been largely downplayed and overshadowed in geopolitics, international relations, and policymaking. Furthermore, dismissing the historical and geopolitical layers of borderlands and border cities, popular debates on the strategies and tactics of urban politics, such as city branding, and commodification, took precedence over geopolitical emotions (Neil 2024; Wyer 2024; Rossini and Nervino 2019). Undoubtedly, Exarcheia became increasingly popular and came under pressures of commodification and gentrification, partly for its progressive politics (Chapter 2). Packaging the activist spirit of the neighborhood as a marketing point, these trends were turning the neighborhood into a hub of Airbnb. My argument about geopolitical emotions does not contradict or deny such urban trends and processes. Similarly, along with their defense of migrants' rights, both Mayor Orlando and the Moltivolti leaders were proudly promoting the municipality as a human rights city. They also openly disagreed with the critics and discontents of tourism, arguing that the poor southern city could benefit from revenue from tourists more than the rich Northern cities do.[4] Hence, the strong association I have drawn between geopolitical emotions and solidarity does not rule out the strategic thinking or acting of the agentic city—the municipality, officials, and activists in solidarity. Rather, drawing such a binary between emotions and strategy is futile, and even reductive of emotional places and geographies. However, dismissing the human dimension by reducing multifaceted (pro) migrant resistance to a business transaction or a market strategy provides an incomplete and inaccurate picture (see, e.g., Neil 2024). Further, disregard for the centrality of geopolitics of emotion undermines a nuanced grasp of native-migrant solidarity, along with its achievements and potential.

The Danger of "Ranking" Hierarchies of Vulnerability and Injustice

In her analysis of "racial hierarchies" in Italy and Europe, Camilla Hawthorne (2022, 175) compares the more "sympathetic" construction of Syrian refugees to Eritrean, Ethiopian, or other Black colonial subjects. She rightly notes that Syrians were perceived as "white" or treated as "white adjacent" and that their arrival with families and children constituted "factors that in practice seemed to *outweigh* any potential institutional Islamophobia" (175). However, these differences in the perception and reception of Muslims and Blacks noted here have nothing to do with Europe's progress to overcome Islamophobia or develop sympathies for Muslims. Bluntly speaking, racism does not outweigh Islamophobia, which is simply another form of racism (De Genova 2018b). The "special" treatment of Syrians was substantiated by Europe's "selective" compliance with refugee status (determined by the 1951 Geneva Convention), but only if Syrians, unlike Ukrainians, managed to step foot on Europe as irregular border-crossers despite infinite obstructions across deadly borders. When pinpointing the problematic "hierarchies of race" between Muslims from the Middle East and African migrants, there is a wide array of issues to take into consideration. First, the identification of Middle Easterners as "Caucasian" or "white adjacent" indicates a deeper racial problem despite its anti-racist façade. As in the case of the United States, the denial of a racial category, such as Muslim Middle Easterners helps only to conceal and deny racial injustices and to prevent a racialized minority from seeking justice and claiming their rights (on the racialization of Muslims, see Barreto and Sindi 2020; De Genova 2018b).

Second, rather than sympathy for Syrians, I observed hostility and mistreatment in Greek islands and Athens, their main entry points, where even their presumably official refugee status was questioned and denied by government officials, anti-immigrant locals, and far-right forces. While their racialization was not much different from that of Afghans and Iraqis, they were indeed held higher on the "civilizational" racial and migration status hierarchies than both Afghans and Black migrants by way of misleading cultural constructs and racial prejudices (Chapter 1). My data, like Hawthorne's, point to the construction of racial hierarchies. But what do these constructed hierarchies convey? The relatively "different" regard for certain racial migrants may partly originate from the historical ties and the geopolitics between host and home country, such as between North African states and Sicily. And partly, the racial hierarchies continue being constructed between older migrant communities that had arrived earlier, such as Turkish migrants, and the newcomer Syrians in Germany. But it is important to remember here that Europe had rampant racism for decades and experimented with failed policies of integration of the guest workers, primarily the Turkish *Gastarbeiter* in Germany (Turam 2015; Hinze 2013), Denmark, and Holland, and North Africans in France (Dikeç 2007).

Third, the reconstruction of these problematic racial hierarchies prevents racialized Middle Easterners and Africans from realizing their shared vulnerabilities and from connecting, cooperating, and forming political alliances (as noted in the absence of North Africans in Palermitan solidarity in Chapter 4). The non-critical adoption and reinforcement of these racial hierarchies between Muslim and Black migrants favors Europe's security regime by further dividing and polarizing the differently racialized groups. Hence, my findings suggest that this unproductive distancing—projected also in the disconnect between research on the eastern and central Mediterranean—is not helpful for fighting racism or for the empowerment of racialized migrants in Europe. Like the critique of the problematic categories of "deserving and undeserving" migrants constructed by Western receiving countries, the solidarity movement could benefit from avoiding the construction of racial hierarchies between racialized migrants.

Fourth, the futile ranking of various forms of vulnerabilities undermines the importance of intersectionality. Injustices committed against migrants take place on a spectrum of multiple vulnerabilities and inequalities. A narrow focus on one form of stratification—for example, racial versus religious—would risk the overlapping impact of the intersecting vulnerabilities. Put differently, if we rank migrants exclusively along one line of discrimination, we are likely to miss the multiplier effect of the juncture of those inequalities. For example, when Bobo admitted that his association could not accommodate a debate on LGBTQ rights because it would cause divides, given Muslim beliefs and homeland traditions, the intersecting impact of racial and religious vulnerability intensifies the marginalization and discrimination against this association in the European context (for prejudices against Muslims, see Duyvendak et al. 2023).

Finally, while racial hierarchies harm Black migrants more than some Muslim Middle Easterners, Europe adamantly insists on staying a Christian club without any compromise (see Chapter 2). Whereas studies increasingly speak of the racial liminality of southern Europe, I have not encountered any concept of religious liminality in my field research in either the eastern or central Mediterranean gateways. While the sense of shared racialization facilitates bonding between Sicilians and Black migrants, I did not observe a similar emotional connection and related shared marginalization with Muslims at Europe's MENA borderlands. Unlike the racial liminalities of Italians, Greeks or other European ethnicities do not historically remember or construct a shared oppression with the Muslims of the Middle East (and North Africa)—but rather harbor prevailing negative feelings toward neighboring Turkey and the imperial predecessor Ottomans.

The geopolitical difference between the two border regions—the eastern Mediterranean facing a former imperial power and the central Mediterranean facing former colonies—has a wide range of unexplored political repercussions for border politics and solidarity. Productive of varying geopolitical emotions—fear and distrust versus familiarity and (for some) responsibility—the two distinctly emotional border geographies have different impacts on solidarity. Strong Black migrant activism in Palermo has thrived from highly securitized border zones, whereas an emergent migrant activism by Afghan migrant women in Athens was capitalized on and interrupted by humanitarian benefactors.

Here, it is important to remember that the solidarity in Athens was empowered against securitization by historically rooted leftist activism and its aversion to fear (Part 1), whereas solidarity in Palermo was facilitated by a shared sense of racialization and marginalization by Europe (Part 2). Uncovering similar modus operandi in both border regions—that is, the dehumanization and securitization of Muslim and Black migrants—this book contextualized (dis)similarities of resistance and solidarity against the same security regime.

Linking Solidarity in Two Entry Points of Europe

One of the findings of this ethnography caught me by surprise. Despite the geographical nearness between them, the solidarity in Athens and Palermo was largely disconnected. As Greece and Sicily were located at the two sides of the Ionian Sea, one would have expected more interaction, communication, and cooperation, or at least some emotional bonding and support. During my trips between Athens and Palermo, I met only a handful of activists who had been to the other border city or met with solidarity actors and networks over there. Except for a few activists in transnational networks and leading pro-migrant politicians, such as Vice Mayor Papagiannakis and Mayor Orlando, the bulk of the local solidarity was not familiar with the situation and challenges faced in the other gateway city.

In the eastern Mediterranean, the most common border security practices have been the pushbacks by Greece and Frontex in the Aegean Sea that separates Turkey and Greece. In the central Mediterranean, on the other hand, pullbacks by Libya and the struggles between the NGO rescue ships and Libyan coastal guards played a major role in securitization of migration and borders. The NGO rescue ships were absent in the Aegean Sea owing to the short distances between the Greek border islands and Turkey as well as Greece's tightly sealed borders. Solidarity in each location seemed overwhelmingly engrained in local struggles and regional border politics not paying much attention to the EU's other arrival geographies in the Mediterranean. For solidarity, the disconnect between the eastern and central Mediterranean was rarely and abruptly interrupted by catastrophic events, such as the Cutro shipwreck in 2023, when the migrant boat traveled from Turkey to Italy bypassing Greece because of its violent pushback practices. As local pro-migrant activists in each arrival city were intensely engaged in their battle with border security, this day-to-day intensity did not seem to leave much space to ponder the solidarity in the other entry point. This relative disinterest was not entirely surprising when we consider that the Greek and Italian states had the jurisdiction in border protocols, which partially "nationalized" the EU's external border politics. The borders with different countries that presented different geopolitical conditions also "regionalized" the challenges in the eyes of local solidarity. These geopolitical circumstances prevented the solidarity in each city from integrating the bigger picture, learning from each other's experiences and collaborating, even though they both were dealing with the same racial security on the two sides of the Ionian Sea. Both solidarity groups focused exclusively on local human flow across the MENA border rather than also looking towards each other.

Importantly, however, the most puzzling aspect of this disconnect for me was not about the solidarity but rapidly growing research on migration and securitization in Europe: scholarship yielded to this regional divide, as researchers focused on and studied the eastern and central Mediterranean separately. In the absence of comparisons or multisited research projects, the (dis)continuities of securitization and resistance between the two major entry points were largely missed. This scholarly divide explains why different racialization of Muslim and Black border-crossers to Europe and distinct peripheralization of Greece and Sicily have been left unnoticed and invisible.

This book has contextualized how and why geopolitical emotions, reactions, and responses to securitization overlapped and differed in each region, even though both were confronting the same mechanisms of racial security. Owing to a different border history and politics with Turkey, Libya, and Tunisia—the EU's different neighboring "third safe" countries—the positionality and sensitivity of solidarity in relation to colonial subjects and colonial powers varied. My ethnography revealed and analyzed the local dynamics of resistance in each geography by situating them in the larger frame of the racial border security of Fortress Europe.

Despite regional differences, native-migrant solidarity thrived in both entry points. Also, both have had in common the legacy of violence—the anarchists of Athens and the mafia of Palermo. Infamous for such home-based illegal activities, both Exarcheia and Ballarò displayed some similar sociospatial patterns: They developed a deeper sense of awareness of a persistent extralegality while regulating and overcoming any related fear. One of the main findings of this book is that migrants became main actors in these urban recoveries, as they played vital roles in the transformation from insecurity and violence to safety and solidarity. In the geopolitics of emotions, they were major (f)actors in overcoming fear, replacing despair with hope, building and leveraging local trust, and thereby moving on from past insecurities into new solidarities. No top-down policy—whether integrationist or multiculturalist or related to border regulations—could accomplish the outcomes documented in this ethnography.

Of course, the legacy and type of local violence in the two entry points are not comparable. Unlike the pro-migrant, anti-authority, and anti-security anarchists of Exarcheia, the mafia of Palermo was racist and anti-migrant. These contrasting cases of home-based crime towards migrants shaped solidarity's stance and perspective. Furthermore, migrants played a role in the ways in which solidarity positioned itself in the legacy of violence and the ways it dealt with its present-day repercussions. Ballarò sheltered a solid native-migrant solidarity that was aligned and entangled with the anti-mafia movement. Despite different vulnerabilities and varying reactions of migrants and natives to insecurity, the shared aversion to violence brought them closer. Exarcheia, on the other hand, displayed coexisting— and at times contrasting—local responses from residents who did not act collectively or in political alliance with one other. Even though humanitarian frontliners, anarchists, and (non)activist locals refused fear and resisted securitization alongside one another, they were clear about their differing political agendas. A pro-refugee agenda shared by the anarchists and pro-migrant locals brought them closer in conditional cooperation, as the anarchists were committed to nonviolence toward all civilians and to protection of migrants.

The analytical linkage between the two entry locations reveals the migrants' dissociation and distancing from violence, crime, and illegality in both arrival cities. Despite their higher vulnerability to violence by both the security regime and local crime, they cultivated peaceful relations and cooperation with pro-migrant actors at multiple scales. As both Mayor Orlando and Alessandra Sciurba stated in their critiques of the EU's migration governance, the security regime was pushing migrants in Italy to illegality and local crime through its closed borders and imposition of residency requirements. Solidarity in both gateway cities has struggled for decriminalization in multiple ways, from legal channels to everyday life.

However, each city responded and coped differently with the electoral defeat of pro-migrant local governments and the rise of conservatives to power (Chapters 2 and 4). Under attack by security forces, solidarity in Athens shrank spatially to migrant-dense pockets of the city, such as Victoria and Exarcheia (for shrinking spaces of solidarity, see Della Porta and Steinhilper 2022). As the national- and municipal-level New Democracy governments targeted Exarcheia, the historically insurgent anarchist neighborhood became a hub not only for migrants but also for activists and frontliners and drew international attention. Unlike Athens, solidarity in the post-Orlando period did not move to a new place or shrink. To the contrary, under Mayor Lagalla, Black activism continued to flourish locally and displayed more leadership in solidarity in Palermo's city center.

Importantly, while the resistance in Athens confronted the conservative municipal government of New Democracy, activists in Palermo did not clash with the anti-migrant right-wing municipality. The disengagement of solidarity with Lagalla's local government was striking in its disregard. Instead, they directed their energies and local efforts to engage in transnational activism and international human rights circles. This difference was partly due to Orlando's legacy, solidified by the Palermo Charter, which the new municipal government avoided criticizing, denouncing, or disrespecting. Put differently, Lagalla's municipality avoided undermining Mayor Orlando's bequest without following in his footsteps, whereas Mayor Bakoyannis's New Democracy came to power by criticizing and promising to put an end to Mayor Kaminis and Syriza's take on refugee issues and desecuritization. Rooted in different historical and (geo)political contexts, the relationship of solidarity with conservative local governments was different in each city: clash in Athens and disengagement in Palermo.

Conclusions

Fear Divides or Unites More Than Ideology Does

Over the last decades, not only Italy, but also the entire world witnessed the decreasing efficacy of the Left in presenting meaningful opposition to the empowerment of conservative forces. The narrowing gap of ideological differences between the Left and the Right evolved parallel to the increasing role of geopolitical emotions in shaping the resistance. Ideological differences have been shrinking in terms of not only governance of migration and borders but also other pressing issues, such as crimes against humanity and genocide. We have witnessed the rising apathy and inertia of the International Left in responding to these crimes and to violence against the vulnerable and the oppressed. Giving in to self-centered, self-interested lives, a puzzling bulk of the International Left could not care less about the suffering of those whose lives have come to be valued less than others. As the Left increasingly collides with the Right on issues that harm minorities and racialize migrants (for nativism of the Left, see Duyvendak et al. 2023), the First World has failed to cultivate meaningful ideological disagreement and political opposition. Subsequently, dehumanization of racially displaced people became normalized. As authoritarian far-right leaders of the First World, such as in Italy and United States, joined non-Western autocrats, the scope of the International Left shrank and became limited to a critique of right-wing parties, instead of generating a self-critique of their own failures, absences, and silences, along with an original politics of their own. (For a compelling critique of social democrats in Italy, see Grossi and Niccolò 2022.)

In some ways, local and national politics in Athens deviated from this global trend, as ideological clashes continued and had an impact on refugee politics and the securitization of borders in Greece. Short-time desecuritization during the leftist Syriza government (Skleparis 2018), followed by intensified securitization under the New Democracy, is a telling example of this. In a small private roundtable conversation in 2025, I participated in a discussion with former prime minister of Syriza, Alexis Tsipras,(2015–2019). Reflecting on his policies during the peak of the refugee flow, he continued defending human rights, a pro-refugee stance, and his refusal of pushbacks.[5] The clash between the neofascist Golden Dawn and the Left had preoccupied local and national politics during the Tsipras administration until Golden Dawn was charged with criminal activity and shut down in 2019.

Unlike in Greece, ideological differences did not seem to make major differences about the governance of borders and migration in Italy. For example, the agreement with Libya to externalize Italy's borders was signed under a coalition government with the Left. Overall, Italy's political landscape has continued to be dominated by right-wing conservative forces.

With the increasing global popularity of right-wing populism and rising levels of corruption over the past couple of decades, a general loss of interest (and trust in some cases) was noted in electoral processes and democratic procedures. Subsequently, widespread violations of human rights, increased racism, and racial violence have culminated in sweeping theories of a general disengagement from politics. Young people, particularly Generation Z, have been judged for their presumed apolitical tendencies and "exhaustion of political imagination" (Furedi 2005, 14–15). Even though I have argued for the fading importance of ideology, my data do not support arguments about the end of history or the decline of political engagement (see, e.g., Fukuyama 2006). To the contrary, the solidarity I observed in the peripheral border regions of the EU and the high-energy activism of young Black migrants, many of whom are Gen-Zers, provides a substantial challenge to the thesis of political exhaustion caused by the fear of uncertainty. Rather than extrapolating the end of history or the demise of political engagement, I have argued that geopolitical emotions have become the modus operandi of resistance and solidarity. An emotion-blind geopolitics or international theory not only overlooks this turn but also turns its back on its unlimited potential and opportunities for change.

Along these lines, I argue that conservatism as an ideology no longer appears to be a distinctive quality of right-wing parties but expands loosely along the ideological continuum from the Left to the Right, especially about the governance of borders and migration. So, if not ideology or party affiliation, what differentiates people's position in the (geo)politics of migration? This book made a strong case about how fear becomes a decisive force that divides and polarizes people on migration and border politics. Accordingly, conservatism is no longer exclusively about conserving the status quo or objecting to change. It is also about giving in to fear of the Other—

refugees, migrants, other races, pandemics, nonbinary genders, religious converts—anything and anybody who does not conform to the dominant power structure. Conservatives from all political fronts from the Left to the Right connect on the basis of the shared fears of these nontraditional "threats" that are then securitized.

Choosing (or not) to be fearful of a place, like Exarcheia, or people, like refugees, is the new determinant of how politics unfold at multiple scales, from the neighborhood to the transnational level. This book has both complicated and concretized the multiscalar geopolitics of fear by demonstrating how, like other geopolitical emotions, fear could be regulated and maneuvered as well as chosen or refused. I, then, revealed how the geopolitics of fear were replaced by migrants and pro-migrant locals with cultivating local trust, carving out safe places, respecting human dignity as a core value, nurturing hope, and so on. Juxtaposed to fear in proximity, these geopolitical feelings that were mindfully brewed and regulated for (geo) political ends empowered solidarity. The dynamics of Black migrant activism achieved by refusing fear, tempering anger, filtering trusting relationships, and championing hope ends my analysis. The primacy of geopolitical emotions was clearly articulated in migrants' refusal to put their trust in a political ideology, political party, or politician, because they thought "all were the same," referring to their indifferent or hostile non-cooperation. Instead, they chose to nurture the geopolitical emotions that strengthened solidarity and to avoid the ones that pushed them towards victimization. I have underlined how these emotions—chosen, regulated, tempered, reinforced, or avoided—were deeply contextual for human beings, communities, and publics. The situated nature of such emotions in geography and history, whether the anti-authoritarian roots of insurgency in Athens or the historical alienation of Sicily from Europe, shape pro-migrant resistance and solidarity against securitization.

However, having testified to the full-force continuation of securitization, my analysis of the geopolitics of emotions is clearly not about "overcoming" the pain or suffering of migrants (Ahmed 2014, 21). Nevertheless, as border violence persists, and as the safety of irregular migrants remains an uphill struggle, an in-depth inquiry of emotional border geographies becomes even more timely and crucial. In this respect, Reece Jones's follow-up discussion to his book *Violent Borders* provides an important insight. Jones delivers an optimistic update, pointing to evidence that, "in spite of the anti-immigrant talk, more people are open to more immigration now." Accordingly, he suggests that "a fertile ground for additional research is on the geography of these different views of immigrants within countries, regions and cities" (Jones, qtd. in Fregonese et al. 2020, 8).[6]

Hence, despite the escalation of anti-Muslim racism (i.e., Islamophobia) and racism against Black migrants, this book has documented the choice to refuse fear. It, thereby, questioned the presumed global inevitability and unavoidability of securitization of migration. The cases of disobedient Exarcheia and Black Ballarò confirm that securitization can be resisted at multiple scales, given that it is mainly a state-framed political mandate with spatial and temporal directives (Mountz and Hiemstra 2014). First, the spatiality of place-based resistance to securitization evokes doubts about how unavoidable "global fear" and securitization can be when some places elude it at the local scale. Second, the brief halt in securitization by the leftist Syriza (preceding the 2016 Turkey-EU agreement) speaks to the temporality of securitization, no matter how short-lived the break might have been.[7] Accordingly, my ethnographic approach sensitive to emotions, spatiality, and temporality has decentered the security regime.

Along with the temporality of securitization, Fassin also warns us about the temporality of political emotions. Surely, some might wonder whether fear aversion, like other intense emotions documented in this book, might persevere beyond "privileged moments of collective redemption" (Fassin 2005, 375). Yet a deeply contextual analysis challenges the elusiveness of geopolitical emotions and shows their rootedness in history, collective memory, and geography. However, Fassin's point is valuable, as there is no point in romanticizing emotions as generative of pro-migrant politics in geographies that massively violate human rights. Instead, this book closely examined the deep inner workings and emotional motives of solidarity. Ethnographic data illuminated their intervening role in interrupting the dialectical relationship between securitization of migration and pro-migration resistance.

This ethnographic approach with an emphasis on contextuality renders a universal model for all borderlands and border cities impossible. One-size-fits-all macro theories will not do justice to deeply situated geopolitics of solidarity. Frankly, the findings of this research cannot be copied and pasted to analyze other highly contested geopolitically strategic gateways across the world. While mapping of a formula for all cases is neither feasible nor recommended, my ethnography provides a conceptual and methodological approach to contextualize the interplay between securitization of borders (and migration) and the resistance to it.

As the racial border regime continues to become increasingly inhumane, ethnographic data have uncovered how border security was breeding its antidote, the native-migrant solidarity in peripheral border geographies. However, instead of depicting peaceful sanctuaries, my analysis showed how migrant-receiving gateway cities turned into zones of heightened contestation. Rather than an ideological opposition, the demonstrated confrontation is between those who feared—who generated, chose, fueled, or gave into fear—and those who looked into the eyes of fear and resisted, refused, fought against, and evaded it.

Hence, I conclude that as long as fear remains the modus operandi for securitization and criminalization, and given that fear aversion is the key to solidarity, the geopolitics of emotion are likely to continue stimulating the dialectic between securitization and resistance to it. At a time when emotions as central components of politics are largely dismissed or looked down upon, and when emotionality is still stigmatized as a weakness in achieving (geo)political ends, the in-depth analysis of the geopolitics of emotion calls for further ethnographic research that digs into and contextualizes everyday responses and reactions to securitization of migration.

NOTES

Preface

1. For an in-depth analysis of the fear of "Muslim invasion" and fear-aversive resistance in the eastern Mediterranean, see Turam (2023). For a cotemporal and similar fear in the central Mediterranean, the fear of "African invasion," see Hawthorne (2022, 13). See also de Haas (2008).

2. See, e.g., Schneider (1998a).

3. Here, the term *First World* points not only to the European colonial powers but also to the settler colonial nations, often referred to as the migrant countries: the United States, Canada, and Australia.

4. Makari's (2021, 11) search for the historical origins of the term *xenophobia* showed that, although the word united two Greek roots, *xenos* and *phobia*, it did not originate in ancient Greece: "The first use of xenophobia in English . . . was from a British magazine in 1909." Pointing to the first use of the term in colonial context, Makari's research makes a clear connection between xenophobia and colonialism by underlining it as a social construct that emerged under specific historical conditions.

5. "As every schoolchild knew, Western civilization commenced in ancient Greece, was transplanted to Rome, and then unfurled in Europe and America" (Makari 2021, 11).

6. Here, it is also helpful to remember that no one is exempt from becoming a refugee under unforeseen conditions (see Aktar 2021).

7. The United States, where I have lived, officially categorizes Middle Easterners, such as Turks, Arabs, and Iranians, as Caucasian, rendering their difference officially unrecognized. This is paradoxical when the post–September 11 geopolitics continue to racialize Muslims and manufacture the fear of the Muslim terrorist as the main target of securitization.

Introduction

1. My choice of terminology for migration status is contextual—and purposely not legalistic. Unlike my contextualized use of the term, a considerable portion of existing works relies on the "universal" definition of a refugee agreed on by the 1951 Geneva Refugee Convention and utilizes mostly quantitative data from the UN High Commissioner for Refugees (UNHCR). However, ethnographic research reveals how the seemingly universal terminology is not only slippery but also does not align with everyday experiences and practices of people for multiple reasons. For example, during my fieldwork, the arbitrarily defined statuses of refugees and asylum seekers were changing frequently, as were indiscriminate application of regulations and the constantly shifting policies of both the host country and the EU. Accordingly, paying attention to the everyday practices and the lived experience of "becoming and being" a refugee or migrant (see Arar and Fitzgerald 2022, 6), I adopted the terms that natives and migrants choose to use in daily life to describe status at a particular moment of the long journey. While acknowledging that the categories of migrants, such as refugees, asylees, and economic migrants are politicized (see Crawley and Skleparis 2018, 49), I consistently use the term *refugee* in the context of Greece (Part One). My choice of *refugee* in the Greek islands and Athens conveys meanings and reflects experiences of migrants in the geopolitics of the eastern Mediterranean in the aftermath of the Syrian civil war. Sidelining legal definitions, I observed (and participated) in the dominant discourse in everyday life that revolved around "the refugee" in Athens and "the migrant" in Palermo. The solidarity in Palermo (Part Two), both migrants and natives, vocally expressed distaste for these categories, arguing that they ranked migrants according to deservedness. Most of my interlocutors in Palermo refused to use these legal categories. Instead, many reminded me that "we were all human beings." Following Mayor Orlando, they repeatedly emphasized that anybody who lived in Palermo was "Palermitan." Overall, this book is focused on *irregular* migrants, which I use as an umbrella term to refer to migrants with different statuses. An immigrant is categorized as "irregular" when their entry to the receiving country is considered in violation of border regulations. The illicit border crossing stigmatizes the migrant, even though refugees and asylum-seekers were given the right to seek asylum by international conventions (Guild 2004).

2. Even though major migrant-sending countries to the Eastern and the Central Mediterranean varied widely, most irregular migrants arrived from Muslim-majority states. The recent influx to Greece was mainly from Syria, Iraq, and Afghanistan via Turkey, but Sicily in the past received migrants from North Africa and South Asia and, more recently, from Sub-Saharan and West African countries, including Nigeria, Senegal, and The Gambia via Libya.

3. Admittedly, Achiume (2022, 449) was not the first to use the term *racial borders*. De Genova (2018b) had already referred to Europe's borders as racial. See also Jones's 2021 *White Borders*.

4. *Politico* (2018). See also Wintour et al. (2018).

5. Pointing to the two aspects of the borders of Greece and Italy, the militaristic and the humanitarian, Chouliaraki and Musaro (2017) argue for the hybridity of these places that produced both fear and care. Considering the criminalization of rescue and solidarity, this book has a different take on these borders, mainly as violent dehumanizing places. I, then, turn to border cities, which generate solidarity (rather than humanitarian aid) and local trust and hope (rather than just care) against the background of inhumane border governance.

6. My analysis is built around two major streams of scholarship centered on human agency and emotions: political geography and critical security studies. The former is central to this book because of political geographers' emphasis on the primacy of geography and space or place in analyzing migration, security, and resistance. I benefited particularly from the contextual depth of work in political geography that parted ways with policy-driven efforts or modeling efforts in conventional security and migration studies. For key texts that integrate the human dimension, see Gökariksel and Secor (2018); Pain and Smith (2008); Pain (2009); İşleyen (2023); Wright (2008); Yuval-Davis et al. (2019); Askins (2016); Danewid (2017); Hawthorne (2022); Giglioli (2021). I engage with critical security studies in exploring resistance to securitization and the criminalization of migrants and solidarity. Recently, more works in this line of scholarship have brought emotions to the fore (see, e.g., Lampredi 2024; Vrabiescu 2022; Vrabiescu and Anderson 2023; Borelli 2022; Rozakou 2024; Milan 2018; Aradau 2004; Hagan and Bachelet 2024; Turam 2023). In addition, I also benefited vastly from critical ethnographies that spatialized fear, safety, and (in)security (e.g., Glück 2017; 2015; Glück and Low 2017; Low and Maguire 2019; Grimson and Renoldi 2019; Maguire, Frois, and Zurawski 2014. Lewek. 2016; Gregory and Pred 2007; Hagmann 2017; Low 1997; Low 2001).

7. For a similar critical approach, see, for example, Yuval Davis et al. (2019), who argue that "bordering processes weave together arenas of social, political and economic configurations in complex and contested ways, which cannot be understood while remaining within the boundaries of more traditional subdisciplines, such as social policy, international relations, migration studies, social identities or race and ethnic studies" (3).

8. Here, the geopolitical emotions are the "intervening" variable that determine the impact of securitized borders (independent variable) on resistance and native-migrant solidarity (independent variable). Put differently, these emotions interrupt, mediate and mold the dialectical relationship between securitization and solidarity by shaping mundane responses, practices, and discourses of resistance.

9. Building upon rapidly growing scholarship on emotions in political geography, my approach views emotions as historically and geopolitically situated. Some scholars in the realm of international politics and international theory define *affect* as historically formed feelings and differentiate it from emotions perceived as personal and instant reactions. For example, Hutchinson and Bleiker (2014) distinguish macro approaches to political emotions that develop "general-

izable propositions" from micro approaches that examine specific emotions in specific circumstances. This book does not make such a distinction, as emotions analyzed in this project are by-products of geopolitics rooted in history and geography.

10. Unlike personal feelings, political fear is understood as a phenomenon arising from "conflicts from within and between societies." Clearly, the repercussions of these emotions are not personal, such as a fear of heights that prevents a person from mountain climbing. On the contrary, political emotions have wide-ranging effects that dictate or reform policy; create or overturn laws; empower, discriminate against, or criminalize certain groups; violate or defend human rights; and enforce or resist violence.

11. The historical memory of my Greek and Sicilian interlocutors are of the colonized rather than the colonial imperial power, even though ancient Greece colonized Sicily in the late eighth century BC and parts of the Black Sea region in the seventh or sixth century BC.

12. In addition to the Ottoman conquest of Istanbul, Turkey's victory in the Greco-Turkish War (1919–22) shaped the emotionally laden Greek imagery of their Muslim neighbor, whereas Italy's annexation of Sicily in 1860 was largely perceived by Sicilians as a colonial act by Italy. This had an impact on the solidarity's positioning towards North Africa, particularly Tunisia, a former French protectorate with which Sicily has had long cross-border exchange, interaction, and familiarity, but also Libya, a former colony of Italy.

13. Critical of the idea of the white-European-led solidarity (Danewid 2017), recent works on the central Mediterranean prefer an understanding of solidarity based on "shared histories of racist injustice and Black struggle across the Mediterranean from colonialism to Fortress Europe" (Hawthorne 2022, 10).

14. For other critical points on integration theories and policies, see for example, Spencer and Charsley 2021; Turam 2023, 2015.

15. For vocal critics of the term *crisis* in the context of migration, see De Genova 2017; 2018b; Squire at al. 2021; Hawthorne 2022.

16. In the aftermath of the Cold War, the concept of security was expanded from territorial defense, war, and the realm of military to include so-called non-traditional security threats (Stivas 2021, 2). For converts as a security threat, see Özyürek (2009), whose work on German converts to Islam analyzes the official declaration of converts to minority religions as threats to national security.

17. The book contributes to a rich, expansive, and interdisciplinary literature on solidarity (e.g., Della Porta and Steinhilper 2022; Della Porta 2018; Dijstelbloem and Walters 2021; Hom 2019; Duarte 2020; Hagan and Bachelet 2024; Cusumano and Bell 2021; Tazzioli and Walters 2019; Raimondi 2019; Moulin 2012; Kolankiewicz and Sager 2021; Nicholls and Uitermark. 2017). However, while engaging this line of scholarship, I build my analysis on studies that center on the role of (geo)political emotions. Focusing on the intimate and daily dimension of social life, Lampredi (2024, 738) argues: "Viewed from this perspective, no aspect of social life remains outside the attempts to govern the moral bound-

aries of nation-states through affectivity." Accordingly, the criminalization of solidarity appears as "an emotional governance strategy" that judges and denounces certain emotions such as safety, trust, empathy, and so on. These emotions come under attack because by empowering pro-migrant resistance (Turam 2023), they disrupt the reproduction of "the material, legal, and moral boundaries through which migration is governed" (Lampredi 2024, 722). While I am inspired by several subfields that incorporate the role of emotions into their analysis on issues, such as citizenship, right-wing ideologies, security, and race (e.g., de Wilde and Duyvendak 2016; Di Gregorio and Merolli 2016; Anderson 2009; Ayata 2019; Salmela and von Scheve 2017; Pesarini 2021), my main interest remains in exploring the role of geopolitical emotions in violent securitized borderlands, specifically border cities, that give rise to meaningful resistance to the securitization of migration. Further, original contribution to the study of emotions from ethnographies must be noted. Özyürek's (2023) *Subcontractors of Guilt* and Parla's (2019) *Precarious Hope* exemplify remarkable research on emotions, migrants, and minorities.

18. See particularly Stivas (2024, 9). Despite ongoing disagreements among EU institutions about the source, nature of the risk, and the threat of the EU's "refugee crisis," Stivas (2024, 9) claims that the disagreements culminated mainly in the variation of *intensity* of securitization narratives. But overall rhetoric, he argues, was "accepted by their *targeted audiences*, the European public and the other EU Institutions." The competing views about the source of the risk and threat ranged from "the inability of the EU to stand firm in its position as the guarantor of human rights" and "the reintroduction of internal border- controls between EU member states" to "the lack of solidarity among the member states in dealing with the refugee crisis" (9). However, despite all these contestations of the nature and risk of the crisis, consensus was reached that "the refugee crisis could develop into a risk to the EU's survival. This made it possible for the EU Institutions and member states to act rapidly and—arguably-effectively to deal with the refugee crisis and the asylum seekers" (9).

19. Here, I benefit from urbanists' argument that securitization creates insecurity by generating fear of the targeted object (Glück 2017; Glück and Low 2017; Low and Maguire 2019). However, the fear-aversive Exarcheia complicates and puzzles such debate.

20. Like the concept of human agency, the term *agentic city* is largely misunderstood in scholarship. Rather than a static quality, an attribute or the essence of a person, place, or city, I use the term *agentic* to highlight the capacity for dynamic transformation. The term brings to the fore the urban will (or the will of the urbanites) to liberate, empower, and grow by embracing challenges from multiple fields—geopolitical, socioeconomic, geographic, and historical (Turam 2015).

21. The UNHCR states, "At the end of 2023, an estimated 117.3 million people worldwide were forcibly displaced due to persecution, conflict, violence, human rights violations and events seriously disturbing the public order. Based

on operational data, UNHCR estimates that forced displacement has continued to increase in the first four months of 2024 and by the end of April 2024 is likely to have exceeded 120 million. The increase to 117.3 million at the end of 2023 constitutes a rise of 8 per cent or 8.8 million people compared to the end of 2022 and continues a series of year-on-year increases over the last 12 years. One in every 69 people, or 1.5 percent of the entire world's population, is now forcibly displaced. This is nearly double the 1 in 125 people who were displaced a decade ago." UNHCR, "Global Trends," https://www.unhcr.org/us/global-trends (accessed March 13, 2025).

22. The EU's Dublin agreement adopted in June 2013 determined that the refugees apply for asylum in the first EU member state that they enter. This EU law put the main responsibility for refugees on the Southern European arrival countries, especially Greece, Italy, and Spain. With the exception of Germany, the EU's destination states have refused to share equal responsibility with arrival states (Ferreira, 2019; Karageorgiou, 2016).

23. The subversive Italian mayors in southern borderlands who stood up to the security regime, such as mayors of Palermo, Naples, Taranto, Messina, and Reggio Calabria, were referred to only rarely in news and in passing in a few academic works. Overall, the highly emotional context in which they fostered the pro-migrant resistance was entirely dismissed. See, e.g., *Politico* 2018; Wintour et al. (2018).

24. Most of these couples are Black men and white women, but this is most likely the outcome of the overwhelmingly Black male migrant population in the city.

25. From my fieldwork in Palermo, May 2024. I met Sofia and her partner in one of several migrant solidarity organizations formed by African migrants over the past couple of years. Sofia had a PhD and an academic job in Britain, where her partner could not travel, even though he had legal status as a refugee. He was one of the first refugees criminalized and prisoned unfairly for human trafficking (for driving the boat) in 2016 for three years. He learned perfect Italian, which impressed Italians, from his cellmate, an old Italian man who taught him the language, the culture, the old and new music genres of the country, and so on.

26. In the age of rising right-wing populism and racism, it does not seem to take much effort for security regimes, political leaders, and professionals to transform the successfully manufactured fear of "the stranger" into collective anxiety, hatred, hostility, and aggression. For the emotional roots of right-wing populism, see Salmela and von Scheve (2017). Contrary to the predominant explanations of the rise of right-wing populism by socioeconomic transformation reinforced by globalization, the authors explain this rise by emotional processes, particularly the link between fear and shame.

27. Even in the rapidly growing body of scholarship on sanctuary cities, little has been said about the geopolitics of emotions (for exceptions, see Bagelman 2013, 2016).

28. The Schengen Acquis—Agreement Between the Governments of the States of the Benelux Economic Union, the Federal Republic of Germany, and the French Republic On the Gradual Abolition of Checks at Their Common Borders, Official Journal L 239, 22/09/2000 P. 0013–0018.

29. Throughout the book, I engage with the broader subfield of "forced displacement" that covers all kinds of involuntary human mobility "in all its manifestations as an alternative to the more narrowly focused 'refugee studies,' which refers only to those who fall under the international legal definition of 'refugee'" (Crepeau et al. 2006, 2–3).

30. For an argument on the interconnectedness of the unification of Europe and a joined European effort to colonize Africa, see Danewid (2017, 1680): "From the beginning of the Pan-European movement in the 1920s to its institutionalisation in the European Economic Community (EEC), European integration was inextricably bound up with the question of Europe's continued dominance over Africa. The 2008 agreement between Italy and Libya, in which Colonel Gaddafi agreed to help curb migration flows in return for colonial reparations, is but a recent example of how the historical reality of colonialism continues to pattern the present."

31. See, e.g., LIFO 2019.

32. IOM collects data on migrant deaths in the Mediterranean and elsewhere through its Missing Migrants project, available at https://missingmigrants.iom .int/.

33. While trafficking involves coercion, exploitation, and kidnapping, such as sex trafficking, smuggling assists in the "irregular" border-crossing by charging the refugee a price. Yet the boundaries between the two experiences often are blurred, as both involve violence to maintain control over refugees. In both cases, human rights violations occur frequently, as refugees are exposed to inhumane conditions, lack of water and food, or being stuck in small, airtight spaces during transportation.

34. See Aru 2023, for the disputes in the Italian Parliament about the rationale of migration policies and Salvini laws. Mr. Salvini was investigated multiple times for blocking the embarkment of rescued migrants on rescue ships, including the *Diciotti* of the Italian Coast Guard in 2018 (see Frazetta and Piazza 2022); *Sea Watch 3* German NGO in January 2019; *Sea Watch 3* in June 2019; *Gregoretti* of the Italian Coast Guard in July 2019; and *Open Arms,* a Spanish NGO in August 2019.

35. The pushbacks were confirmed in my interviews with the spokesperson of the Greek Helsinki Monitor, Panayote Dimitras, September 25, 2022, and multiple interviews with Lefteris Papagiannakis, the director of the Greek Council for refugees. These organizations documented and accumulated numerous cases of pushbacks waiting to be investigated by the courts. See also, investigative journalists, e.g., Simon's (2023) interview with Lydia Emmanouilidou; Fallon et al. (2023); and *The Guardian* (2024).

36. By saying this, I do not by any means argue for a decrease of authority or power of the nation-state in governing securitization and migration. To the contrary, this book illuminates how, at this historical period when states' unjust and arbitrary acts towards vulnerable migrant populations intensified racial security, local politics and municipal governments had leverage to confront injustice and the violations of human rights.

37. My interviewees who were politicians and pro-migrant and human rights advocates included then-member of Parliament Erasmo Palazzotto from Palermo, who at the time also served on NGO boat rescue teams; and member of the European Parliament Pietro Bartolo, who had also served as a doctor in Lampedusa, treating arriving migrants. Similarly, Palermo's five-time mayor Orlando had served as a member of the Italian and the European Parliament (1994–99 and since 2024). On July 29, 2019, I also interviewed an ally of Orlando, Luigi de Magistris, former mayor of Naples (2011–21) and a former member of the European Parliament (2009–11).

Chapter 1

1. For UNHCR refugee statistics, see https://www.unrefugees.org/refugee-facts/statistics/. When the non-registered refugees in the country are added to the refugee population, the refugee population is estimated to amount to more than 3.6 million in Turkey. Compared to the three million refugees accepted to the United States since 1975 (with a rate of some twenty to thirty thousand refugees accepted per year) and the 2.1 million hosted by Germany, the major host in Europe, Turkey's responsibility stands out.

2. For UNHCR data on the irregular crossings of the Turkey-Greece border, see https://data.unhcr.org/en/situations/europe-sea-arrivals/location/24489.

3. See, e.g., Tondo and Stierl (2020). A rescue boat named *Louise Michel*, funded by Banksy, departed secretly on August 18 from the Spanish port of Burriana, near Valencia carrying over 250 refugees. The mayor of Marseilles opened that city's port while European governments refused docking. See also York (2020).

4. This image of Greece as a transitional arrival country changed partly in the next couple of years with the closed borders of EU members and the refusal of countries elsewhere in Europe to accept refugees and to share the burden.

5. With regard to the juxtaposition of rights against security, see Goldstein (2010).

6. Although the politics of and debate on sanctuary cities peaked during Donald Trump's first presidency (2017–21), the term has been used in the United States since the 1980s to refer to the prominent sanctuary cities of the United States, such as Los Angeles and San Francisco.

7. Overall, the term *refugee* (*prosfighas*) has had a negative connotation in Greece. In the late 1970s and 1980s, when Greece was receiving Kurdish political refugees, who were members of the PKK, the Kurdish militant political organization and armed guerillas, the Left in Greece welcomed them, considering the

Kurdish refugees as socialist freedom fighters. Rozakou (2012) argues that this was also a reflection of the tense Greek-Turkish relations. When the migration flow increased significantly in the 1990s, migration and asylum acquired negative connotations and came to be constructed as key political problems. But Greece continued accepting political refugees from Turkey, I was told during my field research, as the border police perceived them as "the enemy of the enemy."

8. The neofascist party Golden Dawn was receiving 8 percent electoral support during this period, and after its closure in 2019, three other ultranationalist parties entered the Greek parliament in 2023. After the 2023 elections, Greece was the only country with three far-right parties in the parliament (Fallon 2023).

9. Rozakou's (2017) ethnographic work shows how the police officers felt deserted by the state with meager resources and no guidance in migration governance.

10. The literature on social movements established that successful protests either might lead to further demonstrations by the same movement or might instigate in time the mobilization and development of a countermovement (Meyer and Staggenborg 1996).

11. While space is socially and politically constructed (Lefebvre 1992), it also shapes social and political processes and power dynamics.

12. For example, interviews conducted in Southern Wales, identified as a city of refuge, show that undocumented people frequently avoided reporting crimes that had happened to them, including attacks and rapes (Hintjens and Puori 2014). Similarly, all my interlocutors agreed that it would be impossible to ensure safety to refugees whether a city qualifies as a welcoming or pro-migrant place or not.

13. For the Athens Coordination Centre for Migrant and Refugee Issues, see https://www.accmr.gr/en/.

14. Most of the achievements in refugee work in Athens (such as access to municipal services) have been in the areas of reception, sheltering, and protection. This focus aligns with the fact that, "refugees are not like other migrants: they are not moving for gain, but they have no choice. They are seeking safety abroad" (Betts and Collier 2017, 1).

15. ECHO (European Community Humanitarian Office) is the largest single collaborator in humanitarian aid to the office of the UNHCR.

16. American sanctuary cities try to enable refugees and immigrants to safely report crime without being fearful of deportation. They do so by claiming that enforcement of immigration law is not their job.

17. The party's leadership, Michaloliakos and six of his deputies, were found responsible for the actions of party members, which included multiple assaults, human trafficking, illegal possession of weapons and explosives, and murder (of Fyssas) (see Kakissis 2020; Baboulias 2020; Kitsantonis and Magra 2020).

Chapter 2

1. Mr. Bakoyannis comes from a family of prominent politicians and political elites. Serving in local governance for more than a decade, he served as the mayor in his hometown Karpenisi and head of the Central Greece region. He holds a PhD from the University of Oxford in international relations and politics, a master's degree in public policy from Harvard University, and a bachelor of arts in international relations and history from Brown University.

2. Despite the overall anti-refugee stance in the country, negative sentiment toward Turkey that is shared widely in Greek political culture figures in the relatively welcoming attitudes toward political refugees fleeing from Turkey in the past and present—previously Kurds and more recently followers of the Gülen movement.

3. Ahmed (2014, 25) points to "the role of fear in the conservation of power, by considering how *narratives of crisis* work to secure social norms in the present, with specific reference to the figure of the international terrorist."

4. Fallon (2022).

5. From the Q&A after his talk "Reinventing Athens: A Conversation with Mayor Kostas Bakoyannis," February 4, 2020, at Minda de Gunzburg Center for European Studies, Harvard University.

6. Exarcheia "offered a viable solution that guaranteed a largely sustainable hospitality" (Cappuccini 2018, x–xi).

7. The minister of public order, Michalis Chrisochoidis, joined Mitsotakis in the project of "taming" Exarcheia as New Democracy's major agenda. See *National Herald* (2019).

8. According to my interviews with municipal officials, 2021.

9. My field research documented distrust, ostracization, and threats to and even physical attacks on humanitarians by locals in border islands of Greece in the aftermath of the 2016 Turkey-EU agreement. In my interview with a frontline worker in Samos in August 2018, he shared with me that he was threatened and physically attacked. Due to ongoing intimidation, the entrance of the office I visited had security locks installed. Similarly, several interlocutors shared with me incidents of physical confrontation between migrants, pro-migrant activists, and anti-migrant islanders during my multiple visits to Leros and Chios between 2018 and 2021.

10. During my fieldwork in 2021, I observed that no one seemed to understand the logic of the EU-funded prison-like buildings erected on the Greek border islands. It became clear only with time that, unlike the previous refugee camps, the goal of the new buildings was the confinement and detainment of refugees and asylum seekers.

11. On my last visit in July 2024, the outer parts of Omonoia Square that accommodated migrants looked chaotic, with prostitution and sex trafficking in the streets. They were unlike Exarcheia and Victoria in their unneighborly and mostly commercial and transactional outlook. As I walked through the streets, I felt uncomfortable but experienced no danger, harassment, or disturbance.

Chapter 3

1. Leoluca Orlando is an Italian politician born in Palermo in 1947. Before his career in politics, he studied law at the University of Palermo and received a graduate degree in philosophy and law in Germany. In addition to his academic position as a professor of constitutional law at the University of Palermo and five mayoral terms in Palermo, he served as a member of the European and Italian parliaments.

2. Sorge's research on other small towns of Sicily captures the anti-immigrant sentiments of locals who align with the far right due to their feelings of estrangement from and criticism of solidarity; they do not share the middle-class values of solidarity and human rights with activists, and they perceive and fear migrants as a threat to societal cohesion and collectively shared values.

3. The IOM collects data on migrant deaths in the Mediterranean and elsewhere through its Missing Migrants project, available at https://missingmigrants .iom.int/. See also Merelli (2017).

4. After the peak flow in 2015–16, the externalization of European borders led to a relative decline of the migrant flow in the central Mediterranean in 2017–18 (Landau 2019).

5. For the historical background of the Northern League's othering of Sicily for its ethnic makeup and racial liminality, see Agnew (2000, 307).

6. The League (Lega) was formerly known as the Northern League (Lega Nord); it originated in the 1990s. Lega Nord defended separation from the underdeveloped South, which the party viewed as a burden on the developed North. The Lega despised southerners as lazy, corrupt, and racially mixed. Eventually, the party expanded its racist and exclusionary reactions from southern Italians to migrants from other countries and mobilized anti-immigrant and Islamophobic sentiments.

7. Originally built in the sixteenth century and renovated in the eighteenth century, the villa hosted the Valguarnera family for three centuries until it was sold to the Commune of Palermo in 1987. Since then, Villa Niscemi has been used as a venue of the mayor's office and the municipal government.

8. A *human rights city* is a municipality that establishes its policies, principles, and programs according to international human rights standards. The term originated in the late 1990s, when an NGO in New York, People's Movement for Human Rights Learning, called for the incorporation of human rights into local governance to improve the lives of vulnerable and excluded groups. See Van den Berg and Oomen (2014, 13).

9. Drawn from my field notes on July 25, 2019. Most of the young migrants were Black Muslim men working in the agricultural sector. The mission was founded in 1991 by Biagio Conte, who passed away in 2023. Famous for his hunger strikes and other acts of protest, Conte staged a mission walk from Palermo to Brussels in the summer of 2019 to make a case for refugees to the European Parliament. Working for a shared purpose, the municipality provided infrastructure, electricity, and water to the charitable mission. Although the mis-

sion had difficulty maintaining hygiene and safety after the peak of the flow, it was recognized internationally for its pro-migrant humanitarian commitments. The situation in the shelters got out of control during the COVID-19 pandemic. See particularly Picone and Giubilaro (2022, 79–91).

10. See the UNHCR's website "Resettlement and Other Forms of Legal and Safe Transfer to Italy," https://help.unhcr.org/italy/resettlement/.

11. Pettrachin (2022) explored the "unexpected" absence of anti-immigrant protests. His analysis pointed to a lack of divisive politicization of migration issues by political party leaders in Sicily.

12. For the text of the Italian constitution, see the website of the Senato della Republica, at https://www.senato.it/documenti/repository/istituzione/costituzi one_inglese.pdf.

13. Similarly, managing the refugee flow as "a crisis" becomes a key strategy targeting refugees and asylum seekers as major threats to security (Bigo and Guild 2005; Guild 2009).

14. *Politico*, 2018; Wintour et al. (2018).

15. For the controversy between Salvini, the prime minister, and the courts, see Giuffrida (2019).

16. Upon the embarkment of *Seawatch*, a German NGO rescue ship, to Lampedusa in 2019, Carole Rackete was arrested and detained for refusing to obey military orders. In a clash with far-right Salvini (then in office), she stated that she was doing her duty to save lives in accordance with the principles of international law. Her case remained under investigation until the court acquitted her in 2021.

17. The situation was quite different in northern cities. For example, even though Trento is a university town, none of the locals I met condemned racial profiling on the streets or questioned the police's discriminatory treatment of Black migrants.

18. In September 2019, the coalition between the Five Star Movement and the Salvini-led Lega was dissolved and replaced by a new coalition between the Five Star Movement and the three left-wing parties—Democratic Party (center-left), Italia Viva (Italy Alive, center-left), and Liberi e Uguali (Free and Equal People, left).

19. Drawn from my interviews in 2021–22. Against the backdrop of his international reputation as a defender of migrants' rights, he was criticized by activists and ordinary locals in Palermo. Some researchers also criticized his undertakings and politics. For example, Orlando's liberal cosmopolitanism was criticized for essentializing multiculturalism as an inherent feature of the city. The critique was developed by using Orlando's Facebook page as the source of data (Wyer 2024). Another single-sited field study that focused on one social enterprise in Palermo problematized Orlando's adoption of the concept of hospitality for city-branding of Palermo (Neil 2024). As these studies are narrowly focused, they largely neglect the complex contextuality in which the border city is situated. They also fail to do justice to Orlando's local and transnational advo-

cacy and political accomplishments in human and migration rights and his civil disobedience to the Italian government. Most importantly, the works entirely dismiss migrants' overwhelmingly positive views and trust of his municipal government.

Chapter 4

1. These identifications of locals seemed to contradict my use of the term *native* to distinguish them from older migrants and newcomers, but they did not provide a compelling reason for me to ignore the differential status and experiences of migrants from nonmigrants. I use the term *native* particularly to highlight different geopolitical emotions of insecurity and safety of natives and migrants.

2. "Many have commented that an explicit discourse about race is often absent or tacit in Latin America; that people deny that racism is a problem (including many black and indigenous people); that they assert that class inequality is the real problem; that overt reference to race somehow goes against the national grain in many countries; and that those who highlight racial identifications—for example, in the name of antiracism—may be accused of being racist" (Wade 2010, 43).

3. Founded in 1897 as one of Europe's finest opera houses, the Teatro Massimo was closed in 1974 for urgent repairs and remained closed until renovations in 1996 (Orlando 2001, 3). When it was founded, it was the third largest opera house in Europe, and it still is the largest one in Italy.

4. See Tamkin (2024). A widely shared source of pride in Palermo is the medieval era during the reign of Roger II (1130–54) that is depicted as a time of cultural exchange with a multiethnic and multilingual society that is argued to be a bridge between the East and the West. See Houben (2013, 21).

5. There is ongoing debate about Palermo's medieval diversity, particularly the Arab-Norman period, and a substantial critique of the tendency to trace the present-day politics of multiculturalism back to that period. My ethnography and interviews with local academics documented some of these critiques. Further, researchers question the factuality of these historical constructs and memories (for a study of the disagreements and debates on Facebook, see Wyer 2024). Others point to the multiplicity of competing historical scripts depending on who is "remembering." As expected, the selective memories of different ethnic groups point to different historical moments. For example, Tunisians recall the ninth century, whereas Sicilians commemorate the eleventh century and Arab-Norman period (Ben-Yehoyada 2017).

6. A portion of solidarity is implicated in this critique directed towards Italy for "recounting a particular history of Italianness" that paints a past of "mixing." Critics argue that it is not enough for many proud Italians "to simply claim that Italy has recently become 'mixed' because of immigration" (Hawthorne 2022, 119).

7. Shot during an art residency in Palermo, the film was produced by True

Tales of the Mediterranean and supported by the French Institute of Palermo.

8. The market of Albergheria at the margins of Ballarò market was represented by Sbaratto, a local association, that defended the market against foreclosure.

9. I purposely refrained from asking about past suffering in my interviews unless the migrant volunteered details.

10. Pinkwashing is a political propaganda strategy that uses LGBTQIA+ rights to create a progressive image that masks human rights violations.

11. In 2023, twelve organizations were cooperating with Moltivolti and using their space for activities.

12. There were about four or five Black migrants in a class of twelve to eighteen students in the high school that Bobo attended.

13. This curatorial text is written by Don Liborio Paeri for Bellina's exhibition of Oriri in Palermo.

14. Bellina, 2022. *Oriri* is a curated catalog of Bellina's photos accompanied by people's stories documented by him.

15. The photographer's words echoed Mayor Orlando's bold statements about the Sicilian affinity for the Islamic World (Mattozzi 2019).

16. The documentary's preview is available on Gravagna's YouTube channel, at https://www.youtube.com/watch?app=desktop&si=SXh99REdFSpILkQe&v=hGYBlTibJXw&feature=youtu.be.

17. I used a snowball sampling method through which migrants introduced me to their friends who were migrants. When I was introduced to my first Black migrant interlocutors, the migrants were often hesitant to meet with me. Some shied away, and others were suspicious, even after I explained the principle of confidentiality and my research goals. As we created bonds in daily life beyond the confines of a formal interview process, they started to relax and communicate less cautiously. For example, Bobo did not respond to my first request for an interview for a week. And then when we met for the first time, he was very guarded. He carefully checked out my personality and asked me a few questions to test the parameters of my politics and my agenda. Over the following two years, Bobo trusted me enough to talk for many hours about multiple aspects of his past and present life, his politics, his family back in the homeland, his emotions, the challenges he faced, and his future plans.

18. Categorically denied for refugee status, Tunisians have experienced deportations and tend to be more distrustful of strangers, including researchers.

19. There is an absence of research on older Arab migrant groups in Palermo and Sicily (for an exception, see Giglioli 2021). As the explicit hierarchy of power between North and Sub-Saharan Africans is an important part of the racial dynamics in the Mediterranean, these call for in-depth research.

Conclusions

1. For example, Danewid (2017) critically assesses Butler's (2004) call for a new critical humanism based on common bodily vulnerability of all human

beings—our vulnerability to external or material forces. Danewid disagrees with Butler's ontological approach because of the absence of historical contextuality. Butler's work on vulnerability and mourning, she argues, is a failed attempt to recover the humanist project of bonding humanity. Instead, the project "results in a fetishisation of the stranger and a consequent erasure of history . . . by an ideological discourse that removes from view the history of colonialism and the way in which it continues to structure the present" (Danewid 2017, 1676).

2. For the text of the pact, see the European Commission's website "Pact on Migration and Asylum," https://home-affairs.ec.europa.eu/policies/migration -and-asylum/pact-migration-and-asylum_en.

3. The spokesperson of the German rescue NGO Seawatch referred to the new regulation as the EU's "legalization of human right abuses." Alessandra Sciurba, professor of human rights and a founding member of the Legal Clinic for Human Rights, responded to the EU pact on social media: "They have 'made history,' they speak of 'an epoch-changing,' while they have . . . legitimized the worst policies that have been going on for decades and have produced illegality, insecurity, and human trafficking." Calling for safe and legal entry channels, Sciurba rebuffed the EU's intensified securitization of migration through "widespread detention of asylum seekers in extraterritorial areas, deportations, violation of freedoms, biometric checks even for children, and declaration of states of emergency."

4. Drawn from my interviews in 2022–24. While city branding appears as the major qualifier of richer cities of northern Italy and Europe, such as Milan, Florence, and Paris (see, e.g., Rossini and Nervino 2019, 68; Capone and Lazzeretti 2016), some locals questioned why branding is problematized in the context of poor southern cities.

5. The round-table conversation with former Prime Minister Tsipras was by invitation only and took place at Minda de Gunzburg Center for European Studies, Harvard University, April 8, 2025.

6. "While media narratives often focus on the rise of the far right, and there were indeed substantial increases in their support in countries ranging from Sweden to Austria, very few of these parties won elections. . . . In the US, for example, a 2019 Pew survey found 62% of Americans said that immigrants make the country stronger, the highest number to date. In 1994, the same survey found only 34% agreed with that statement" (Jones, in Fregonese et al. 2020, 8). It is to be seen how the aggressively anti-migrant rule by President Trump will impact these results in the near future.

7. In contrast to New Democracy, Syriza warned that police repression and violence against refugees "would lead Europe to a dead-end." See Stivas (2021, 8–11).

BIBLIOGRAPHY

Abel, Richard L. 2018. *Law's Wars: The Fate of the Rule of Law in the US "War on Terror."* Cambridge University Press.

Achiume, E. Tendayi. 2022. "Racial Borders." *Georgetown Law Journal* 10 (13): 446–88.

Ackleson, Jason. 2005. "Constructing Security on the U.S.–Mexico Border." *Political Geography* 24(2): 165–84.

Agnew, John. 2000. "Italy's Island Other: Sicily's History in the Modern Italian Body Politic." *Emergences: Journal for the Study of Media & Composite Cultures* 10 (2): 301–11.

Ahmed, Sara. 2014. *The Cultural Politics of Emotion.* New ed. Edinburgh University Press.

Ahmed, Sara. 2000. "Who Knows? Knowing Strangers and Strangerness." *Australian Feminist Studies* 15 (31): 49–68.

Aktar, Cengiz. 2021."Notes for the Anti-Refugee and Anti-Migrant" (Mülteci ve Göçmen Karşitlarina Notlar), *Ahval,* 167, July 21.

Ali, Nadya, and Ben Whitham. 2020. "Racial Capitalism, Islamophobia, and Austerity." *International Political Sociology* 15 (2): 190–211.

Altınordu, Ateş. 2021. "Uncivil Populism in Power: The Case of Erdoganism." In *Populism in the Civil Sphere,* edited by Jeffrey C. Alexandre, Peter Kivisto, and Giuseppe Sciortino. Polity Press.

Ambrosini, Maurizio. 2013. "Immigration in Italy: Between Economic Acceptance and Political Rejection." *Journal of International Migration and Integration* 14 (1): 175–94.

Anderson, Ben. 2009. "Affective Atmospheres." *Emotion, Space and Society* 2 (2): 77–81.

Andersson, Ruben. 2016. "Europe's Failed Fight Against Irregular Migration: Ethnographic Notes on a Counter-Productive Industry." *Journal of Ethnic and Migration Studies* 42 (7): 1055–75.

Antonsich, Marco. 2022. "The Diversity Continuum: Blurring the Boundaries Between Internal and External Others Among Italian Children of Migrants." *Political Geography* 96: 102602

Aradau, Claudia. 2004. "The Perverse Politics of Four-Letter Words: Risk and Pity in the Securitisation of Human Trafficking." *Millennium* 33 (2): 251–77.

Arampatzi, Athina. 2017a. "Contentious Spatialities in an Era of Austerity: Everyday Politics and 'Struggle Communities' in Athens, Greece." *Political Geography* 60 (September): 47–56.

Arampatzi, Athina. 2017b. "The Spatiality of Counter-Austerity Politics in Athens, Greece: Emergent Urban Solidarity Spaces." *Urban Studies* 54 (9): 2155–71.

Arci Porco Rosso and Alarm Phone. 2021. *From Sea to Prison: The Criminalization of Boat Drivers in Italy.* https://www.borderline-europe.de/sites/default/files/background/from-sea-to-prison_arci-porco-rosso-and-alarm-phone_october-2021.pdf.

Arar, Rawan, and David Scott Fitzgerald. 2022. *The Refugee System: A Sociological Approach.* Polity Press.

Armenta, Amada. 2017. "Racializing Crimmigration: Structural Racism, Colorblindness, and the Institutional Production of Immigrant Criminality." *Sociology of Race and Ethnicity* 3 (1): 82–95.

Aru, Silvia. 2023. "Battleship at the port of Europe': Italy's closed-port policy and its legitimizing narratives," *Political Geography* 104:102902

Askins, Kye. 2016. "Emotional Citizenry: Everyday Geographies of Befriending, Belonging and Intercultural Encounters." *Transactions of the Institute of British Geographers* 41 (4): 515–27.

Ayata, Bilgin. 2019. "Affective Citizenship." In *Affective Societies*, edited by Jan Slaby and Christian von Scheve, 330–39. Routledge.

Baboulias, Yiannis. 2020. "How to Beat the Nazis in 2020." *The Atlantic*, October 8. https://www.theatlantic.com/international/archive/2020/10/golden-dawn-greece-far-right/616642/.

Bacharach, Michael, and Diego Gambetta. 2001. "Trust in Signs." In *Trust in Society*, edited by Karen S. Cook. Russell Sage Foundation.

Bagelman, Jennifer. 2013. "Sanctuary: A Politics of Ease?" *Alternatives: Global, Local, Political* 38 (1): 49–62.

Bagelman, Jennifer. 2016. *Sanctuary City: A Suspended State.* Palgrave Macmillan.

Balzacq, Thierry, and Sergio Carrera. 2016. *Security Versus Freedom. A Challenge for Europe's Future.* Routledge.

Barreto, Amílcar, and Omar Sindi. 2020. "From Nearly White to Brown: Nation, Identity, and the Racialization of Muslim Americans." *Culture and Religion* 21 (4): 409–27.

Başaran, Tuğba. 2014. "Saving Lives at Sea: Security, Law and Adverse Effects." *European Journal of Migration and Law* 16 (3): 365–87.

Bauder, Harald. 2017. "Sanctuary Cities: Policies and Practices in International Perspective." *International Migration* 55 (2): 174–87.

Bauder, Harald. 2021. "Urban Solidarity: Perspectives of Migration and Refugee Accommodation and Inclusion." *Critical Sociology* 47 (6): 875–89.

Bauder Harald, and Lorelle Juffs. 2020. " 'Solidarity' in the Migration and Refugee Literature: Analysis of a Concept." *Journal of Ethnic and Migration Studies* 46 (1): 46–65.

Bayat, Asef. 2013. *Life as Politics: How Ordinary People Change the Middle East*. Stanford University Press.

Bazurli, Raffaele. 2019. "Local Governments and Social Movements in the 'Refugee Crisis': Milan and Barcelona as 'Cities of Welcome.' " *South European Society and Politics* 24 (3): 343–70.

Bazurli, Raffaele, Tiziana Caponio, and Els de Graauw. 2022. "Between a Rock and a Hard Place: Mayors, Migration Challenges and Multilevel Political Dynamics." *Territory, Politics and Governance* 10 (2): 2–10.

Bazurli, Raffaele, and Carlos Delclós. 2022. "Crimmigration and Solidarity in the Global City: The Case of Barcelona's Street Vendors." In *Contentious Migrant Solidarity: Shrinking Spaces and Civil Society Contestation*, edited by Donatella della Porta and Elias Steinhilper. Routledge.

BBC News. 2013. "Italy Boat Sinking: Hundreds Feared Dead Off Lampedusa." October 3. https://www.bbc.com/news/world-europe-24380247.

BBC News. 2018. "Italy Migrants: Matteo Salvini Calls for End to Sicily 'Refugee Camp.' " June 3. https://www.bbc.com/news/world-europe-44346084.

Beerli, Monique. 2018. "Saving the Saviors: Security Practices and Professional Struggles in the Humanitarian Space." *International Political Sociology* 12 (1): 70–87.

Bellina, Francesco. 2022. *Oriri*. Forward Edizioni.

Ben-Yehoyada, Naor. 2011. "The Clandestine Central Mediterranean Passage." *Middle East Research and Information Project (MERIP)* (261), 18–23.

Ben-Yehoyada, Naor. 2017. *The Mediterranean Incarnate: Region Formation Between Sicily and Tunisia Since World War II*. University of Chicago Press.

Berger, Miriam. 2021. "Italy's Ex-interior Minister Is on Trial for Blocking a Migrant Boat from Docking: Actor Richard Gere Is a Witness." *Washington Post*, October 24. https://www.washingtonpost.com/world/2021/10/24/matteo-salvini-richard-gere-migrant-boat-kidnapping/.

Bessant, Judith, and Rob Watts. 2022. "The Criminalisation of Solidarity: Asylum-seekers and Australia's Illiberal-democracy." In *Contentious Migrant Solidarity: Shrinking Spaces and Civil Society Contestation*, edited by Donatella della Porta and Elias Steinhilper. Routledge.

Besteman, Catherine, and Hugh Gusterson. 2010. *The Insecure American: How We Got Here & What We Should Do About It*. University of California Press.

Betts, Alexander, and Paul Collier. 2017. *Refuge: Rethinking Refugee Policy in a Changing World*. Oxford University Press.

Biancalana, Cecilia. 2020. "Four Italian Populisms." In *Multiple Populisms:*

Italy as Democracy's Mirror, edited by Paul Blokker and Manuel Anselmi. Routledge.

Bigo, Didier. 2014. "The (in)Securitization Practices of the Three Universes of EU Border Control: Military/Navy—Border Guards/Police—Database Analysts." *Security Dialogue* 45 (3): 209–25.

Bigo, Didier. 2016. "Liberty, Whose Liberty? The Hague Programme and the Conception of Freedom." In *Security Versus Freedom? A Challenge for Europe's Future*, edited by Thierry Balzacq and Sergio Carrera. Routledge.

Bigo, Didier, and Elspeth Guild. 2005. *Controlling Frontiers: Free Movement into and Within Europe*. Ashgate.

Bilgiç, Ali. 2013. *Rethinking Security in the Age of Migration*. Routledge.

Bloemraad, Irene. 2006. *Becoming a Citizen Incorporating Immigrants and Refugees in the United States and Canada*. University of California Press.

Blokker, Paul. 2020. "The Populist Assault on the Constitution." In *Multiple Populisms: Italy as Democracy's Mirror*, edited by Paul Blokker and Manuel Anselmi. Routledge.

Blokker, Paul, and Manuel Anselmi, eds. 2020. *Multiple Populisms: Italy as Democracy's Mirror*. Routledge.

Blokker, Paul, and Chris Thornhill, eds. 2017. *Sociological Constitutionalism*. Cambridge University Press.

Body-Gendrot, Sophie. 2012. *Globalization, Fear, and Insecurity: The Challenges for Cities North and South*. Palgrave Macmillan.

Borderline Sicilia. 2022. "The African Migrants Who Italy Accuses of People Smuggling." *Borderline Sicilia*, April 28. https://www.borderlinesicilia.it/en/news-en/the-african-migrants-who-italy-accuses-of-people-smuggling/.

Borelli, Lisa Marie. 2022. "Tracing the Circulation of Emotions in Swiss Migration Enforcement: Organizational Dissonances, Emotional Contradictions and Frictions." *Identities* 31 (1): 47–64.

Boyce, Geoffrey A. 2018. "Appearing Out of Place: Automobility and the Everyday Policing and Suspicion on the IS/Canada Border." *Political Geography* 64: 1–12.

Briskman, Linda, and Lucy Fiske. 2016. "Creating Criminals: Australia's Response to Asylum Seekers and Refugees." In *The Immigrant Other: Lived Experiences in a Transnational World*, edited by Rich Furman, Greg Lamphear, and Douglas Epps. Columbia University Press.

Bubola, Emma, and Elisabetta Povoledo. 2024. "Matteo Salvini Acquitted After Blocking Rescue of Migrant Boat in Italy." *The New York Times*, December 20.

Burrell, Kathy, and Kathrin Hörschelmann. 2019. "Perilous Journeys: Visualizing the Racialized 'Refugee Crisis.'" *Antipode: A Radical Journal of Geography* 51 (1): 45–65.

Butler, Judith. 2004. *Precarious Life: The Powers of Mourning and Violence*. Verso.

Bibliography

Buzan, Barry, Ole Waever, and Jaap De Wilde. 1998. *Security: A New Framework for Analysis*. Lynne Rienner Publishers.

Caldeira, Teresa P. 2000. *City Walls: Crime, Segregation and Citizenship in São Paulo*. University of California Press.

Calhoun, Craig. 1993. *Habermas and the Public Sphere*. MIT Press.

Capone, Francesco, and Luciana Lazzeretti. 2016. "Fashion and City Branding. An Analysis of the Perception of Florence as a Fashion City." *Journal of Global Fashion Marketing* 7 (3): 166–80.

Cappuccini, Monica. 2018. *Austerity and Democracy in Athens*. Palgrave Macmillan.

Castelli Gattinara, Pietro. 2016. *The Politics of Migration in Italy: Perspectives on Local Debates and Party Competition*. Routledge.

Cesari, Jocelyne. 2012. "Securitization of Islam in Europe." *Die Welt Des Islams* 52 (3–4): 430–49.

Charlton, Joseph. 2013. "Greek Anti-Fascist Rapper Murdered by 'Neo-Nazi' Golden Dawn." *The Independent*, September 19. https://www.independent.co.uk/news/world/europe/greek-antifascist-rapper-murdered-by-neonazi-golden-dawn-supporter-8824664.html.

Christopoulou, Nadina, and Mary Leontsini. 2017. "Weaving Solidarity: Migrant Women's Organisations in Athens," *Journal of Intercultural Studies* 38 (5): 514–29.

Chouliaraki, Lilie, and Pierluigi Musaro. 2017. "The Mediatized Border: Technologies and afeects of Migrant Reception in the Greek and Italian Borders." *Feminist Media Studies* 17 (4): 535–49.

Ciucci, Alessandra. 2022. *The Voice of the Rural: Music, Poetry, Masculinity Among Migrant Moroccan Men in Umbria*. University of Chicago Press.

Collingwood, Loren, and Benjamin Gonzales O'Brien. 2019. *Sanctuary Cities: The Politics of Refuge*. Oxford University Press.

Côté, Adam. 2016. "Agents Without Agency: Assessing the Role of the Audience in Securitization Theory." *Security Dialogue* 47 (6): 541–58.

Crabapple, Molly. 2020. "The Attack on Exarcheia, an Anarchist Refuge in Athens." *New Yorker*, January 20. https://www.newyorker.com/news/dispatch/the-attack-on-exarchia-an-anarchist-refuge-in-athens.

Crawley, Heaven, and Dimitris Skleparis. 2018. "Refugees, Migrants, Neither, Both: Categorical Fetishism and the Politics of Bounding in Europe's 'Migration Crisis.'" *Journal of Ethnic and Migration Studies* 44 (1): 48–64.

Crepeau, François, Delphine Nakache, Michael Collyer, Nathaniel H. Goetz, Art Hansen, Renu Modi, Aninia Nadig, Sanja Spoljar Vrzina, and Loes H. M. van Willingen. 2006. *Forced Migration and Global Processes*. Rowman and Littlefield.

Cronache di Ordinario Razzismo (Chronicles of Ordinary Racism). 2016. "Mafia Extortion Aggravated by Racism: Arrests and Confiscations in Palermo." November 8.

Cusumano, Eugenio, and Flora Bell. 2021. "Guilt by Association? The Criminalisation of Sea Rescue NGOs in Italian Media." *Journal of Ethnic and Migration Studies* 47 (19): 4285–4307.

Cusumano, Eugenio, and Marianne Riddervold. 2023. "Failing Through: European Migration Governance Across the Central Mediterranean." *Journal of Ethnic and Migration Studies* 49 (12): 3024–42.

Cuttitta, Paulo. 2018. "Repoliticization Through Search and Rescue? Humanitarian NGOs and Migration Management in the Central Mediterranean." *Geopolitics* 23 (3): 632–60.

Danewid, Ida. 2017. "White Innocence in the Black Mediterranean: Hospitality and the Erasure of History." *Third World Quarterly* 38 (7): 1674–89.

D'Angelo, Alessio. 2018. "Italy: The 'Illegality Factory'? Theory and Practice of Refugees' Reception in Sicily." *Journal of Ethnic and Migration Studies* 45 (12): 2213–26.

Darling, Jonathan, and Harald Bauder, eds. 2019. *Sanctuary Cities and Urban Struggles: Rescaling Migration, Citizenship, and Rights.* Manchester University Press.

De Genova, Nicholas. 2010. "Migration and Race in Europe: The Trans-Atlantic Metastases of a Postcolonial Cancer." *European Journal of Social Theory* 13 (3): 405–19.

De Genova, Nicholas. 2013. "Spectacles of Migrant Illegality: The Scene of Exclusion, the Obscene of Inclusion." *Ethnic and Racial Studies* 36 (7): 1180–98.

De Genova, Nicholas. 2017. *The Borders of Europe: Autonomy of Migration, Tactics of Bordering.* Duke University Press.

De Genova, Nicholas. 2018a. "Europe's Racial Borders." *Monitor Racism*, January.

De Genova, Nicholas. 2018b. "The 'Migrant Crisis' as Racial Crisis: Do Black Lives Matter in Europe?" *Ethnic and Racial Studies* 41 (10): 1765–82.

De Graauw, Els. 2016. *Making Immigrant Rights Real: Non-Politics and the Politics of Integration in San Francisco.* Cornell University Press.

De Haas, Hein. 2008. "The Myth of Invasion: The Inconvenient Realities of African Migration to Europe." *Third World Quarterly* 29 (7): 1305–22.

De Vries, Leonie Ansems, and Elisabeth Guild. 2018. "Seeking Refuge in Europe: Spaces of Transit and the Violence of Migration Management." *Journal of Ethnic and Migration Studies* 45 (12): 2156–66.

Delgado, Melvin. 2018. *Sanctuary Cities, Communities, and Organizations: A Nation at a Crossroads.* Oxford University Press.

Della Porta, Donatella. 2018. *Solidarity Mobilizations in the "Refugee Crisis": Contentious Moves.* Palgrave Macmillan.

Della Porta, Donatella, and Elias Steinhilper, eds. 2022. *Contentious Migrant Solidarity: Shrinking Spaces and Civil Society Contestation.* Routledge.

De Tocqueville, Alexis. (1856) 2008. *The Ancien Régime and the French Revolution.* Edited and translated by Gerald Bevan. Penguin.

De Wilde, Mandy, and Jan W. Duyvendak. 2016. "Engineering Community

Spirit: The Pre-Figurative Politics of Affective Citizenship in Dutch Local Governance." *Citizenship Studies* 20 (8): 973–93.

Dezalay, Sara. 2020. "Introduction: Wars on Law, Wars Through Law? Law and Lawyers in Times of Crisis." *Journal of Law and Society* 47: S1–S13.

Di Gregorio, Michael, and Jessica L. Merolli. 2016. "Introduction: Affective Citizenship and the Politics of Identity, Control, Resistance." *Citizenship Studies* 20 (8): 933–42.

Di Maio, Alessandra. 2021. "The Black Mediterranean: A View from Sicily." *Transition* 132: 34–53.

Dijstelbloem, Huub, and William Walters. 2021. "Atmospheric Border Politics: The Morphology of Migration and Solidarity Practices in Europe." *Geopolitics* 26 (2): 497–520.

Dikeç, Mustafa. 2007. *Badlands of the Republic: Space, Politics and Urban Policy*. Wiley.

Diken, Bülent. 2004. "From Refugee Camps to Gated Communities: Biopolitics and the End of the City." *Citizenship Studies* 8 (1): 83–106.

Di Rosa, Roberta T., and Giuseppina Tumminelli. 2022. "Diversification of Diversity: Migrations, Cultural Pluralism and Urban Transformations in Palermo (Italy): A Case Study." *Current Sociology Monograph* 70 (2): 275–90.

Duarte, Melina. 2020. "The Ethical Consequences of Criminalizing Solidarity in the EU." *Theoria* 86 (1): 28–53.

Duneier, Mitchell, Philip Kasinitz, and Alexandra Murphy, eds. 2014. *The Urban Ethnography Reader*. Oxford University Press.

Duyvendak, Jan W., Josip Kešić, and Timothy Stacey. 2023. *The Return of the Native: Can Liberalism Safeguard Us Against Nativism?* Oxford University Press.

Dzenovska, Dace. 2017. "We Want to Hear from You,' Reporting as Bordering in the Political Space of Europe." In *The Borders of "Europe": Autonomy of Migration, Tactics of Bordering*, edited by Nicholas De Genova. Duke University Press.

Einashe, Ismail. 2016. "Meet the Migrants Who Are Helping Italians Take on the Sicilian Mob." *International Business Time*, October 14.

Einashe, Ismail. 2020. "How Sicily Inspires African Love Ballads and New Stars." *BBC News*, December 12. https://www.bbc.com/news/world-africa-55257978.

Ellermann, Antje. 2006. "Street-Level Democracy: How Immigration Bureaucrats Manage Public Opposition." *West European Politics* 29 (2): 293–309.

El Qadim, Nora, Beste İşleyen, Leonie Ansems de Vries, Signe S. Hansen, Sibel Karadağ, Debbie Lisle, and Damien Simonneau. 2021. "(Im)Moral Borders in Practice." *Geopolitics* 26 (5): 1608–38.

Enroth, Henrik. 2017. "Fear as a Political Factor." *International Political Sociology* 11 (1): 55–72.

Fabini, Giulia. 2017. "Managing Illegality at the Internal Border: Governing

Through 'Differential Inclusion' in Italy." *European Journal of Criminology* 14 (1): 46–62.

Fallon, Katy. 2022. "It Is an Atrocity Against Humankind: Greek Pushbacks Blamed for Double Drowning." *The Guardian*, February 17.

Fallon, Katy. 2023. "'Very Worrying': Three Far-Right Parties Enter Greek Parliament." *Al Jazeera*, June 30. https://www.aljazeera.com/news/2023/6/30/very-worrying-three-far-right-parties-enter-greek-parliament.

Fallon, Katy, and Ans Boersma. 2020. "'There Is No Future': The Refugees Who Became Pawns in Erdoğan's Game." *The Guardian*, May 8. https://www.the guardian.com/global-development/2020/may/08/erdogan-turkey-refugees -pawns-game.

Fallon, Katy, Giorgos Christides, Julian Busch, and Lydia Emmanouilidou. 2023. "Greek Shipwreck: Hi-Tech Investigation Suggests Coastguard Responsible for Sinking." *The Guardian*, July 10. https://www.theguardian.com/global-de velopment/2023/jul/10/greek-shipwreck-hi-tech-investigation-suggests-coast guard-responsible-for-sinking.

Fassin, Didier. 2005. "Compassion and Repression: The Moral Economy of Immigration Policies in France." *Cultural Anthropology* 20 (3): 362–87.

Fassin, Didier. 2011. *Humanitarian Reason: A Moral History of the Present*. University of California Press.

Fassin, Didier. 2020. "Introduction: Connecting Borders and Boundaries." In *Deepening Divides*, edited by Didier Fassin. Pluto Press.

Fekete, Liz. 2009. *A Suitable Enemy: Racism, Migration, and Islamophobia in Europe*. Pluto Press.

Feldman, Gregory. 2011. *The Migration Apparatus: Security, Labor, and Policymaking in the European Union*. Stanford University Press.

Feldman, Gregory. 2019. *The Gray Zone: Sovereignty, Human Smuggling, and Undercover Police Investigation in Europe*. Stanford University Press.

Ferreira, Susana. 2019. *Human Security and Migration in Europe's Southern Borders*. Palgrave Macmillan.

Fischer, Leandros, and Martin Bak Jørgensen. 2021. "'We Are Here to Stay' Vs. 'Europe's Best Hotel': Hamburg and Athens as Geographies of Solidarity." *Antipode* 53 (24): 1062–82.

Fossum, John E., Riva Kastoryano, Tariq Modood, and Ricard Zapata-Barrero. 2023. "Governing Diversity in the Multilevel European Public Space." *Ethnicities* 24 (1): 3–30.

Frazzetta, Federica, and Gianni Piazza. 2022. "Emotions in Shrinking Spaces for Migrant Solidarity: The Protest Campaign in the 'Diciotti Ship Affair.'" In *Contentious Migrant Solidarity: Shrinking Spaces and Civil Society Contestation*, edited by Donatella Della Porta and Elias Steinhilper. Routledge.

Fregonese, Sara, Beste İşleyen, Jonathan Rokem, and Nando Sigona. 2020. "Reading Reece Jones's Violent Borders: Refugees and the Right to Move." *Political Geography* 79: 2–9.

Fukuyama, Francis. 2006. *The End of History and the Last Man.* Free Press.

Furedi, Frank. 2005. *Politics of Fear.* Continuum.

Furedi, Frank. 2007. *Invitation to Terror: The Expanding Empire of the Unknown.* Continuum.

Gambetta, Diego. 1993. *The Sicilian Mafia: The Business of Private Protection.* Harvard University Press.

Giglioli, Ilaria. 2017. "From 'A Frontier Land' to 'A Piece of North Africa in Italy': The Changing Politics of 'Tunisianness' in Mazara del Vallo, Sicily." *International Journal of Urban and Regional Research* 41 (5): 749–66.

Giglioli, Ilaria. 2021. "On Not Being European Enough: Migration, Crisis, and Precarious Livelihoods on the Periphery of Europe." *Social & Cultural Geography* 22 (5): 725–44.

Giuffrida, Angela. 2019. "Italian PM Resigns with Attack on 'Opportunist' Salvini." *The Guardian*, August 20. https://www.theguardian.com/world/2019/aug/20/italian-pm-expected-resign-giuseppe-conte.

Giuffrida, Angela. 2021. "Matteo Salvini Objects to Richard Gere as Witness in Kidnap Trial." *The Guardian*, October 23. https://www.theguardian.com/world/2021/oct/23/matteo-salvini-goes-on-trial-for-kidnap-over-blocked-migrant-ship.

Glück, Zoltán. 2015. "Piracy and the Production of Security Space." *Environment and Planning D: Society and Space* 33 (4): 642–59.

Glück, Zoltán. 2017. "Security Urbanism and the Counterterror State in Kenya." *Anthropological Theory* 17 (3): 297–321.

Glück, Zoltán, and Setha Low. 2017. "A Sociospatial Framework for the Anthropology of Security." *Anthropological Theory* 17 (3): 281–96.

Gökariksel, Banu, and Anna Secor. 2018. "Affective Geopolitics: Anxiety, Pain, and Ethics in the Encounter with Syrian Refugees in Turkey." *EPC: Politics and Space* 38 (7–8): 1237–55.

Goldstein, Daniel M. 2010. "Toward a Critical Anthropology of Security." *Current Anthropology* 51 (4): 389–490.

Gowayed, Heba. 2022. *Refuge: How the State Shapes Human Potential.* Princeton University Press.

Gozzi, Laura. 2024. "Europe Approves Major Overhaul of Migration Rules." *BBC*, April 10.

Gramsci, Antonio. (1995) 2009. *The Southern Question.* Guernica.

Gregory, Derek, and Allan Pred, eds. 2007. *Violent Geographies: Fear, Terror, and Political Violence.* Routledge.

Grigolo, Michele. 2011. "Incorporating Cities into the EU Anti-Discrimination Policy: Between Race Discrimination and Migrant Rights." *Ethnic and Racial Studies* 34 (10): 1751–69.

Grimson, Alejandro, and Brigida Renoldi. 2019. "Borderization and Public Security in Argentina." In *Spaces of Security: Ethnographies of Security Scapes, Surveillance and Control*, edited by Setha Low and Mark Maguire. New York University Press.

Grossi, Tommaso, and Niccolò Barca. 2022. "Italy's Social Democrats Are Adrift." *Politico.eu*, October 19. https://www.politico.eu/article/italy-social-democrats -are-adrift/.

The Guardian. 2019. "Migrant Ship Heads for Italy's Waters After Judge Over-rules Salvini." August 14. https://www.theguardian.com/world/2019/aug/14/ migrant-ship-heads-for-italys-waters-after-judge-overrules-salvini.

The Guardian. 2019. "Greece to Replace Island Refugee Camps with 'Detention Centres.'" November 20. https://www.theguardian.com/global-development/ 2019/nov/20/greece-to-replace-island-refugee-camps-with-detention-centres.

The Guardian. 2024. "The Brutal Truth Behind Italy's Migrant Reduction: Beatings and Rape by EU-funded Forces in Tunisia." September 19. https://www .theguardian.com/global-development/2024/sep/19/italy-migrant-reduction -investigation-rape-killing-tunisia-eu-money-keir-starmer-security-forces.

Guild, Elspeth. 2004. "Who Is an Irregular Migrant?" In *Irregular Migration and Human Rights: Theoretical, European and International Perspectives*, edited by Barbara Bogusz, Ryszard Cholewinski, Adam Cygan, and Erika Szyszczak. Brill.

Guild, Elspeth. 2006. "Protection, Threat and Movement of Persons: Examining the Relationship Between Terrorism and Migration in EU Law After September 11." In *Forced Migration and Global Processes*, edited by François Crepeau et al. Rowman and Littlefield.

Guild, Elspeth. 2009. *Security and Migration in the 21st Century*. Polity Press.

Hagan, Maria, and Sebastien Bachelet. 2024. "Insidious Harassment: Criminalisation, Solidarity, and Migration in France and Morocco." *Antipode* 56: 1308–28.

Hagmann, Jonas. 2017. "Security in the Society of Control: The Politics and Practices of Securing Urban Spaces." *International Political Sociology* 11 (4): 418–38.

Hall, John A. 1992. "Trust in Tocqueville." *Policy, Organisation and Society* 5 (1): 16–24.

Hall, John A. 2013. *The Importance of Being Civil: The Struggle for Political Decency*. Princeton University Press.

Harvey, David. 2003. "The Right to the City." *International Journal of Urban and Regional Research* 27 (4): 939–41.

Harvey, David. 2008. "The Right to the City." *New Left Review* 53: 23–40.

Hawthorne, Camilla. 2022. *Contesting Race and Citizenship: Youth Politics in the Black Mediterranean*. Cornell University Press.

Heller, Charles. 2021. "(Un)Contentious Solidarity at Sea: The Shifting Politics of Nongovernmental Rescue Activities in the Mediterranean." In *Contentious Migrant Solidarity: Shrinking Spaces and Civil Society Contestation*, edited by Donatella Della Porta and Elias Steinhilper. Routledge.

Heller, Charles, and Lorenzo Pezzani. 2017. "Liquid Traces: Investigating the Deaths of Migrants at the EU's Maritime Frontier." In *The Borders of "Europe": Autonomy of Migration, Tactics of Bordering*. Duke University Press.

Hernández, Tanya Katerí. 2013. *Racial Subordination in Latin America: The Role of the State, Customary Law, and the New Civil Rights Response.* Cambridge University Press.

Herzfeld, Michael. 1987. *Anthropology Through the Looking-Glass: Critical Ethnography on the Margins of Europe.* Cambridge University Press.

Heyer, Karl. 2022. "Keeping Migrants at the Margins. Governing Through Ambiguity and the Politics of Discretion in the Post 2015 European Migration and Border Regime." *Political Geography* 98: 102643.

Hintjens, Helen, and Ahmed Puori. 2014. "Toward Cities of Safety and Sanctuary." *Peace Review: A Journal of Social Justice* 26 (2): 218–24.

Hinze, Annika M. 2013. *Turkish Berlin: Integration Policy and Urban Space.* University of Minnesota Press.

Hirschon, Renée, ed. 2003. *Crossing the Aegean: An Appraisal of the 1923 Compulsory Population Exchange between Greece and Turkey.* Berghahn Books.

Hom, Stephanie Malia. 2019. *Empire's Mobius Strip: Historical Echoes in Italy's Crisis of Migration and Detention.* Cornell University Press

Horowitz, Jason. 2019. "Palermo Is Again a Migrant City Shaped Now by Bangladeshis and Nigerians." *New York Times*, May 22.

Houben, Hubert. 2013. "Between Occidental and Oriental Cultures: Norman Sicily as a 'Third Space?'". In *Norman Tradition and Transcultural Heritage*, edited by S. Burkhardt and T. Foerster. Taylor & Francis.

Hutchison, Emma, and Roland Bleiker. 2014. "Theorizing Emotions in World Politics." *International Theory* 6 (3): 491–514.

Işin, Engin. 2018. "Mobile Peoples: Transversal Configurations." *Social Inclusion* 6 (1): 115–23.

İşleyen, Beste. 2023. "Affective Politics of Migration Control: A Postcolonial Approach." *European Security* 32 (3): 367–84.

Jasper, James. 2011. "Emotions and Social Movements: Twenty Years of Theory and Research." *Annual Review of Sociology* 37 (August): 285–303.

Johnson, Corey, Reece Jones, Anssi Paasi, Louise Amoore, Alison Mountz, Mark Salter, and Chris Rumford. 2011. "Interventions on Rethinking 'the Border' in Border Studies." *Political Geography* 30 (2): 61–69.

Johnson, Heather. 2012. "Moments of Solidarity, Migrant Activism and Non-Citizens at Global Borders: Political Agency at Tanzanian Refugee Camps, Australian Detention Centers and European Borders." In *Citizenship, Migrant Activism, and the Politics of Movement*, edited by Peter Nyers and Kim Rygiel. Routledge.

Jones, Gavin. 2018. "Italy Will No Longer Be 'Europe's Refugee Camp,' Vows New Government." Reuters. https://www.reuters.com/article/idUSKCN1J017N/.

Jones, Reese. 2012. *Border Walls: Security and the War on Terror in the United States, India and Israel.* Zed Books.

Jones, Reece. 2016. *Violent Borders: Refugees and the Right to Move.* Verso.

Jones, Reece. 2018. "Violence in Asian Borderlands." In *Routledge Handbook of*

Asian Borderlands, edited by Alexander Hostmann, Martin Saxer, and Alessandro Rippa. Routledge.

Jones, Reece. 2021. *White Borders: The History of Race and Immigration in the United States from Chinese Exclusion to the Border Wall.* Beacon Press.

Jones, Reece, and Corey Johnson. 2014. *Placing the Border in Everyday Life.* Routledge.

Kakissis, Joanna. 2020. "Golden Dawn: Greek Court Delivers Landmark Verdicts Against Neo-Nazi Party." NPR, October 7.

Karageorgiou, Eleni. 2016. "Solidarity and Sharing in the Common European Asylum System: The Case of Syrian Refugees." *European Politics and Society* 17 (2): 196–214.

Karakoulaki, Marianna. 2019. "Framing Solidarity as Terrorism: Greek Media and Refugee Squat Evictions in Athens." Media Diversity Institute.

Karyotis, Georgios. 2012. "Securitization of Migration in Greece: Process, Motives, and Implications." *International Political Sociology* 6 (4): 390–408.

Karyotis, Georgios, and Dimitris Skleparis. 2016. "Resistance to the Criminalization of Migration: Migrant Protest in Greece." In *The Immigrant Other: Lived Experiences in a Transnational World,* edited by Rich Furman, Greg Lamphear, and Douglas Epps. Columbia University Press.

Kasaba, Reşat. 2009. *A Moveable Empire: Ottoman Nomads, Migrants and Refugees.* University of Washington Press.

Kayaoğlu, Ayşegül. 2022. "Do Refugees Cause Crime?" *World Development* 154: 105858.

Kingsley, Patrick. 2018. " 'Better to Drown': A Greek Refugee Camp's Epidemic of Misery." *New York Times,* October 2. https://www.nytimes.com/2018/10/02/world/europe/greece-lesbos-moria-refugees.html.

Kirchgaessner, Stephanie. 2015. "From Mafia City to a Haven for Refugees: Palermo Moves on from Its Criminal Past." *The Guardian,* December 27. https://www.theguardian.com/world/2015/dec/27/palermo-rejects-mafia-safe-haven-refugees-sicily-mayor-leoluca-orlando.

Kitsantonis, Niki, and Iliana Magra. 2020. "Golden Dawn Found Guilty of Running Criminal Organization in Greece." *New York Times,* October 7. https://www.nytimes.com/2020/10/07/world/europe/golden-dawn-guilty-verdict-greece.html.

Koizumi, Koichi, and Gerhard Hoffstaedter. 2018. *Urban Refugees: Challenges in Protection, Services and Policy.* Routledge.

Kolankiewicz, Marta, and Maja Sager. 2021. "Clandestine Migration Facilitation and Border Spectacle: Criminalisation, Solidarity, Contestations." *Mobilities* 16 (4): 584–96.

Komporozos-Athanasiou, Aris, and Nina Papachristou. 2018. "Migration and Citizenship in 'Athens of Crisis': An Interview with Vice Mayor Lefteris Papagiannakis." *Migration and Society Advances in Research* 1: 127–35.

Kuntz, Kathrin. 2022. "A Parliament of Exiled Afghan Women in Athens." *Der Spiegel,* February 8. https://www.spiegel.de/international/europe/athens-parli

ament-of-exiled-afghan-women-making-their-voices-be-heard-a-67c41c9d
-9f76-47eb-bef8-330bc3bbef46.

Lampredi, Giacomo. 2024. "The Intimate Life of Criminalization: Affective Governance Contentious Migrant Solidarity." *Ethnic and Racial Studies* 47 (4): 721–41.

Landau, Loren B. 2019. "A Chronotope of Containment Development: Europe's Migrant Crisis and Africa's Reterritorialisation." *Antipode* 51 (1): 169–86.

Lee, Matthew T., and Ramiro Martinez. 2009. "Immigration Reduces Crime: An Emerging Scholarly Consensus." *Sociology of Crime, Law and Deviance* 13: 3–16.

Lee, Matthew T., Ramiro Martinez, and Richard Rosenfeld. 2001. "Does Immigration Increase Homicide? Negative Evidence From Three Border Cities," *Sociological Quarterly* 42 (4): 559–80.

Lefebvre, Henri. 1992. *The Production of Space*. Translated by Donald Nicholson-Smith. Wiley Blackwell.

Lefebvre, Henri. 2017. *Everyday Life in the Modern World*. Routledge.

Léonard, Sarah, and Christian Kaunert. 2019. *Refugees, Security and the European Union*. Routledge.

Léonard, Sarah, and Christian Kaunert. 2022. "De-centring the Securitisation of Asylum and Migration in the European Union: Securitisation, Vulnerability and the Role of Turkey." *Geopolitics* 27 (3): 729–51.

Lewek, Mirjam. 2016. "Spaces of Fear and their Exclusionary Consequences: Narratives and Everyday Routines of Sub-Saharan Immigrants in Berlin." In *Creating the Unequal City: The Exclusionary Consequences of Everyday Routines in Berlin*, edited by Talja Blokland, Carlotta Giustozzi, Daniela Krüger, and Hannah Schilling. Routledge.

LIFO. 2019. "Πώς ο δήμος Αθηναίων έγινε ευρωπαϊκό παράδειγμα για τη διαχείριση του προσφυγικού" (How the Municipality of Athens Became a European Example for Handling the Refugee Crisis). April 24.

Lipsky, Michael. 1980. *Street-Level Bureaucracy: Dilemmas of the Individual in Public Services*. Russell Sage Foundation.

Low, Setha. 1997. "Urban Fear: Building the Fortress City." *City and Society* 9 (1): 53–71.

Low, Setha. 2001. "The Edge and the Center: Gated Communities and the Discourse of Urban Fear." *American Anthropologist*, n.s., 103 (1): 45–58.

Low, Setha. 2003. *Behind the Gates: Life, Security, and the Pursuit of Happiness in Fortress America*. Routledge.

Low, Setha, and Mark Maguire, eds. 2019. *Spaces of Security: Ethnographies of Securityscapes, Surveillance, and Control*. NYU Press.

MacAllan, Sarah. 2019. "Object Study: The Tombstone of Anne: A Case Study of Multilingualism in Twelfth Century Sicily." *ANU Historical Journal* 2 (1): 179–89.

Maffeis, Stephania. 2021. "The Palermo Charter Process. Towards the Recognition of Migration as a Human Right Movements." *Journal for Critical Migration and Border Regime Studies* 6 (1).

Maguire, Mark, Catarina Frois, and Nils Zurawski, eds. 2014. *The Anthropology of Security: Perspectives from the Frontline of Policing, Counterterrorism and Border Control.* Pluto Press.

Makari, George. 2021. *Of Fear and Strangers.* W. W Norton and Co.

Mamo, Alessio, and Lorenzo Tondo. 2018. " 'We Have Found Hell': Drawings Reveal Children's Trauma at Lesbos Camp." *The Guardian*, October 3. https://www.theguardian.com/global-development/2018/oct/03/trauma-runs-deep-for-children-at-dire-lesbos-camp-moria.

Mancina, Peter. 2013. "The Birth of a Sanctuary City: A History of Governmental Sanctuary in San Francisco." In *Sanctuary Practices in International Perspectives: Migration, Citizenship and Social Movements*, edited by Randy K. Lippert and Sean Rehaag. Routledge.

Mansouri, Fethi, and Tariq Modood. 2020. "The Complementarity of Multiculturalism and Interculturalism: Theory Backed by Australian Evidence." *Ethnic and Racial Studies* 44 (2): 1–20.

Marchetti, Chiara. 2020. "Cities of Exclusion: Are Local Authorities Refusing Asylum Seekers?" In *Migration, Borders, and Citizenship: Between Policy and Public Spheres*, edited by Maurizio Ambrosini, Manlio Cinalli, and David Jacobson. Springer International.

Mattozzi, Savin. 2019. " 'Sicilians Have Affinity for the Islamic World in Their DNA.' " *Al Jazeera*, May 13. https://www.aljazeera.com/features/2019/5/13/sicilians-have-affinity-for-the-islamic-world-in-their-dna.

McKernan, Bethan, and Daniel Boffey. 2020. "Greece and Bulgaria Crack Down on Turkish Borders as Refugees Arrive." *The Guardian*, February 28. https://www.theguardian.com/world/2020/feb/28/tensions-rise-between-turkey-and-russia-after-killing-of-troops-in-syria.

Megoran, Nick. 2005. "The Critical Geopolitics of Danger in Uzbekistan and Kyrgyzstan." *Environment and Planning D: Society and Space* 23 (4): 555–80.

Merelli, Annalisa, and Gianfranco Rosi. 2017. "Rescuing Refugees Is a Matter of Common Sense for the Paradisiacal Mediterranean Island of Lampedusa." *Quartz*, February 3. https://qz.com/678164/in-the-mediterranean-paradise-of-lampedusa-rescuing-refugees-and-migrants-is-a-matter-of-common-sense.

Meyer, David S., and Suzanne Staggenborg. 1996. "Movements, Countermovements, and the Structure of Political Opportunity." *American Journal of Sociology* 101 (6): 1628–60.

Mezzadra, Sandro, and Brett Neilson. 2013. *Border as Method; or, the Multiplication of Labor.* Duke University Press.

Migdal, Joel S. 2001. *State in Society: Studying How States and Societies Transform and Constitute One Another.* Cambridge University Press.

Milan, Chiara. 2018. "Emotions That Mobilise: The Emotional Basis of Pro-Asylum Seeker Activism in Austria." In *Solidarity Mobilizations in the "Refu-*

gee Crisis": *Contentious Moves*, edited by Donatella della Porta. Palgrave Macmillan.

Modood, Tariq. 2005. *Multicultural Politics: Racism, Ethnicity and Muslims in Britain*. Edinburgh University Press.

Modood, Tariq. (2007) 2013. *Multiculturalism: A Civic Idea*. Polity.

Mollenkopf, John, and Manuel Pastor, eds. 2016. *Unsettled Americans: Metropolitan Context and Civic Leadership for Immigrant Integration*. Cornell University Press.

Monroe, Kristin V. 2016. *The Insecure City: Space, Power, and Mobility in Beirut*. Rutgers University Press.

Montesquieu. (1721) 1973. *Persian Letters*. Translated by C. J. Betts. Penguin.

Montesquieu. (1748) 1977. *The Spirit of Laws*. University of California Press.

Morgan, Kimberly J., and Ann S. Orloff, eds. 2017. *The Many Hands of the State: Theorizing Political Authority and Social Control*. Cambridge University Press.

Moulin, Carolina. 2012. "Ungrateful Subjects: Refugee Protests and the Logic of Gratitude." In *Citizenship, Migrant Activism, and the Politics of Movement*, edited by Peter Nyers and Kim Rygiel. Routledge.

Mountz, Alison. 2020. *The Death of Asylum: The Hidden Geographies of Enforcement Archipelago*. University of Minnesota Press.

Mountz, Alison, and Nancy Hiemstra. 2014. "Chaos and Crisis: Dissecting the Spatiotemporal Logics of Contemporary Migrations and State Practices." *Annals of the Association of American Geographers* 104 (2): 382–90.

Müller, Jan-Werner. 2016. *What Is Populism?* University of Pennsylvania Press.

National Herald. 2012. "New Democracy Will Clean Out, Cleaning Up Exarchia." August 12. https://www.thenationalherald.com/new-democracy-will-clean-out-clean-up-exarchia/.

Nee, Victor, and Jimmy Sanders. 2001. "Trust in Ethnic Ties: Social Capital and Immigrants." In *Trust in Society*, edited by Karen S. Cook. Russell Sage Foundation.

Neil, Margaret. 2024. " 'We Welcome Migrants and the Tourists Come': Postmodern Hospitality in Palermo, Sicily." *Journal of the Royal Anthropological Institute*: 1–18.

New York Times. 2020. "There's a New Game of Thrones in the Mediterranean." August 31. https://www.nytimes.com/2020/08/30/opinion/turkey-greece-oil-gas.html.

Nicholls Walter. 2015. "Policing Migrants as Politicizing Immigration: The Paradox of Border Enforcement." *ACME, An International Journal of Critical Geographies* 14 (2): 512–21.

Nicholls, Walter J., and Justus Uitermark. 2017. *Cities and Social Movements: Immigrant Rights Activism in the US, France, and the Netherlands, 1970–2015*. Wiley Blackwell.

Norris, Pippa, and Ronald Inglehart. 2019. *Cultural Backlash: Trump, Brexit, and Authoritarian Populism*. Cambridge University Press.

O'Brien, Benjamin Gonzalez, Loren Collingwood, and Stephen Omar El-Khatib. 2017. "The Politics of Refuge: Sanctuary Cities, Crime, and Undocumented Immigration." *Urban Affairs Review* 55 (1): 3–40.

Orlando, Leoluca. 2001. *Fighting the Mafia and Renewing Sicilian Culture*. Encounter Books.

Örs, Ilay Romain. 2021. *Diaspora of the City: Stories of Cosmopolitanism from Istanbul and Athens*. Palgrave.

Osborne, Samuel. 2019. "Italy Passes Law to Fine People Who Rescue Refugees at Sea." *The Independent*, June 12. https://www.independent.co.uk/news/world/europe/italy-refugee-rescue-fine-emergency-decree-fine-boats-matteo-salvini-a8954986.html.

Özyürek, Esra. 2007. *The Politics of Public Memory in Turkey*. Syracuse University Press.

Özyürek, Esra. 2009. "Convert Alert: German Muslims and Turkish Christians as Threats to Security in the New Europe," *Comparative Studies in Society and History* 51 (1): 91–116.

Özyürek, Esra. 2018. Rethinking Empathy: Emotions Triggered by the Holocaust Among the Muslim-Minority in Germany. *Anthropological Theory* 18 (4): 456–77.

Özyürek, Esra. 2023. *Subcontractors of Guilt: Holocaust Memory and Muslim Belonging in Postwar Germany*. Stanford University Press.

Pain, Rachel. 2001. "Gender, Race, Age and Fear in the City." *Urban Studies* 38 (5–6): 899–913.

Pain, Rachel. 2009. "Globalized Fear? Towards an Emotional Geopolitics." *Progress in Human Geography* 33 (4): 466–86.

Pain, Rachel, and Susan Smith, eds. 2008. *Fear: Critical Geopolitics and Everyday Life*. Ashgate.

Palm, Anja. 2017. "The Italy-Libya Memorandum of Understanding: The Baseline of a Policy Approach Aimed at Closing All Doors to Europe?—EU Immigration and Asylum Law and Policy." *EU Migration Law* (blog). https://eumigrationlawblog.eu/the-italy-libya-memorandum-of-understanding-the-baseline-of -a-policy-approach-aimed-at-closing-all-doors-to-europe/.

Palmas, Luca Queirolo. 2020. "Back to the Sicilian Landing Sites: Exploring a Borderland Through a Refugee Gaze." *Journal of Contemporary Ethnography* 49 (6): 853–80.

Panebianco, Stefania. 2022. "Migration Governance in the Mediterranean: The Siracusa Experience." *Geopolitics* 27 (3): 752–72.

Papagiannakis, Lefteris. 2024. "The Cost of the Tough but Fair Policy." *Rosa*, June 28. https://www.rosa.gr/prosfygiko/to-kostos-tis-skliris-alla-dikaiis-politikis/?fbclid=IwZXh0bgNhZW0CMTAAAR0Mn9sXqPUFnbgZglrvuuC9Wc5YtgKOk2iWIkSWoBHNMzbBNHcR5s5YPBw_aem_OL1pgktKoM67ed0CmQL12A.

Parekh, Serena. 2020. *No Refuge: Ethics and the Global Refugee Politics*. Oxford University Press.

Bibliography

Parla, Ayşe. 2019. *Precarious Hope: Migration and the Limits of Belonging in Turkey*. Stanford University Press.

Parsanoglou, Dimitris. 2020. "Volunteering for Refugees and the Repositioning of State Sovereignty and Civil Society: The Case of Greece." *Citizenship Studies* 24 (4): 457–73.

Pesarini, Angelica. 2021. "When the Mediterranean 'Became' Black: Diasporic Hopes and (Post)colonial Traumas." In *The Black Mediterranean: Bodies, Borders and Citizenship*, edited by Gabriele Proglio et al. Palgrave Macmillan.

Pettrachin, Andrea. 2022. "The Unexpected Dynamics of Politicisation of Migration: The Case of the Refugee Crisis in Sicily." *Mediterranean Politics* 27 (1): 29–56.

Pezzani, Lorenzo, and Charles Heller. 2013. "A Disobedient Gaze: Strategic Interventions in the Knowledge(s) of Maritime Borders." *Postcolonial Studies* 16 (3): 289–98.

Picone, Marco, and Chiara Giubilaro. 2022. "Migrations, Populisms and Emergencies: A Sicilian Case Study." In *Values, Cities and Migrations: Real Estate Market and Social System in a Multicultural City*, edited by Grazia Napoli, Giulio Mondini, Alessandra Oppio, Paolo Rosato, and Simona Barbaro. Springer International Publishing.

Politico. 2018. "Italian Mayors Rebel Against Salvini's Order to Block Migrant Ship." June 11.

Ponce, Aaron. 2023. "Ethnoracist Exclusion and Anti-immigrant Sentiment in Europe: A Hybrid Model Analysis Using the European Social Survey, 2002–2016." *Ethnicities*: 24 (1): 31–26.

Pradella, Lucia, and Rossana Cillo. 2021. "Bordering the Surplus Population Across the Mediterranean: Imperialism and Unfree Labour in Libya and the Italian Countryside." *Geoforum* 126: 483–94.

Proglio, Gabriele, et al. 2021. *The Black Mediterranean: Bodies, Borders and Citizenship*. Palgrave.

Purcell, Mark. 2003. "Excavating Lefebvre: The Right to the City and Its Urban Politics of the Inhabitant." *GeoJournal* 58.

Rabrenovic, Gordana, and Bunar Nihal. 2021. "Special Issue: Refugees and the City." *Journal of Urban Affairs* 43 (6).

Raimondi, Valeria. 2019. "For 'Common Struggles of Migrants and Locals': Migrant Activism and Squatting in Athens." *Citizenship Studies* 23 (6): 559–76.

Ramakrishnan, Karthick, and Tom Wong. 2010. "Partisanship, Not Spanish: Explaining Municipal Ordinances Affecting Undocumented Immigrants." In *Taking Local Control: Immigration Policy Activism in U.S. Cities and States*, edited by Monica Varsanyi. Stanford University Press.

Ridgley, Jennifer. 2008. "Cities of Refuge: Immigration Enforcement, Police, and the Insurgent Genealogies of Citizenship in U.S. Sanctuary Cities." *Urban Geography* 29 (1): 53–77.

Ridgley, Jennifer. 2013. "The City as a Sanctuary in the United States." In *Sanctuary Practices in International Perspectives: Migration, Citizenship and*

Social Movements, edited by Randy K. Lippert and Sean Rehaag. Routledge.

Roberts, Gillian. 2015. *Discrepant Parallels: Cultural Implications of the Canada-US Border*. McGill-Queen's University Press.

Robin, Corey. 2004. *Fear: The History of a Political Idea*. Oxford University Press.

Rossini, Francesco, and Esterina Nervino. 2019. "City Branding and Public Space: An Empirical Analysis of Dolce & Gabbana's Alta Moda Event in Naples." *Journal of Public Space* 4 (4): 61–82.

Rozakou, Katerina. 2012. "The Biopolitics of Hospitality in Greece: Humanitarianism and the Management of Refugees." *American Ethnologist* 39: 562–77.

Rozakou, Katerina. 2017. "Nonrecording the 'European Refugee Crisis' in Greece: Navigating Through Irregular Bureaucracy." *Focaal* 77: 36–49.

Rozakou, Katerina. 2024. "Ambivalent Feelings: 'Filotomo' in the Greek Migration Regime." *Identities* 31 (1): 31–46.

Sajed, Alina. 2012. "Securitized Migrants and Postcolonial (In)difference: The Politics of Activisms Among North African Migrants in France." In *Citizenship, Migrant Activism and the Politics of Movement*, edited by Peter Nyers and Kim Rygiel. Routledge.

Salmela, Mikko, and Christian von Scheve. 2017. "Emotional Roots of Right-Wing Political Populism." *Social Science Information* 56 (4): 567–95.

Scheppele, Kim Lane. 2017. "The Social Lives of Constitutions." In *Sociological Constitutionalism*, edited by Paul Blokker and Chris Thornhill. Cambridge University Press.

Schneider, Jane. 1998a. "The Dynamics of Neo-Orientalism in Italy (1848–1995)." In *Italy's "Southern Question": Orientalism in One Country*, edited by Jane Schneider. Bloomsbury Academic.

Schneider, Jane, ed. 1998b. *Italy's "Southern Question": Orientalism in One Country*. Berg Publishers.

Sciurba, Alessandra. 2017. "Categorizing Migrants by Undermining the Right to Asylum: The Implementation of the 'Hotspot Approach' in Sicily." *Etnografia e Ricerca Qualitativa* 1: 97–119.

Selod, Saher. 2016. "Criminalization of Muslim American Men in the United States." In *The Immigrant Other: Lived Experiences in a Transnational World*, edited by Rich Furman, Greg Lamphear, and Douglas Epps. Columbia University Press.

Selod, Saher. 2019. "Gendered Racialization: Muslim American Men and Women's Encounters with Racialized Surveillance." *Ethnic and Racial Studies* 42 (4): 552–69.

Sennett, Richard. 1998. *The Spaces of Democracy*. College of Architecture and Urban Planning, University of Michigan.

Shils, Edward. 1975. *Center and Periphery: Essays in Microsociology*. Chicago University Press.

Simon, Scott. 2023. "New Report Shows the Greece Coast Guard's Role in Boat

Capsizing that Killed Hundreds." NPR, July 15. https://www.npr.org/2023/ 07/15/1187929840/new-report-shows-the-greece-coast-guards-role-in-boat -capsizing-that-killed-hund.

Skleparis, Dimitris. 2016. "(In)Securitization and Illiberal Practices on the Fringe of the EU." *European Security* 25 (1): 92–111.

Skleparis, Dimitris. 2017. "The Politics of Migrant Resistance amid the Greek Economic Crisis." *International Political Sociology* 11 (2): 113–29.

Skleparis, Dimitris. 2018. " 'A Europe Without Walls, Without Fences, Without Borders': A Desecuritisation of Migration Doomed to Fail." *Political Studies* 66 (4): 985–1001.

Smith, Helena. 2013. "Greek Golden Dawn Member Arrested Over Murder of Leftwing Hip-hop Artist." *The Guardian*, September 18. https://www. theguardian.com/world/2013/sep/18/greece-murder-golden-dawn.

Sorge, Antonio. 2021. "Anxiety, Ambivalence, and the Violence of Expectations: Migrant Reception and Resettlement in Sicily." *Anthropological Forum* 31 (3): 256–74.

Spencer, Sarah, and Katharine Charsley. 2021. "Reframing 'Integration': Acknowledging and Addressing Five Core Critiques." *Comparative Migration Studies* 9 (18).

Squire, Vicki, and Jonathan Darling, "The 'Minor' Politics of Rightful Presence: Justice and Relationality in *City of Sanctuary*," *International Political Sociology* 7 (1): 59–74.

Squire, Vicki, Nina Perkowski, Nick Vaughan-Williams, and Dallal Stevens. 2021. *Reclaiming Migration: Voices from Europe's Migrant Crisis.* Manchester University Press.

Steil, Justin P., and Ion Bogdan Vasi. 2014. "The New Immigration Contestation: Social Movements and Local Immigration Policy Making in the United States, 2000–2011." *American Journal of Sociology* 119 (4): 1104–55.

Stierl, Maurice. 2016. "Contestations in Death: The Role of Grief in Migration Studies." *Citizenship Studies* 20 (2): 173–91.

Stierl, Maurice. 2017. "Excessive Migration: Excessive Governance: Border Entanglements in Greek-EU-rope." In *The Borders of Europe: Autonomy of Migration, Tactics of Bordering*, edited by Nicholas De Genova. Duke University Press.

Stivas, Dionysios. 2021. "Greece's Response to the European Refugee Crisis: A Tale of Two Securitizations." *Mediterranean Politics* 28 (1): 49–72.

Stivas, Dionysios. 2024. "Variations in the Intensity of the Securitization Narratives at the EU Level: Securitizing the European Refugee Crisis." *Frontiers in Political Science* 6: 1460531.

Stolle, Dietlind. 2001. "Clubs and Congregations: The Benefits of Joining. An Association." In *Trust in Society*, edited by Karen S. Cook. Russell Sage Foundation.

Sziarto, Kristin M., and Helga Leitner. 2010. "Immigrants Riding for Justice:

Space-time and Emotions in the Construction of a Counterpublic." *Political Geography* 29 (7): 381–91.

Tamkin, Emily. 2024. "Deep Dive: Palermo Patchwork." *Inkstick*, August 15. https://inkstickmedia.com/deep-dive-palermo-patchwork/.

Tarchi, Marco. 2015. "Italy: The Promised Land of Populism?" *Contemporary Italian Politics* 7 (3): 1–13

Tazzioli, Martina, and William Walters. 2019. "Migration, Solidarity and the Limits of Europe." *Global Discourse: An Interdisciplinary Journal of Current Affairs* 9 (1): 175–90.

Telles, Edward E. 2004. *Race in Another America: The Significance of Skin Color in Brazil*. Princeton University Press.

Thompson, Debra. 2013. "Through, Against and Beyond the Racial State: The Transnational Stratum of Race, March." *Cambridge Review of International Affairs* 26 (1).

Tondo, Lorenzo, and Sam Jones. 2024. "Italian Deputy PM Acquitted of Charges over Refusal to Let Migrant Ship Dock." *The Guardian*, December 20.

Tondo, Lorenzo, and Maurice Stierl. 2020. "Banksy Funds Refugee Rescue Boat Operating in Mediterranean." *The Guardian*, August 28. https://www.theguardian.com/world/2020/aug/27/banksy-funds-refugee-rescue-boat-operating-in-mediterranean.

Triandafyllidou, Anna. 2019. "The Migration Archipelago: Social Navigation and Migrant Agency." *International Migration* 57 (1): 5–19.

Triandafyllidou, Anna. 2022. "Decentering the Study of Migration Governance: A Radical View." *Geopolitics* 27 (3): 811–25.

Tsavdaroglou, Charalampos. 2024. "Homeless Migrants' Commoning Practices. 'Our House' Solidarity Project in Athens' Omonoia Square." *European Journal of Geography* 15 (1): 54–66.

Tsavdaroglou, Charalampos, and Maria Kaika. 2021. "The Refugees' Right to the Centre of the City: City Branding Versus City Commoning in Athens." *Urban Studies* 59 (6): 1130–47.

Turam, Berna. 2015. *Gaining Freedoms: Claiming Space in Istanbul and Berlin*. Stanford University Press.

Turam, Berna. 2021. "Refugees in Borderlands: Safe Places Versus Securitization in Athens, Greece." *Journal of Urban Affairs* 43 (6): 756–80.

Turam, Berna. 2023. "The Geopolitics of Fear: Pro-refugee Resistance to Europe's Racial Security." *Political Geography* 109: 103047.

Valentine, Gill. 1989. "The Geography of Women's fear." *Area* 21 (4): 385–90.

Vallet, Elisabeth, ed. 2014. *Borders, Fences, Walls: A State of Insecurity*. Ashgate.

Van den Berg, Esther, and Barbara Oomen. 2014. "Towards a Decentralization of Human Rights: The Rise of Human Rights Cities." In *The Future of Human Rights in an Urban World: Exploring Opportunities, Challenges, and Threats*, edited by Doutje Lettinga and Thijs Lindert. Amnesty International Netherlands.

Van der Zee, Renate. 2017. "He Fought the Mafia and Won: Now This Mayor Is Taking on Europe over Migrants." *The Guardian*, April 18. https://www. theguardian.com/global-development-professionals-network/2017/apr/18/he -fought-the-mafia-and-won-now-this-mayor-is-taking-on-europe-over -migrants.

Varsanyi, Monica. 2010. *Taking Local Control: Immigration Policy Activism in U.S. Cities and States*. Stanford University Press.

Vicino, Thomas, J., Hanlon, Bernadette, and Short, John Rennie. 2011. "A Typology of Urban Immigrant Neighborhoods." *Urban Geography* 32 (3): 383–405.

Vrabiescu, Ioana. 2022. "Detention Is Morally Exhausting: Melancholia of Detention Centres in France." *Identities* 31 (1): 123–39.

Vrabiescu, Ioana, and Bridget Anderson. 2023. "Affective Control: The Emotional Life (En)Forcing Mobility Control in Europe." *Identities* 31 (1): 1–13.

Vradis, Antonis. 2020. "Spatial Politics and the Spatial Contract in Exarcheia, Athens, Greece (1974–2018)." *Transactions of the Institute of British Geographers* 45 (3): 542–58.

Vradis, Antonis, Evie Papada, Joe Painter, and Anna Papoutsi. 2019. *New Borders: Hotspots and the European Migration Regime*. Pluto Press.

Wade, Peter. 2010. "The Presence and Absence of Race." *Patterns of Prejudice* 44 (1): 43–60.

Waever, Ole. 1998. "Securitization and Desecuritization." In *On Security*, edited by Ronnie D. Lipschutz. Columbia University Press.

Wimmer, Andreas, and Thomas Soehl. 2014. "Blocked Acculturation: Cultural Heterodoxy among Europe's Immigrants." *American Journal of Sociology* 120 (1): 46–86.

Wintour, Patrick, Lorenzo Tondo, and Stephanie Kirchgaessner. 2018. "Southern Mayors Defy Italian Coalition to Offer Safe Port to Migrants." *The Guardian*, June 11. https://www.theguardian.com/world/2018/jun/10/italy -shuts-ports-to-rescue-boat-with-629-migrants-on-board.

Wright, Sarah. 2008. "Practicing Hope: Learning from Social Movement Strategies in the Philippines." In *Fear: Critical Geopolitics and Everyday Life*, edited by Rachel Pain and Susan J. Smith. Ashgate.

Wyer, Sean. 2024. "Palermo Is a Mosaic": Cosmopolitan Rhetoric in the Capital of Sicily." *Modern Italy* 29 (4): 1–20.

York, Joanna. 2020. "Marseille Mayor Welcomes Banksy Rescue Boat Refugees." *The Connexion*, August 31. https://www.connexionfrance.com/news/ marseille-mayor-welcomes-banksy-rescue-boat-refugees/424894.

Yuval-Davis, Nira, Georgie Wemyss, and Kathryn Cassidy. 2019. *Bordering*. Polity Press.

Zardo, Federica, and Sarah Wolff. 2022. "Decentering the Study of Migration Governance in the Mediterranean." *Geopolitics* 27 (3): 687–702.

INDEX

The authorized representative in the EU for product safety and compliance is:
Mare Nostrum Group
B.V Doelen 72
4831 GR Breda
The Netherlands

www.ingramcontent.com/pod-product-compliance
Lightning Source LLC
Chambersburg PA
CBHW020845270326
41928CB00006B/559